ART/COMMONS

This exchange of information through stories about what had just happened was a primary factor in the survival of the human species in a world in which nearly all creatures were either bigger, stronger or faster than human beings. So, I imagine that at first humans exchanged stories to acquire knowledge as a survival strategy, to learn to anticipate the many threats and dangers in their world. Considerable details and vivid descriptions were essentials to the telling; the most important actions in a story might be repeated to make sure the listeners remembered what to do to survive in a similar situation. I like to imagine that the listeners took solace but also pleasure in hearing these stories told by survivors – amazing stories with happy endings.

– Leslie Marmon Silko

The Storyteller

ART/COMMONS

Anthropology beyond Capitalism

Massimiliano Mollona

ZED

Zed Books
Bloomsbury Publishing Plc
50 Bedford Square, London, WC1B 3DP, UK
1385 Broadway, New York, NY 10018, USA
29 Earlsfort Terrace, Dublin 2, Ireland

BLOOMSBURY and Zed Books are trademarks of Bloomsbury Publishing Plc

First published in Great Britain 2021

ISBN: HB: 978-1-7869-9698-5
         PB: 978-1-7869-9699-2
       ePDF: 978-1-7869-9701-2
       ePUB: 978-1-7869-9700-5

Series: In Common

Typeset by Integra Software Services Pvt. Ltd.

To find out more about our authors and books visit www.bloomsbury.com
and sign up for our newsletters.

CONTENTS

ACKNOWLEDGEMENTS

The ideas generated in this book come from conversations about and experimentations around art and capitalism I have had with artists, curators, scholars, activists and students in the last ten years. To all of them, I am deeply indebted. I want to thank especially the comrades from the Institute of Radical Imagination – Sara Buraya, Elena Lasala, Gabriella Riccio, Margherita D'Andrea, Giuseppe Micciarelli, Manuel Borja-Villel, Marco Baravalle, Emanuele Braga, Raúl Sánchez Cedillo, Anna Longoni, Mabel Tapia, Dmitry Vilensky, Jasmina Metwaly, Philip Rizk, Theo Prodromidis, Jesus Carrillo, Olga Egorova, Alexey Penzin, Ivet Ćurlin, Dević, Nataša Ilić and Sabina Sabolović – for teaching me how to care for and learn from the commons; my friends from the Laboratory for the Urban Commons (LUC) Xenia Kalpaktsoglou, Antonis Papangelopoulos, Stavros Stavrides and Pegi Zaly for the wonderful job LUC is doing in Athens; my Freethought friends Irit Rogoff, Adrian Heathfield, Luis Moreno, Stefano Harney and Nora Sternfeld for the polyphonic work we are doing together; Max Haiven for the generous feedback on the first draft of this book, and together with Cassie Thornton for the friendship; Massimo de Angelis for sharing with me his inspirational vision on commons; Elizabeth Povinelli and Denise Ferreira da Silva for their deep thinking around art, anthropology, and black and indigenous politics; Suzanne Lacy for the wonderful collaborations and dialogues around working-class politics; Leo Panitch for the political wisdom and warmth; Xenia and Poka-Yio for the intensity; Catherine Wood for her dedication to the open politics of performance art; Daria Martin for sharing her artist's point of view; and Sofia Mollona for the precious help on the first draft of the manuscript. Lastly, I deeply thank the students of the Master of Visual Anthropology (MAVIS) cohort 2019–20, to whom this book is dedicated.

Part I

TOWARDS AN ANTHROPOLOGICAL THEORY OF ART/COMMONS

PROLOGUE

This text discusses the conditions of life under capitalism and art's contribution to it. I define capitalism as a movement of systematic abstraction and reification of life culminating in its capture by the commodity form (that is, in the monetization of all that is human and non-human) and in a class system polarized between those who make a living out of other people's labour and those who survive by selling their labour power. Entangled with imperialism and colonialism, capitalism is a violent process of occupation, devalorization and annihilation of life based on the social construction of a racialized and sexualized 'other'. That is to say, every capitalism is racial and patriarchal.

I frame the relationships between art and political economy through anthropology, particularly Alfred Gell's seminal book *Art and Agency* which looks at art as a system of social actions and considers artefacts *like* people, that is, endowed with the power to affect and be affected and hence as relational beings. Going beyond a certain Western anthropocentrism, I discuss art in terms of 'flow of matter', partly outside human control,[1] multisensory and embodied in different human and non-human media.[2] I define Western art as a historical attempt to bypass the conditions of life under capitalism (La Berge, 2019) – by replacing ugliness with beauty, material enslavement with abstract contemplation, competition with a hierarchical system based on spiritual enlightenment – but one which, in fact, provides the conditions for capital's social reproduction.

The aim of the book is to sketch a general theory of commons, agency and art, based on some practices and ontologies of movement, creativity and beauty celebrated by non-Western societies and in black radical philosophy, to mount a critique of the alienated political economy of life under capitalism, and to sketch the contours of a non-alienated and 'good' life.[3]

Movement is the way humans come to valorize, understand and reproduce life. In movement we hunt and are hunted; return home and become strangers; communicate with our parents when still in the womb; relax, work, trade in the market, and generate images of each other in fleeting encounters. Dwelling in movement, resisting it slightly and folding it into patterns that return, we carve out practices and forms of living. But countering movement are the enclosures – physical or immaterial – set up by those in power with the aim of extracting value from them. The issue of how to animate, immobilize and choreograph people was once the domain of gods, then of kings in their thinking around questions of sovereignty and limits to their subjects' autonomy, and lastly of the bourgeoisie, who had the opposite problem of how to enforce movement and make it productive.

Western epistemology and historical forms of 'governmentality' revolve around constructed hierarchies between agents endorsed with different degrees of animacy.[4] During infancy we learn that humans are superior to objects because the latter lack the power to move on their own. We cease to be transported and moved by them and use them just instrumentally, as tools or commodities. We also learn that we are separate individuals with a separate capacity for movement from our parents and siblings and from the other entities that exist outside our bodies, which we call environment. We learn that this disembodied and lifeless environment is a limitless resource to be exploited and used carelessly. Moreover, through movement we learn to control our emotions. By moving closer and travelling into other bodies we identify and empathize with the other. By pulling back we cut social relations and create emotional distance.

Thus, under capitalism we gain agency, by disentangling, distancing and severing ourselves from life's sensuous movement, and simultaneously, internalizing, entrapping and enclosing this movement within our individual bodies. In other words, we become free by neutralizing and immobilizing all that surrounds us.

I argue that by abstracting, extracting and freezing life through systematic enclosures of humans and non-human entities, capitalism is a speculative process which creates value negatively and through its opposite: that is, through waste and annihilation. Examples of capitalist enclosures that devalue what they enfold are factories, private land, prisons and intellectual patents. The negative and speculative logic of capital is also the logic of Western art, which de-functionalizes, neutralizes and renders inoperative everyday objects and social relations by turning them into abstract – material or mental – images/commodity forms, with the aim of reproducing existing class relations. If the violent physical enclosure of objects, nature and people is the precondition for primitive accumulation, it is through the abstraction of art and the unpaid labour of artists that capitalism 'puts the soul of the beholder/proletariat to work'. A royal portrait by Titian beautifies the colonialist; a monument to the unknown soldiers justifies imperial expansion; a photo of a working-class slum legitimizes its clearance. Hence, I consider art as 'capitalism's double' – the bourgeois ideology of aesthetics as a separate realm of life is the double of the bourgeois ideology of the separate realm of economics and the figure of the artists is the double of the *Homo economicus*.

But with Adorno, I am also intrigued by the magical power of Western art in constructing fictional spaces in which images are entrapped, neutralized and frozen – and yet they also appear to be in motion. Thus, I consider Western bourgeois art to be the magical technology of entrapment of movement associated with the capitalist mode of production. Moreover, I locate the origins of 'modern' bourgeois art and economics in the encounter between capitalism and colonialism when, as well as the development of the North being premised upon the stillness and underdevelopment of the South, the material and cultural resources extracted from the South re-enchanted and animated the European world.

The supposedly neutral realm of aesthetics, as envisaged by Kant, in fact transposed indigenous categories into figures of European modernity against the backdrop of racial domination.[5] Sublime works of art mediated between the magical fetish of indigenous communities,[6] with the power to animate or freeze people, *and* the capitalist commodity; the de-commodified regime of the circulation of art mediated between the free circulation of objects in indigenous gift-giving *and* the free market; the 'unproductive' labour of the artist mediated between slavery *and* 'free' wage labour; the aristocratic virtuosity of the *artist/master* mediated between the magical power of Amerindian shamans or the Afro-Atlantic priests – which animated the inanimate or conversely made people stand still like sculptures or objects – *and* the capitalist master; the ethnographic museum mediated between the regime of production of the plantation *and* the Taylorist factory.

Of course, the whole idea of kings, managers and artists having the power to control the movement of their subjects and beholders is not only authoritarian but also ethnocentric. In a non-capitalist and non-Western world, value is relational and does not stem from autonomous and individual gestures. On the contrary, personhood is dividual and fractal rather than individual and self-contained, and individual gestures are interruptions of movement – holes in the communal texture.

Indeed, countering the movement of capital are the acts of commoning, the pooling and sharing of resources for the reproduction of life in common. I call this socialist and postcolonial space where knowledge, gestures and social relations go towards the reproduction of the commons 'art/commons'. Art/commons is the reproductive labour of shamans, storytellers or priests, revealing the continuous and unbroken temporality and the unfolding social texture out of which humanity emerges.

Movement and the political economy of life

'A man, running along the street, stumbles and falls; the passers-by burst out laughing. They would not laugh at him, I imagine, could they suppose that the whim had suddenly seized him to sit down on the ground. They laugh because his sitting down is involuntary.'

– Bergson, H. *Laughter, an Essay on the Meaning of the Comic*

How many times have we stumbled, slipped or fallen and, in the act of falling, noticed the suppressed laughter of the occasional witness?

For Bergson, laughter is the automated response to witnessing someone moving clumsily, mechanically and inelastically and losing control of his or her body. It is a detached echo without feeling – purely mechanical – that reverberates contagiously and generates 'its own closed community'.

Indeed, life under capitalism demands that our bodies be continuously in sync, tense and infinitely elastic – as consumers, producers, friends, parents or partners. To lose control, to stumble, to grind to a halt – like a broken machine – is punished with laughter. Unlike Kleist's puppets or the automata of classical antiquity, whose fall had a precise arc of movement and a weightless grace, the fall of the exhausted capitalist individual is laughable because it always contains an attempt to resist, a barely perceptible countermovement, which is then suppressed in the act of falling. Charlie Chaplin, the anti-hero of modern cinema, falls, lags behind and moves in awkward quivers and spasms, jamming and jarring, together with vagrants, children, women and the lumpen, against the smooth flow of industrial capitalism in cuts, close-ups and fades which, as Walter Benjamin observed, keep the audience in a state of irritable suspension.

It seems that the great political controversies of our time – the unrestrained flow of migrants and refugees, or the free movement of suspected terrorists; labour and capital deregulation; forced exile, intergenerational mobility and anti-immigration borders; intellectual property rights, economic protectionism and cultural appropriation; mass incarceration, gentrification and slummification – are fundamentally struggles over *movement* – that is, over the real or imagined consequences of the unrestricted flows of objects, people and knowledge in an environment that is also continually moving and transforming. For some, movement, or the lack of it, underpins a new kind of global class polarization, pitting a mobile, cosmopolitan, multiculturalist and financialized elite against a socially and geographically bounded working class which is also increasingly localist, nativist and xenophobic.[7]

In a polemical exchange with Toni Negri, the philosopher Giorgio Agamben argues that the (ab)use of the term 'movement' by left-wing scholars betrays their lack of trust in democratic institutions including the role of 'the people'.

But I argue quite the opposite: that the emergence of capitalist institutions – centralized states, factories, land, money, machines, finance, markets, nuclear families and even some versions of 'the people' as fictitious political subject – marks the end of political movement. These institutions lead to violent physical and mental enclosures and a stasis that goes against life. Beyond its fictitious ideologies of movement, autonomy and freedom, the world of capitalism is enclosed, frozen and solidified.

I also argue that outside capitalism, the human condition is experienced as a relational flow, whereby the lives of people and those of non-humans and their environments are deeply entangled. But as much as humans strive to enter 'the flow', they also fear oblivion and self-annihilation and develop institutions and support structures – families, clans, congregations, markets, armies or states – that make their 'selves' unique, memorable and even immortal; hence, they block the flow and cut the social network. But it is the interests of the rich that these institutions are built to protect. The autonomy and freedom of people and the closure and fixity of their institutions are in constant tension so that the outlines of personhood and human agency need constant redefinition through the lenses of religion, art or economics.

Anthropological literature shows that throughout history, commons have strived to challenge, break and socialize the ossified human institutions of kinship, clans and states (the phantasmatic embodiments of capital) and their control by male elders, and that countering such movement of commoning, colonial capitalism has imposed even stronger and more violent boundaries and enclosures locally, through various versions of the market ideology.

The anthropologist Marcel Mauss understood that movement is a central component of how societies are organized – of the 'political economy of life'. In the non-capitalist societies he describes in his book *The Gift* (1950) it is believed that all organic and inorganic beings are endowed with movement and that objects and people should circulate openly and freely. In this context, gestures of permanence – gestures which put things and people back into circulation and keep the flow open – are more valued than gesture of impermanence – that is, the 'productive' gestures that carve objects, wealth and individuals out of the relational flow of life. But these impermanent gestures and their agents remain invisible, as they partake to a world in movement. In other terms, in non-capitalist societies, there is no separation between productive and reproductive labour, since they are part of the same principle of productivity – or 'vital energy' (*hau*) – of social relations.[8] In these non-capitalist zones, life is relational and in *motion* but experienced as a 'steady state' (Bateson, 1942) and without hierarchies.

Unlike those societies, capitalist societies set a high value on those impermanent – 'productive' – gestures that freeze movement, block circulation, cut relationships, and build borders and boundaries. This forced separation between productive and reproductive gestures creates an inverted relationship[9] between humans and things. Capital (money, land, machines or commodities) is the invisible energy that puts humans in motion and gives to the bourgeoisie the power to compartmentalize life, freeze movement, and make and cross thresholds. Labour consists of those humans who – disentangled from circulation, emptied out of life, excluded from relations and left without movement – exist only in the abstract and lifeless commodity form.

Thus, the dialectic of movement and stasis and the social construction of hierarchies based on differential forms of animacy and 'geontopower' (Povinelli, 2016) are the central dimensions of the political economy of life under capitalism. The living machines, commodities and money of the capitalist cosmos push people and nature violently into the background as they forcibly move to the foreground. Alienation is the state of consciousness where objects, machines and money attack humans with overbearing force – rendering them motionless, helpless and abstracted. This splitting between a frozen humanity and a moving capitalist cosmos is never resolved. Existing in-between hollowed-out existences and enchanting virtual realities, the capitalist 'individual'[10] oscillates between depression and aggression, hard work and overconsumption, acceleration, impotence and stasis.

Under the capitalist spell, the inanimate becomes animate and the animate dies out. Ossified humans, objects and organic matter circulate in remote markets, while capital parasitically roots itself in the micro-texture of everyday life, becoming increasingly vibrant. The more capital embeds itself in the material texture of life, the more extreme is its movement of objectification, dehumanization, expulsion and abstraction, in the forms of xenophobia, sexism and homophobia. The greater the dehumanization, the stronger the force of expulsion and the broader the trajectories of capital circulation. Capital's enclosures are holes in the relational texture of life out of which value originates negatively as 'anti-value' (Harvey, 2018). The dazzling movements and the vitalism of capitalism are nothing more than an optical illusion generated by the fall (often mistaken for progress or self-determination) of the capitalist subject through the holes, cuts and rips in the web of life.

Yet, for Castoriadis (1994), human imagination has a magmatic logic – egalitarian, utopian and anti-capitalist – that continuously strives to destroy human enclosures, consolidations and institutions and to restore movement (Haiven, 2018). The figure of the magma prefigures revolutionary societies – based on forms that are also formless, closures that remain open, collectives sharing autonomy and a movement that never ceases or disperses. The magma is the threshold between movement and stasis – between the flow that erases differences and liberates people, and the institutions that protect them but also occupy their spaces and freeze their development. For Castoriadis, humanity's magmatic logic is tragic, as humans are the only living creatures who can imagine the horizon of their own destruction.

COMMONS

Commons are worlds in movement (Stavrides, 2016). They are communities that create forms of life in common and that together produce and share and are continuously transformed. The term 'commons' can signify three things: (1) a pool of natural and/or human resources, (2) a community of people with reciprocal and sharing relations and (3) acts of working together towards the reproduction of the community (De Angelis, 2017). It is only when these three dimensions come together that we have real commons. 'Commons' also implies specific forms of participatory governance (collective monitoring and conflict resolution, self-determination and nested levels of authority) reflecting the practical urgencies, the grassroots knowledge and the embodied skills of the commoners. In spatial terms commons are neither private nor public – neither collective nor individual. They are relational thresholds and spaces of radical openness reflecting the autonomy of the collective. Affectively, they refuse ideological forms of identification and belonging and the cynicism or 'cruel optimism' of capitalism. They demand fugitive attachments, precarious affects; silent, sensuous and embodied knowledge production and continuously shifting and co-evolving relations.

The movement of the commons wants to break the ossified life enclosures produced by the capitalist institutions of money, work, property and market consumption and the associated ideologies of scarcity, competition and self-interest. But commons cannot exist in isolation from capitalism (Stavrides, 2016). For instance, the egalitarian societies described by anthropologists Clastres (1974), Overing (1975) and Graeber (2004) or the Zapatistas communities are not *outside* capitalism and the bourgeois state; rather, they have carved zones of self-organization and autonomy *within* them. Likewise, as a mode of production and circulation capitalism needs commons in order to spread and grow – the socialization of productive labour by workers, of reproductive labour by women, or state redistribution.

Commons are enclosures which remain open, by resisting the disciplinary integration of capitalism.[11] I will explore the tensions, conflicts and mutual entanglements between capitalism and commons at the threshold of art and political economy, from the postcolonial and Marxist perspectives. I call the entanglement of capitalism and commons as 'post-capitalism', which is the generalized condition of the contemporary world.

By the term 'post-capitalism' I also mean the prefigurative political economy and anthropological imagination of those socialist Western philosophers, such as Peter Kropotkin, William Morris and the Marx of the *Ethnographic Notebooks*, who considered small-scale societies on the margins of Europe to be models for instituting commons and post-capitalist forms of life in the present. I also apply the term 'post-capitalism' to Cedric Robinson's (2001) anthropological project of denaturalizing and deconstructing the narrow, narcissistic and 'capitalo-centric' Western bourgeois episteme. In solidarity with the black radical tradition, I define post-capitalism as a non-ethnocentric and non-Eurocentric socialist ontology free from the Enlightenment and Western Judaeo-Christian ideologies of catharsis and revolution. My idea of post-capitalism is not the return of the colonial project of ethnographic salvage of disappearing 'others'. Rather, it is an invitation to use the anthropological imagination to prefigure and bring into life utopian life projects, radical worlds and alternative modes of instituting.

Anthropology shows that the institution of the commons is universal and cross-cultural and that although commons have been endangered throughout history by colonialism, imperialism and capitalism, they have nonetheless resisted, and not only on the basic logic of survival or sustainability. On the contrary, they have developed powerful ontologies of beauty, excess and luxury in countering the dehumanizing and belittling logic of capitalism. In fact, lurking in the background of the bourgeois ideologies of artistic beauty and economic progress is a dry and desolate landscape in which the vast majority of people put up with a destitute, dull and ugly existence. With the notion of art/commons I want to reclaim an aesthetic and political vision of plenty for the future.

In imaging the end of capitalism at the hand of the commons, I also suggest a post-capitalism that goes beyond the dehumanizing techno-accelerationism of Western intellectuals and connects instead to suppressed non-white modes of existence, forms of counter-humanism (Wynter, 2015) and ontologies of movement, and envisions the beginning of history from the South.

Capitalism and abstraction

Abstraction is the forceful drawing away, removal and disposal (from Latin *ab-traere*) of difference with the aim of mechanical comparison, generalization and quantification. It is the severing of social connections, the reduction of depth to the simplicity of the plane, the crystallization of movement and the vampiric extraction of vital essence that freezes life into the commodity form.

In the 1844 Manuscripts, Marx describes abstraction as the dehumanizing process which accompanies the operations of capital. All human beings acquire self-consciousness through the activity of production, which is therefore always also a process of self-production via the mediation of the objects produced. But under capitalism, labour takes up the abstract and alienated form of the commodity which confronts humans, as an external, estranged and hostile entity – that is to say, as a 'practical abstraction'.

The abstract commodity form creates an inverted relationship between humans and things. Money, land and machines are fetishes – humanized objects with their own agency and life energy. Unlike these fetishes, humans are emptied out of life, excluded from social relations, and exist only in the abstract and lifeless commodity form. According to Marx, the fetishism of commodities is like 'a camera obscura'. It literally turns the world upside down (1976).

Lukács develops Marx's 'ocular' depiction of alienation further in his theory of reification as a form of detached spectatorship. In *Reification and Consciousness of the Proletariat*, he describes reification under capitalism as an abstract and naturalized perception of reality in which humans seem to have no agency vis-à-vis the world and can relate to it only passively, as distant observers. Reified consciousness is a spectatorial, contemplative and dissociated consciousness.[12] It is the experience of a frozen and fragmented world of pure forms, which captivates and captures us from a distance. Hidden underneath this world is the living totality of social relations, which can be accessed only through the painstaking labour of mediation, weaving back together, and reconnecting atomized fragments of reality 'in movement' – that is, scattered across different temporal and spatial zones. Thus, for Lukács human consciousness emerges dialectically, reflexively and relationally – that is to say, by dissolving the reified point of view of the bourgeois individual into the point of view of the totality. Revolutionary workers and storytellers, according to Lukács, have the creative gift of seeing themselves through the eyes of the totality.

Philosopher George Simmel, a contemporary of Lukács, is more ambivalent towards 'abstraction' under capitalism. On the one hand, he considers abstraction as a flight, a journey of critical distance, a liberating unsettling of experiential and material boundaries, cognitive illusions and oppressive social relations leading to self-awareness. On the other hand, he argues that abstraction leads to stasis, senselessness, individualism and alienation.

Like Lukács and Marx, Simmel claims that self-consciousness can exist only in mediated form – that is, through external objects to which the human imagination attaches itself to. But unlike Lukács and Marx, who see the process of acquiring self-consciousness as a linear path of the proletariat intended as a collective subject, for Simmel, self-consciousness implies a circular, contradictory and uneven process of boundary-making and boundary-breaking. Stepping outside the physical and mental boundaries of our bodies through the *media* of texts, images or money, we see ourselves from the outside and, hence, experience and transcend finitude. But because the experience of being outside our bodies is frightening, we then attach ourselves to these media and, through them, we draw new boundaries to ourselves. With time these outer boundaries become material enclosures and appendages (for instance, money) with lives of their own. For this reason, Simmel describes the experience of self-transcendence also as one of progressive objectification, externalization and abstraction of life into autonomous and external forms, media and institutions – that is, of self-alienation.

But under normal conditions, the process of self-transcendence continues. Human imagination breaks down boundaries again, tears down ossified institutions, and discards established media inventing new and open ones so that life re-emerges as flow. We can imagine this in terms of dialectical movements. The movement of breaking through and stepping out of self-transcendence is followed by a countermovement of institutional consolidation and material confinement that blocks and freezes movement and generates alienation. Simmel's view of human consciousness is dialectic. The self-transcendence and abstraction achieved through boundary-breaking is dialectically entangled with the self-alienation arising from the making and fixing of new boundaries. Ultimately, for Simmel, the human condition is tragic, because self-consciousness can be achieved only through self-alienation.

Indeed, the wider the *cultural* movements of mediation and abstraction, the more self-consciousness is lost to self-alienation. Under capitalism, according to Simmel, the process of mediation reaches its apex due to the social technology of money. From being a simple tool of valorization of individual actions – a mediator of value – under capitalism money is valuable in itself and circulates independently from social relations. By extracting value as it circulates, money blocks the flow of life and turns people into dead abstractions, flickering surfaces, hypermediated subjects and hollow vessels of wealth and labour. Hence, for Simmel, the modern capitalist metropoles have an eerie quality because they are inhabited by ghost people who, following the flow of money, circulate in the form of flat cinematic and mediatic images, dehumanized stereotypes, and fragmented, isolated and competitive individuals. Moreover, financialization further increases the abstraction of capital, as relationships between individuals are mediated by additional social relations – the 'derivative' promise to pay – rather than by physical money. Here it is social relations, rather than commodities, that are monetized.

What these theorists of reification share is the association of the commodity form with visual art – that is, with still or moving images – and, more broadly, of art with capitalism, as they consider aesthetic *media* functional to both capitalism's abstractions (the transformation of the real into the commodity form) and its concretizations (the materialization of absolute value in the concrete instances of labour, money and land). For Adorno, the mediation effect of the artwork could be inverted. The reification of art could be used against capitalism (see below).

Capitalism and art are historically entangled not only because the emergence of art as an autonomous realm reflects the commodification of life in bourgeois society, but, more importantly, because art is the social technology that produced the abstract realm of the commodity form and the capitalist subject in the first place. As Adorno shows, art is the contradictory and phantasmatic space where movement meets stillness and abstractions and concretization – the immaterial and the material; alienation and freedom – meet in their 'absolute form'.[13] It is the bourgeois 'technology of enchantment'[14] – a mixture of magic and productivity – which made possible the transformation of the religious passions of the old regime into the abstract economic interest of the new one.

For instance, Elizabethan theatre, with its popular realism, plays-within-plays and melodramatic plots, prefigured – even enacted – the modern world of capitalism; this was a new liminal, voyeuristic and performative space inhabited by market swindlers, upwardly mobile entrepreneurs and greedy merchants with split personalities, and alienated and fragmented selves, whose life trajectories were dictated by the capricious forces of the market.[15] How can we read Mayhew's book *The Laboring Poor* if not as an ethnographic rendering of the capitalist market as a theatre and a real-life circus in which performative gestures and tricks of the trade may or may not turn into money as the labouring poor make up rules as they go along, until they hit the jackpot? Or think of Diderot's reflection on the paradox of the actor, whose greatest qualities are emotional detachment and indifference and whose affective labour plays out the split consciousness of the Western possessive individual to the point that 'the player in private and the player on the boards become as two different personages'.[16]

Cinema went even further. It turned the Western 'persona' – with its clear-cut boundaries between the visible and 'artificial' outside and the invisible and true soul within – inside out, unfolding its inner self into a machine-animated surface. In the chrono-photographic work 'hands' by physician Étienne-Jules Marey (a series of photographic still frames of moving hands mapped in spatial metrics) we see hands opening and closing in jarred sequences. We see the cuts and holes on the film sheet opening up the other dimension, where the ghostly power of the labouring hand resides and gathers energy. The early capitalists discovered that the magic forces of electricity and thermodynamics that animated the cosmos also powered the bodies of industrial workers and that the energy of the working class was both immensely dangerous and immensely productive if it was harnessed through the technological apparatuses of the factory and of cinema. The Taylorist assembly line can be thought of as a performative and cinematic space in which commodity fetishism and the vitalism of capital are concretized through the movement of anthropomorphic machines and negatively, by the dematerialization of labour into labour power.

Moreover, cinema transformed the aristocratic technologies of magic lanterns, phantasmagorias and shadow plays, veiled in mystical style and magical aura, into commercial spectacles of mass entertainment. Film is the animist technology of capitalism, which takes life away and reconstructs it as flat cinematic sequences. Industrial capitalism is a cinematic mode of production and cinema is a powerful technology of human abstraction, the artistic equivalent of money.[17] Like money, cinematic images have the power to freeze, abstract and equalize human actions across different spatio-temporal planes. They capture the soul and create their own economy of attention. The magic technology of cinema reproduces the commodity form by force of projection and identification – proximity and distance. We strive to come close and touch the commodity (the film star, the hero or the villain), and at the same time, we indulge in the weightless and distant pleasure of looking. Cinema's 'unproductive' fictions encouraged the expansion of the commodity form and capital's early transformations. As the Lumiére Brothers presciently showed, industrial workers were already leaving the factories when cinema was invented. Where were these workers going? To the museum and to the call centre (Steyerl, 2009).

In fact, industrial capitalism is also a mode of performance;[18] the synchronized movement of the proletariat was first neutralized in Russian constructivist dance and then deconstructed by bourgeois European modern dance. Or we may trace immaterial labour back to the Duchampian aesthetic gesture which produces its own economy of attention, captures value and freezes ordinary acts (such as peeing) out of the flow of life. The more the modernist artistic avant-garde developed forms of abstraction aimed at dissolving capitalist enclosures and the material boundaries of bourgeois personhood, the more these abstract gestures were recycled into the material apparatus of capitalist realism.

The emergence of aesthetics as a separated realm of life can be traced back to the bourgeois revolution in France (Groys, 2016), when the revolutionary government de-functionalized and depoliticized the objects of the old regime by putting them in the museum. But the depoliticization, de-functionalization, externalization and abstraction of life in the space of the museum and of the gallery were primarily a violent act of colonialism. Just as industrial capitalism was a replica of the labour regime of the Caribbean sugar plantation, bourgeois art dates back to the colonial appropriation of indigenous culture and artefacts and their abstraction, decontextualization and commodification on the shop floors of European ethnographic museums. Entities – neither object nor subjects – who had travelled in intercontinental *kularings*[19] carrying with them the spirit of their makers, of their chiefs and of their communities and who had brought together in reciprocity people of different languages and lineages, were emptied of their reproductive power, imprisoned in white spaces and displayed as primitive artworks. The intangibility and vitalism of primitive forms gave a new lease of life to the white canvasses of the European avant-gardes feeding their melancholic search for 'the new' and their vampiric quest for movement and self-regeneration.[20]

Museums brought different rituals of social aggregation from those of theatre and cinema, casting the new public in the mould of modern nation states and of Western capitalism's productivist and object-obsessed teleology of growth (Hantelmann, 2019). Sanitized, de-territorialized and atemporal, the modern museum is a space of mysticism, ascetism and mourning for all white society has lost in the midst of continuous growth and over-accumulation. Capitalism *is* the artistic mode of production. Like money, markets, factories and commodities, artworks, museums, cinemas and art galleries are powerful social technologies which abstract, cut, recompose and redraw the boundaries of personhood and set the horizons of human agency: synchronizing, accelerating or bringing movement to a standstill. Forcedly extracted and abstracted from the flow of life, objects exhaust their movement as works of art.

For anthropologist James Carriers, the central feature of alienation under capitalism is the experience of split consciousness and separation – between production and reproduction; between objects and commodities; between use value and exchange value; and between homes and factories. My contention is that such schizophrenic dualism is made possible by the existence of a third realm, that of the artistic *medium* – photos/cinema/performances mediate between mental images and commodities; artistic labour mediates between production and reproduction; conceptual labour mediates between use value and exchange value; 'contemporary art' museums mediate between factories (work) and homes (leisure); and ethnographic museums between the West and the rest. This bourgeois realm of art is premised upon social hierarchies of perceived humanity built against the backdrop of the back body.

Following his mentor Simmel, art historian Wilhelm Worringer (1908) discusses aesthetics in terms of emotions triggered by artworks. Naturalistic artworks trigger feelings of empathy and identification, and, at the opposite emotional end, abstract art creates distance and detachment. Empathy is a drive to self-affirmation, entanglement with nature and the organic realm, and over-identification with the (art) object, leading to the feelings of exhaustion, absorption, outflow of vital energy from the empathic subject's body, and loss of self. Thus, the dark side of empathy and solidarity is self-alienation. Abstraction is the opposite impulse: to sever oneself from the contingencies, entanglements, relationships and movement of everyday life, critically gaze from a distance, and seek refuge in simplified patterns and minimal forms of existence. Empathy and abstraction can be described as affective movements – one is a drive *towards* life, leading to loss and self-annihilation; the other is a movement *away from* life which generates critical detachment, self-transcendence and, at the same time, a sense of inter-relatedness.

Worringer argues that these affective movements are as much political as they are aesthetic. Animist and egalitarian societies tend to identify with abstract forms. Their world views of the deep entanglement between humans and non-humans, in the context of the dizzyingly moving cosmos, generate a will to abstract and take a distance from the immediate – a longing to return to the primitive and undifferentiated totality and dwell on the crystalline surface rather than in the depth of social relations. Likewise, abstraction characterizes the 'deep consciousness' of Eastern civilizations, symbolized by the pure geometry of the line. The will to empathy comes from the opposite feeling of confidence in and communion with the external world, the appreciation of the beauty of organic forms, and the anthropomorphic identification with nature, which characterizes Western capitalist societies. The empathic, reifying and self-alienating naturalism that Worringer attributed to Western societies is also central to Lukács's critique of bourgeois naturalist literature, which lacked the sense of interconnectedness, totality and critical distance of revolutionary literature.

But Worringer was not in favour of rigid cultural polarizations. He saw the 'primitive' impulse towards the abstract also in German expressionism, in the forms and volumes emerging in Cézanne's liquid landscapes and, more generally, in modernism's search for regularities in the hallucinatory world of capitalism – akin to the literary form of the allegory for Walter Benjamin or Lukács' reification process – whereas Simmel associated immediatism and empathy with primitive societies, and abstraction with capitalist ones.

But the distinction between abstraction and empathy is not clear-cut outside Western capitalism. Take for instance how Brazilian artist Lygia Clark 'reverses' the Western abstract canon[21] by 'concretizing' and humanizing the geometric abstractions of Malevich and Mondrian in animated psychic lines, organic borders, margins, edges and small polymorphous and multitemporal everyday objects – such as paper-cuttings, matchboxes and light metallic folding structures – functioning as sites of empathy and dwelling.

Here I use Worringer's affective theory for the appreciation of the hallucinatory and schizophrenic world of capitalism, rather than an anthropological theory of art, by comparing the affective movements of abstraction and empathy triggered by the artwork to the affective movement triggered by the capitalist commodity. On the one hand, this is a movement of dematerialization, depersonalization and distancing that takes place when human labour is reduced to abstract value; on the other hand, it is a movement of identification, concretization and materialization, associated with the realization of market value. Besides, with Worringer, I consider art as a form of experiential politics based on affective movements, solidarities and psychic exchanges between humans and non-humans mediated by the objects/artworks.

From anthropology we know that in societies living at the margins of capitalism, humans and objects exist only relationally, as afterlives of distributed and invisible agencies. Instead of value emerging from just one medium (money), one sense (visual) and one type of social relation (wage relation), as under capitalism, human value embodies, synaesthetically and polyphonically, multiple mediums and regimes of values – economic, artistic, magical and political. The aesthetic merges with the magical, the technical and the political. Politics takes the form of public and performative gestures embedded in everyday life and open to public contestation, negotiation and co-poiesis. Artworks are temporary stages in the lives of objects. Afterlives of the political.

In this context, artistry entails the mastery of movement for two reasons. First, because artworks unveil the relational network out of which value emerges and openly circulates; that is, it reveals the vitalism and productivity of social relations. Second, because artworks literally contain and entrap the movement – through symmetric decorations that trigger animation; sacred icons that touch us from afar; and fractal woodwork carvings that both magnify and dissolve personhood – pushing the spectator into a double movement of identification and doubt, fusion and distance, empathy and abstraction. To entrap movement is different from representing it, as futurist paintings do, or from the Adorno's attempt to unify dialectically what is divided. Rather, it is a way of entangling the frame with the movement of what is absent; re-embedding the artwork within the productivity of the collective; and generating value conversions between aesthetics, economics and politics.

Anthropologist Alfred Gell (1996) describes artworks as 'mind-traps' – artefacts or actions that embody complex intentionalities and agencies and trigger perceptual illusions, cognitive dissonance, disorientation, experiential displacement, fear or vertigo. For instance, the self-surrendering mesmeric motion of ritual swinging among the Muria of Madhya Pradesh (India); the 'brilliance' of Yolngu paintings that 'flutter, dazzle, shimmer and blur or reverse figure and ground';[22] or the shining headdresses of the Wahgi of Papua New Guinea (O' Hanlon, 1992), considered as maternal second skins that transfix the men who wear them.

Or with Léopold Senghor, we can appreciate how movement is captured and transformed in the rhythm of lines, cones, ridges and edges of African masks, revealing the vital force that bursts out like drums and brasses in music,[23] or we can look at the rhythms of the stories in the sand of the Walbiri Australian aboriginal people, whose circular patterns embody the mythical movement, from waterhole to waterhole, that organizes their nomadic life and echoes the movement of the cosmos (Munn, 1973). The politics of movement is central to black radical aesthetics, for instance, in Fred Moten's notion of 'the break' – not the in-between but the moment just after the beat – and of blackness as a place of gathering of matter, chromatic energy and under-commons. Black radical politics is the pattern of animation and counterinsurgency that inspired C. L. R. James, going beyond the Western master-slave dialectics and expanding to other modes of perception – multisensorial rather than just visual or haptic. Black radical art is the art of bodies in movement – the rhythm, pitch and frequency of gestures 'carried around in the nervous system.'[24]

Art's capture of movement – the object's 'abduction' of human agency – is political because, unlike the animism of commodities, which renders humans passive recipients of movement, here the personification and animation of non-humans are initiated by humans, be they shamans or storytellers, as a way to establish social equilibrium within the cosmos.

In this context, art is experienced as a journey across bodies and boundaries, a merging of foreground and background, a forest of shining words, a fractal multiplications of skins and body parts, a becoming infinitely small and at the same time, embracing the point of view of the gods, a double movement of abstraction and materialization, a momentary standstill, an entrapment between closeness and distance. Under capitalism, however, art is a social technology that traps, immobilizes, divides, ossifies, occupies and compartmentalizes life into flat moving images, museums, choreographed actions and conceptual speculations that reproduce the dead commodity form and its fictitious movements.

For art historian Ernst Gombrich (1960), the great achievement of Western art is to have mastered movement with sophisticated optical techniques creating an illusory naturalistic space of fixity, stillness and 'constancy' in the midst of the anarchic flux of life and in which the critical perspective of the modern beholder is accommodated. Such power of Western art to create a singular point of view out of difference and movement, albeit fleeting and illusory, coincides, according to Gombrich, with the West's other great achievement: democracy. For the art historian, such sophisticated reflexivity of the Western beholder differs from the direct identification of non-Western societies. Barely hiding his amusement, he describes how the Native American chief Little Bear was deeply upset by the portrait made of him by the painter Caitlin in 1838, reading the shadowing on half of his face as if it had been eaten by ghosts and demons. In fact, we can appreciate how the artificial zone of stability and stillness described by Gombrich – the negation of human movement generated by the animism of capital – goes against the real democracy that comes from embracing a world in flux.

In this section I have used art as a space to reflect on the human condition, conceptualized as sets of material and ontological entanglements, enclosures and movements between humans and non-humans, leading to the experiences of 'good' life or 'alienation'. Under capitalism the function of the artwork and of the 'exhibitionary complex'[25] (museums, cinemas, galleries, schools and curators) is to create physical, mental and affective separations between people, objects and environments and to 'abduct' the agency of humans in the same magical and mysterious way as the commodity form does.

In fact, I have also argued that commodity fetishism is generated by the fetishism of the artwork (that is, by the power of abstraction of the artistic medium) rather than the other way around.

Secondly, I have argued that unlike colonial capitalism, under conditions of art/commons, the making and circulation of objects are aimed at concretizing, making visible and surrendering agency to the expanded, multimodal and abstract relational network in which human value is said to reside. In the next section, I will discuss the issues of agency, relationality and movement in relation to labour.

Art, labour, slavery and the actions that make the world alive

The notion of labour is difficult to define because it applies to virtually all human activities – material and immaterial – through which societies reproduce themselves: the physical labour of steelworkers or of parents who raise their children; the immaterial labour of employees in call centres and IT firms; the production of symbols, stories and ideologies by priests, shamans and politicians; and the 'affective' labour of nannies, nurses and maids. Because labour is both symbolic and material – affective and pragmatic – we are often confused as to how to value it.

For Marx, labour is a relational process, which involves both the production of objects and the making of people. I define labour as actions or gestures that can take two value-forms – one productive, one reproductive. I call reproductive labour those kinds of actions that go into the reproduction of people in the present life and the afterlife (food, childcare, clothing, education, mourning) and productive labour those actions that produce objects and wealth – which also include war, oratory or elaborated rituals of gift exchange.[26] The different orders of morality associated with these spheres of labour create inequalities between those who perform them. The handling of money, wages or gifts or the involvement in war, government and diplomacy is called 'work' and performed by people (often men) with high status and rank in public, often ostentatiously. The activities that go into the reproduction of people are normally performed by women and children in the domestic or informal realms; they are considered less valuable and defined 'labour'. Under capitalism on the one hand *work* acquires nearly a near-supernatural value and is considered a magic and transformative power possessed by talented individuals or an inalienable property that gives its 'owners' the rights to citizenship or the dignity of personhood. On the other hand, *labour* is considered a source of alienation, material dependence and social exclusion. This is evident in the way connections are often made between black, unregulated and illegal labour and foreigners or marginal people.

Moreover, unlike economists who consider labour solely as a material and utilitarian activity, Marx considers it also as an imaginative one, involving the production of foundational myths, organizing narratives, moralities and ideologies, which embody the interests of the dominant classes but are presented as the interests of the whole of society. They dictate which human action is deemed valuable and which valueless. Different ideologies legitimize different forms of extraction of social labour by the powerful classes at the expenses of the exploited classes. The elder kinsman commands the labour of juniors and women in the name of kinship; Brahmins command the labour of untouchables in the name of the cosmic principle of *dharma*; the lord exploits his serfs in the name of the law of the kingdom; and the capitalists exploit wage workers in the name of profit.

Ideologies are not external but internal to the experience of labour. They are a kind of ethics or moralities of labour that makes it both opaque and acceptable. Like cosmologies and myths, ideologies of labour are both contextual and universal. Compelling ideologies often concern forces such as 'productivity', 'energy' or 'motion' that are counter-intuitive and go against 'common sense', for instance, because they animate the inanimate or make the invisible visible. Examples of such magical technologies under capitalism are the self-generative and invisible movement of finance or the 'effortless labour' of the fully automated production line. Ideologies are 'mind traps'. They seem to create equivalences between different orders – for instance, between gods and humans, capitalists and workers, or hunters and prey.[27] But even as they bring these orders into a dangerous intimacy, at the same time, they reveal the impossibility of their equivalence. For this reason, they expose the 'tragic' human condition. For instance, among the Fang of the Cameroonian rainforest, animal traps are considered channels of communication between hunters and prey, and hence, they prefigure a world in which animals and humans are in solidarity. In fact, the knowledge of how to produce animal traps is controlled by a priestly caste so that traps come to signify that, just as priests are more powerful then ordinary humans, relationships between animals and humans cannot truly be equal.

As I said above, the comparative analyses of Marx and Mauss describe the same tension between those relational actions and gestures that facilitate the open circulation and sharing of resources and *reproduce* people *in their* totality, and those self-contained and quantifiable actions and gestures that *produce* objects and wealth, the performance of which confers individual freedom and autonomy *from* the totality. This tension between gestures of permanence and gestures of impermanence – between productive and reproductive labour – is at the very core of 'the human condition' (Arendt, 1958). Class relations between productive and reproductive workers also exist in non-capitalist societies. Just as the capitalist wage deprives workers of their means of subsistence and makes them dependent upon undervalued domestic labour, the reproductive power of women is devalued and appropriated by male elders in kinship societies.

Nonetheless, most societies cope with this tension by keeping these two spheres of labour separated into different moral orders[28] and by rituals that reconcile them. In Malaysia, the cash produced through the labour of male fishermen can be used for the household only after women have purified it by cooking it on the household hearth;[29] in Benares, India, Brahmin priests performing death rituals accept money only after an elaborate ritual of refusal performed to avoid spiritual pollution;[30] in imperial Rome, the labour of slaves was kept separate from the work of artisans through their ritual dehumanization and 'social death'.

Under capitalism, however, these two productive and moral orders are confused leading to a peculiar split consciousness. One part is made of fragmented objects, people and environments and impersonal forces called profit, utility, success. Generally, this part is associated with the workplace. The other part is made of intimate connections – between objects, people and places – personal and meaningful social relations and a benign environment, generally associated with the realm of 'home' (Carrier, 1992). Such split consciousness is reflected in the wage system. This valorizes only those forms of *work* that take place inside the productive realm of the factory and devalues the reproductive (and 'unproductive') *labour* that goes into the reproduction of people. On the other hand, however, the wage relation devalues productive work too – to such an extent that it makes workers dependent on the supposedly non-capitalist realm of kinship for survival.

Silvia Federici (2012), in particular, argues that the reproductive and affective labour performed overwhelmingly by women is systematically devalued and exploited under capitalism and that the sphere of social reproduction is one of the many human commons that is constantly under threat of occupation by capital (De Angelis, 2017). For Cathi Weeks (2011), it is precisely by expanding the de-commodified condition of reproductive labour to the whole edifice of work that women can lead the broader process of de-commodification of capitalist society.

Elsewhere[31] I have analysed the structural and multi-scalar entanglements between productive and reproductive labour through the work of anthropologist Claude Meillassoux, particularly, his focus on the entanglement of capitalism and kinship both among traditional pastoral communities and contemporary Western societies. In both contexts, wage contracts deprive workers of their means of subsistence, making them dependent both on domestic labour and on commodity markets.

After the French colonization of Guroland (Ivory Coast), foreign food and agricultural companies destroyed the local self-subsistence agriculture, employing local peasants as wage workers and underpaying them, thus forcing them to rely on the domestic labour of their kin for survival. As well as incorporating the family system into the capitalist system, colonial industrialization created masses of dispossessed peasant proletarians who migrated circularly between factories and villages to survive. For Meillassoux (1964: 58), the forced circular migration of the Guro people was akin to that of the impoverished rural workers in the early capitalist Europe. For the French anthropologist, labour mobility is a central prerequisite for capitalist accumulation in the centre, too. For instance, he presents ethnographic evidence of how a big share of the workforce of a French multinational corporation consisted of underpaid African workers on short-term and precarious contracts, surviving on domestic and informal labour.

Moreover, anticipating the reality of contemporary flexible capitalism, Meillassoux (1981: 92) highlights how South-to-North circular migration of wage workers is central to the functioning of capitalism. North African migrant workers employed in the French company were paid three times less in indirect wages than French workers, and this wage differential was justified through racialized categorization.

Thus, Meillassoux reworks anthropologically Trotsky's notion of 'combined and uneven development', unveiling ethnographically the historical, spatial and ideological oscillatory entanglements between production and reproduction. He shows that capitalism cannot be separated from imperialism, intended as brutal movement of colonization and occupation of the sphere of reproduction, and in fact is structurally but unevenly related to underdevelopment in those parts of the world where extraction of reproductive labour is possible. Besides, in his book on African slavery, Meillassoux (1986) shows how slavery, capitalism and war form a unique and interconnected economic system and how, in addition to class relations being reproduced in non-capitalist societies, capitalism is *internally* constructed through the non-capitalist relations of kinship, war and slavery.

We can now appreciate how capital operates speculatively: by disconnecting geographically, temporally and morally the sites of production from those of reproduction, so that movement, relationality and agency experienced in the former realm translate into stillness, atomization and impotence in the latter, and the abstract, de-territorialized and structural conflicts between labour and capital are localized, humanized and culturally re-embedded. We can also appreciate how the polarization between productive and unproductive labour reproduces itself on several levels: at the level of the individual (between selfishness and generosity), the household (between men and women), the city (between factories and households), the region (between city and countryside) and at the global level (between the global North and the global South).

As well as progressive separation, labour alienation under capitalism can be read in terms of progressive stasis and loss of potency. Factory production breaks the relationships that workers have with each other in the workplace, with their environment and with the objects they produce by constraining their movements inside factories, the movement of their hands and bodies inside machines, and the movement of the objects they produce inside markets. Excluded from the dense texture of exchanges, circulations and movements that normally accompanies human relations, capitalist workers experience their lives in terms of exhaustion, impotence, precariousness and temporal stasis. Their strength and energy appear to have been taken from them, incorporated into the movements of the industrial machines, which Veblen described as 'parasites' sucking the workers' energies[32] and Marx as gigantic anthropomorphic monsters whose mechanical limbs, tools and movements incorporated and replicated those of the workers but on a much bigger scale.

In the current, post-industrial capitalist era, labour takes the immaterial form of general intellect and is extracted at the infrastructural, rather than superstructural, and biopolitical levels. This shift from material to immaterial labour does not alter the fundamental relationship between labour and capital. Instead, it makes the former even more impotent, immobile and spectral vis-à-vis the infinite mobility and animism of the latter.

Thus, if outside capitalism labour partakes in the political economy of life, merging the realm of production with that of reproduction, the wage contract reduces human actions to gestures of impermanence and breaks the vital flow that connects people with their kin, their objects and their environments.

It is wrong to assume that in zones of non-capitalism the tension between production and reproduction is absent. All societies go through an inner conflict between passion and interest, money and gifts, inside and outside, self and other and between the individualism that comes from the fear of death and the egalitarianism that comes from embracing the prospect of self-annihilation. But under capitalism these unconscious emotions and impulses are repressed and compartmentalized into separate realms, and their connection obscured. In non-capitalist zones, however, unconscious drives are openly acknowledged through often violent and terrifying rituals and cosmologies. In other words, the unconscious is productive,[33] and social cohesion emerges precisely from the collective framing, unveiling, reworking and negotiation of these unconscious drives and emotions.

These collective rituals and co-poietic practices are 'reproductive labour' – that is to say, they are actions that remove blockages, mend ruptures, reinstate the commons and populate the world with new social relations. They make the world come alive again.

Take, for instance, the *Naven* ceremony among the Iatmul of Papua New Guinea, a male puberty ritual analysed by anthropology Bateson.[34] *Naven* gives voice to the fears and anxieties associated with inequalities between sexes and generations and re-enacts gender and intergenerational conflicts to the point of rupture, where the community sees the possibility of its own self-annihilation. *Navens* are performed in celebration of the acts and achievement of the *laua* (sister's child) who is symbolically adopted by their maternal uncle. In their more elaborated form *Navens* involve collective transvestism, in which men and women compete in caricaturing each other.

First, the mother's *laua* strips naked. Then, the mother's brother (*wau*) appears, dressed in broken, dirty and grotesquely exaggerated female costumes. The *wau* offers his nephew food in exchange for precious shells. With this offer the *wau* becomes the *laua*'s mother. Then the *laua* disappears. The *wau* looks for him everywhere. This is terrifying for the *laua*. As soon as the *wau* finds him, he performs heavily homoerotic gestures on his nephew's body, in exaggerated sexual gestures. This is so humiliating for the *lauas* that they often burst out crying. Then all the women become powerful and aggressive men, dressed up in beautiful warrior-like costumes. The paternal aunt becomes 'the father' and beats the *laua* up. The *laua*'s older brother's wife becomes his older brother, also beating him up. The *laua's* sister becomes his brother and dresses up in colourful male costumes. *Naven* is a statement of solidarity between the ego and his maternal clan, an affirmation of the principle of affinity in a small society dominated by the patrilinear logic which exposes the fragility of the existing male-dominated order. At the same time, it is a theatre where all identities are grotesquely negated and reversed, but empathy for 'the other' and solidarity across sexes and generations is established.

For example, the artificiality of the solidarity between the *wau* and the *laua* is emphasized when they become wife and husband. There is a fundamental equality and symmetry between men that cannot be denied. On the other hand, the *Naven* shows that relationships between fathers and sons are based not only on competition but also on identification and generosity. The *wau* helps the *laua* only symbolically – by transmitting ritual knowledge, holding him during the ritual of scarification and being proud of his new status. But he does so with an expectation of return. Thus, the *laua* and the *wau* are in a relation of reciprocal exchange, not of generosity. Unlike maternal uncles, fathers help their sons economically and without any expectations of return. It is the father, for instance, who pays the bride wealth or who gives the *laua* the goods to repay the flamboyant offer of the *wau*. In the *Naven*, the father/son relation is competitive, but free and disinterested. There is an implicit understanding that the son will take the father's place and that the two roles will never overlap. The father encourages the son to progress and to take his place; the son defends the dignity of the father. Unlike the normal Iatmul ethos, where older men are ostentatious boasters, in the ritual it is the sons who boast for their fathers.

What kind of gender roles does the *Naven* ritual re-enact? The father is humble and puts himself down. He must be defended by his proud son. The uncle is an exaggerated, violent and loud transgender individual who takes advantage of the younger nephew. Iatmul society has no chiefs or fixed rules and is constantly open to fissions. In this context, self-realization and flamboyance are paramount. But the *Naven* ceremony reveals the flaws and fragility of male ostentatiousness and theatricality, and men's material dependence on the labour of women. The men's exaggerated and theatrical behaviour is both exposed and overpowered by the women's strength and warrior-like beauty. Moreover, women give up their normal role of main producers[35] and become boasters and idle like Iatmul men. Fictionalized and made public, male attitudes look ridiculous, sterile and mean.

Balancing the opposite psychic forces of competition and solidarity, hierarchy and egalitarianism, *Naven* is a collective and theatrical reflection on the productivity of social relations, the actions that erase roles and institutions, and the infinitively fluid psychic and physical boundaries of communities which, according to Bateson, ramify and branch out 'like rhizomes of a lotus' (Bateson, 1942: 249).

I call these reproductive gestures and rituals that re-introduce movement and openness into fixed and static human institutions – such as kinship, gender, states or work – and socialize knowledge and emotions, art/commons.

That non-Western art is a form of reproductive labour is evident in the way the reified notions of 'aesthetics' or 'artwork', or the special agency of the artist, are absent. Among the Yolngu of New Guinea,[36] for example, individuals gain no reward or status for their work as artists, and individual creativity has no positive role. The *mardayn* paintings, which take days, even months, to make are often destroyed or covered within hours, even minutes, of their completion. Made at important moments for the community – burials, marriages or puberty – these paintings are not intended to represent the ancestors, but to reproduce their magical designs (which give access to the land's sacred geography and invisible patterns of ownership) and convey their ancestral power. Indeed, the best indigenous craftsmen can trigger dizziness, extreme happiness or intoxication with their shimmering cross-hatching patterns, carnal bright-red colours, intricate mazes and pulsating lines. These paintings are reproductive inasmuch they establish a common space between ancestors, craftsmen and the community, socialize sacred and restricted knowledge, and externalize the strong emotions associated with moments of loss, love or self-enrichment.

Likewise, for the Piaroa people of the Amazonian Orinoco Basin, aesthetics is a political and ethical category associated with those gestures and artefacts that negate hierarchy and reproduce the community. Aesthetics is constitutive of how people care for each other and keep at bay the poisonous productive and individualistic forces of the cosmos, so that beauty is normally associated with collective work or with the reproductive labour of the shamans, whose beautiful deep-red necklaces are 'beads of life' fallen from the gods' crystal boxes (Overing, 1989). Another example is the poetry and storytelling of the Pintupi-speaking Aborigines of the Australian western desert, through which multiple claims over the land are accommodated and which are 'looked after' by the elders and passed down, in the form of gift, to the next generation (Myers, 1991).

Thus, non-Western art is reproductive and prefigurative in that it opens an imaginary, cooperative, participatory and performative space which corresponds to the political notion of the commons highlighted above. And inasmuch they allow one to travel outside one's body, seeing oneself from afar and entering into other people's bodies; move in and out the sacred land of the Dreaming; beautify others; magnify their potency and build solidarity between humans and non-humans, these reproductive gestures are also magical. And although they cannot be defined as artistic or aesthetic in the Western sense, all these gestures share the same technical mastery, a specific form of framing, dwelling and telling which creates a 'threshold' space which prefigures – in public, unmediated, cruel, raw and dramatic ways – the universal struggle between the movement of identification with the collective (which blurs differences and inequalities and creates solidarity) and the movement of detachment through which individuals mark their existence autonomously from the group. In this magical space where artefacts, artwork and images with complex intentionalities and enchanting power are produced and made to circulate, the human struggle between entrapment, containment and freedom is replayed and socialized. It is through the collective re-enactment of these superstructural and superhuman forces that post-capitalist societies reproduce the commons.

Under capitalism, in contrast, art and economy operate as separate and complementary institutions of objectification, externalization and ossification of life as aesthetic value and exchange value construe each other in a specular way in the imaginary space where life exceeds itself. Western art reproduces capitalism's split consciousness. On the one hand it is the unproductive and de-commodified gesture par excellence, whose value exists only aesthetically and immaterially and is actualized in the public realm; that is to say, in its contribution to the 'high' intellectual and spiritual spheres of societies. On the other hand, it is a unique, precious and authorial gesture, material and materialistic enough, embodied in dead artefacts whose monetary value is concretized in private markets and stored in private homes, museums and galleries.

Artwork is central to the whole capitalist edifice because it embodies both 'what money cannot buy' (that is, the capitalist ideology of scarcity that negates the 'liberal illusion'[37] that money is a social leveller) and extreme commodification in the form of purely abstract value, akin to financial value. Bourgeois art sustains and reproduces capitalist schizophrenia through the dialectic of commodification of the artwork and de-commodification of artistic labour; de-functionalization and sacralization; mental abstraction and market extraction. In this schizophrenic space, where the absolute commodity meets the absolute artwork, what gets lost is human agency. So that every time we think we are dwelling in the spiritual realm of beauty, as makers or beholders, we forget that our capture by images, themselves entrapped and enslaved, bears witness to capitalism's regressive history of human and non-human enslavement, and to the timeless agency of the master. We forget the nexus between art, entrapment and slavery.[38]

In fact the history of Western art is marked by the progressive neutralization of the power of images to haunt us, move us and displace us, and come alive – a history of exorcism, containment and immobilization within sacred and political superstructures – and by the experience of a stable world under constant threat by some freak underground movement, like the uncontrolled gush of red paint flowing from the cushion of Vermeer's lacemaker; the foam rising around Icarus's crushing body, as he fell to his death, affecting and infecting Brueghel's haunting vision; the electric colour condensations in the clouds of Turner, or in Van Gogh's stars, or Rodin's sculptures whose form, according to Simmel, was carved out of the commodity's unbound movements and the melting away of matter – an image that inspired Leon Trotsky to imagine the communist revolution as a similar liquid transfiguration of matter into movement.

The struggle of images against the static, autonomous and ossified realm of the commodity form, and for the reconnection of art and life, was the task taken up by the Western historical avant-garde: in the celebration of everyday objects and chance events by Duchamp and the surrealists; the blurring of form and content in Malevich's black square (and of figure and ground in Mondrian's open matrixes); the fragments, fissures and collages of Eisenstein's cinema and the jumps, cuts, imperfect annotations and cruel associations (*Kriegsfibel*), in Brecht's notebooks, suspended between empathy and detachment, and where images *take position* in front of the beholder (Didi-Huberman, 2018).

For some art historians, the main achievement of the historical avant-garde was to open up a grey zone, neither productive nor reproductive, which, even if did not completely negate, at least suspended the logic of capitalism. Duchamp's ready-made existed in such a grey zone – fluidly navigating between 'art' and 'life'; the commodity and the object; and the museum, the market and the rubbish dump (the schizophrenic space I described above). Moreover, the work of the readymade negated the productive skills of the professional artist and the manual worker and valorized instead the speculative, conceptual and immaterial labour of the non-commercial and non-professionalized artist – a labour which was neither individual and personal, nor acquired value in the artist's private studio, but emerged performatively, regardless of the author's agency, from the encounter between the artwork and the public (Roberts, 2007).

The Western avant-garde's critical engagement with capitalism rested on the appropriation of non-Western ontologies of movement – for example, in certain Cubist paintings or Futurist sculptures.[39] It is in the field of performance, a 'minor art' par excellence, that the fluid and ritual politics of movement of non-capitalist societies becomes a powerful critique of the commodity form – in the cabaret nihilism of the Zurich branch of Dada; Tino Seghal's social games; Yvonne Rainer's deconstructions of capitalist labour or the cruel assemblies of Anne Imhof (Wood, 2018). But even if public assemblies, Situationist *détournements*, socially engaged choreographies and direct actions performatively subvert the existing social canon, they do so within temporally and spatially demarcated and segregated spaces – the enclosures of art and politics – with the objective of challenging if not neutering, state violence and re-enacting their coming together as egalitarian communities. Unlike these, in the tragic and often violent non-capitalist rituals, communities face the horizon of their own annihilation, and this experience of self-annihilation is foundational for the construction of the egalitarian order.

Adorno believed that art had such power of movement outside the commodity form and that by 'separating itself from what it developed out of' (1970: 5) – like a larva bursting out of its shell – it could prefigure life outside capitalism (Roberts, 2015b). But this existence outside the status of objecthood was short-lived and circumscribed – just 'an afterimage of empirical life'. Thus, Western avant-garde artists are at best tragic heroes (Bürger, 1974) whose experiments were successful only insofar as they showed the limits of their utopian horizon, their dysfunctional existence within capitalism, their inability to exist beyond the imaginary and bring about real change in the form of collectivization of the means of production, anarchy or social revolution.

For Adorno, such temporary and critical detachment of art from capitalism was triggered by the power of negative dialectics. In fact, with the exception of Marx, who knew how to think about movement, Western dialectics is merely an optical illusion stemming from the eternal return of schizophrenic divisions, oppositions and polarizations and the longing to go back to the lost original unity. The Western artist is a juggler, an illusionist creating dioramas of moving objects and spectacles of connectedness, out of stasis, separation and stillness. The non-capitalist artist, in contrast, is a shaman weaver, seamlessly mending holes and reconnecting the broken threads to the totality all around.

But it can also be argued that the avant-garde artist is the neoliberal subject par excellence (Vishmidt, 2018) – the self-promoting entrepreneur, the multi-skilled team worker, the speculative social capitalist. In fact, what the speculative and immaterial labour of the conceptual artist of the early twentieth century prefigured and pre-enacted was not life outside capitalism, but the operation of finance and the abstraction of the general intellect which were already in full swing in the 1920s[40] and which culminated in the new spirit of capitalism of the 1980s. It was under the system of mass production that the de-commodified, non-alienated (=creative) and abstract labour of the conceptual artist and the bohemian genius became the ideological blueprint for the intellectual labour of managers and skilled workers – under which the workers' souls 'were made to work'.

Indeed, Duchamp challenged and negated not only the capitalist notion of productive or useful labour, but also the figure of the wage worker whose lives depended on selling labour power to the capitalists. Instead of selling labour-power in exchange of wages, the Duchampian artists sells ideas, even their persona, for a fee, whose opaque economy follows criteria of age, gender, race and class and is sustained by a complex apparatus of 'pimping' (Rolnik, 2006) – curators, museum directors and critics – whose function is, in fact, to un-aestheticize and repress human vulnerability and put creativity, autonomy and the senses in the service of capital. But if the figure of the curator as pimp may hold true, that of the artist as prostitute is disingenuous, if not romantic and self-aggrandizing.[41]

The contemporary artist is closer to the figure of the overexploited service worker or the slave than to that of the prostitute, although these roles historically often overlapped. To begin with, let us consider the continuities between slavery and capitalism.[42] Both are ideologies of production of social aliens and of systematic devaluation and extraction of their reproductive labour. Secondly, slaves, like precarious workers, are 'outsiders' – social aliens and quasi-humans who don't belong to the community and whose inferiority is ritually constructed, publicly performed and branded upon their very bodies, most often in racial terms. Thirdly, precarious workers, like slaves, are often forced migrants, and once they have settled, they are captives. Their movements are predetermined and restricted. Fourthly, they are rendered impotent that is, separated from their kin, unable to give life and to reproduce themselves. Lastly, unlike the insider members of the community, for whom social entanglement is desirable, slaves aspire to social freedom – through manumission, escape, personal enrichment or revolutions.

Present in all societies at all times, slavery becomes 'a system' only under capitalism. Class distinctions under capitalism not only reinforce pre-existing forms of slavery, labour extraction and social alienation. They make these permanent and naturalized in the form of institutionalized racism and patriarchy so that the bodies of women and of people of colour can be systematically occupied and violated; their power to give life systematically negated, and their movements are forcibly regulated to maximize capital's profits. The first great wave of capitalist expansion in the sixteenth century coincided with the Atlantic slave trade and the inquisition, two forms of institutionalized enslavement and biological management of people of colour and of women.[43]

In the plantations of Brazil or the US south in the nineteenth century, the most common reason for slaves' manumission was their ability to entertain their masters, by playing some instruments, acting or dancing. For Hartman (1997), the fact that slaves' subjection was linked to their master's artistic pleasure discredited the black pained body and 'defamiliarized negro enjoyment'. At the same time, art was a fundamental skill for slaves' survival – just as was their command of skilled crafts such as carpentry or weaving. In its idealized depictions of distant gods and kings, Western art in pre-capitalist times was reproductive labour too akin to slavery, but in the gentler form of aristocratic patronage.

There are striking similarities between the figure of the slave, the lumpenproletariat and the contemporary artist. Artists and lumpenproletarians work for a master – the often male, curator, dealer or the patron – who controls their lives and whose own life is enhanced or enriched by their slaves' labour. Moreover, the work of artists, like that of slaves and the lumpenproletarian, is wageless since the vast majority of artists don't make a living out of their work. But they dream of emancipating themselves one day and becoming free. Like slaves, artists are considered social aliens, and their reproduction, especially for women artists, is considered inimical to work production. Their only permitted kinship is among their own community or with the male curator or gallerist (the ringmaster, pimp or patriarch) who may grant them conditional freedom. The figures of the artist, the slave and the lumpenproletarian embody the generalized human condition of extreme imposed precarity, flexibility and casualization of labour and neo-bondage under contemporary capitalism. Thus, as for those runaway slaves who set up egalitarian and autonomous communities (*quilombos*), the artist's withdrawal of labour has the potential to undermine the entire capitalist and colonialist edifice. My question is not 'What can art do to end work?' but 'How can art end slavery? That is to say: put an end to the generalized commodification of our bodies – their abstraction and extraction by capitalism?'

We now understand that the refusal of wage work by the historical avant-garde reflected the privileged position of the affluent cosmopolitan male white bourgeoisie who was spared the destitution of manual jobs. But its hatred of manual labour and ethos of autonomy and freedom, encapsulated so well in Kant's writings, were neither aristocratic nor anti-capitalist, *pace* Beech (2019). In fact, quite the opposite. The bourgeois tropes of beauty and freedom emerged at a time of slave rebellions and abolitionism, when it was clear that Western capitalism, in order to survive, had to incorporate slavery *inside* itself, instead of keeping it hidden in the colonies.

Thus, the white middle classes experienced the ideologies of freedom, idleness and beauty in the context of extreme insecurity and fear, and through the prism of slavery, although this fear and terror of enslavement were repressed and disguised under the supposedly autonomous realm of art.[44] Indeed, between the playful creativity of the bourgeoisie and the industriousness of the proletariat stood the artfulness of the lumpenproletarian and the surplus population, whose tricks, swindles and struggles to reproduce life anew everyday embodied the generalized conditions of capitalism and the haunting presence within it of slavery. The Romantic poet Friedrich Schiller's indignant attitude towards both the idleness of the wealthy and the painful labour of the proletariat was the last cry of the 'fine artist', before they were swallowed up by the mechanical reproduction, the prosthetic imagination and the wageless life of the Duchampian avant-garde.

Moreover, does not the male refusal of productive labour negate also the value of reproductive labour, as some feminist artists have argued for some time? In what ways can the reproductive function of art be rescued from slavery and put in the service of the commons? What would it mean to reimagine reproductive labour as a form of art?

To liberate and decolonize the political imaginary, the first task for the contemporary artist is that of undoing mastery (a Western capitalist concept), embracing those reproductive practices historically performed by slaves, outcasts, enemies, carers – mostly women, black or ethnic-minority precarious workers – and opening up relational spaces where co-emergence, co-dependency and mutualism are valued, not despised. That is to say: the revolutionary avant-garde must reflect on the conditions for the possibility of the abolition of both capitalism and colonialism.

Abstraction and the avant-garde: A historical interlude

I have argued that abstraction is the aesthetic movement that both transcends and reproduces the commodity form under capitalism. Following Worringer, I have also emphasized that under capitalism abstraction is entangled with the opposite movement of concretization and that it is through this productive tension that capital is prefigured and realized in the realms of art and the economy.

I will now sketch a brief history of the relationship between the Western avant-garde and political economy. In contextualizing the political avant-garde within the broader development of capitalism, I argue that every artistic gesture[45] of abstraction and detachment from capital generates a countermovement of concretization and identification with it. Thus, I frame my narrative in terms of the tension between, on the one hand, artistic and curatorial gestures aimed at transcending the logic of capitalism and the commodity form, and on the other, the work of capital which captures, appropriates and concretizes these gestures, turning them into concrete manifestations of profit which are alien to the artists' original intents. Artist Liam Gillick describes the Sisyphean struggle of abstraction as follows: '[T]he endurance of abstraction is rooted in this desire to keep showing the impossibility and elusiveness of the abstract. At the same time, it reveals the process of manipulation that takes place within the unaccountable realm of capital – the continual attempt to concretize abstract relations in the service of capital' (2011: 25).

'Ethnographic surrealism' (Clifford, 1981) – intended as a movement of defamiliarization of the familiar and of intimate proximity with the other: a movement of critique and proposition – was one of such modernist anti-capitalist avant-gardes, consisting of artists and anthropologists. Anthropologists travelled to far distant societies looking for those forms of human organizations that maximized social creativity and self-expression. Outside the West they found cooperative work, fluid clan structures, shamanism, co-housing, gift-giving and intellectual commons which radically challenged the oppressive capitalist institutions of states, churches, families, parties and corporations. Following the opposite movement, surrealist artists created powerful ethnographies of industrial cities, showing the cosmological and irrational basis of the capitalist economy, the terror of modern states, the repressed sexuality generated by nuclear families and the human body as dream machine, alienated social technology and medium of exchange. Eli Lotar's cruel photographs of urban slaughterhouses showed the wild side of capitalist mass consumption, while capitalism's ideologies of scarcity, competition and self-interest were being challenged by the economies of excess, waste and generosity of Maori gift-giving and the Kwakiutl potlatch.

In addition, the familiarity with strangers and the detachment from the familiar felt by the European avant-garde reflected the traumatic experience of the First World War, when its 'civilization' seemed on the brink of extinction. The machine fragments, defaced bodies and human prostheses depicted by Futurist and Cubist artists functioned as '*anaesthetic*'[46] cure that sealed, isolated and repressed the traumatic memory of that conflict. More than in terms of victory or failure, the history of the Western avant-garde can be described as one of melancholy, repression, repetition and recuperation of what was lost with the end of history and of modern(ist) capitalism (Foster, 1995).

My periodization of the end of modern(ist) capitalism and the beginning of late (or postmodern) capitalism is the late 1960s – a time of counterculture, Third World power and deep economic restructuring. But the reason is also autobiographical. I was born two weeks before the astronaut Neil Armstrong touched the surface of the moon, and also a few days before the death of my paternal grandfather. I remember my father saying that these were confusing times, when we were all a bit 'floating in a limbo'. Growing up in Milan – where high fashion, de-industrialization, stock-market capitalism, yuppiedom, neo-fascism and the clan structure of the Sicilian Mafia all converged in the grotesque characters of Berlusconi – the feeling of being afloat in a foreign medium, and of confusion between the celebration of the new and the mourning of the old, never ceased. This feeling continues until the present days, when the world seems still to be under the lunar spell, daydreaming and suspended in the twilight zone, between light and darkness.

First movement: Between the moon and the desert

On 25 July 1969, the issue of *Time* titled 'Man on the Moon' comes out, with its cover image of the first man ever to walk on the moon. Inside it, the article 'A Giant Leap for Mankind' describes the cosmonaut Neil Armstrong as he slowly descends the ladder of the Apollo 11, looking like as white as a ghost, tentatively extends his left foot, as if to test the water in a pool, and then leaps into the dark space in a gesture of self-annihilation. By zooming in on the cosmonaut's abstract gestures – similar to those of a painter drawing a line on a blank canvass – the article conveys the feeling of mastery, displacement and wonder of a humanity which, by entering into an unknown space, was becoming alien to itself.

On page 55 of the same magazine, an article entitled 'The Original Affluent Society' describes the life of the !Kung people of the Kalahari Desert in South Africa. The !Kung are nomadic hunters and gatherers who, in their simple tribal life, have developed communist practices and a strong anti-capitalist ethos. The !Kung have limited wants; hence, they spend only a small part of their day in productive activities. Moreover, lacking complex technologies of production, they have no social hierarchies or gendered divisions of labour. Their nomadic economy, unlike agriculture or industry, is neither private nor public but based on commoning and sharing and mutual psychic and material exchanges between animals, humans and the environment. On the one hand, these hunters and gatherers embodied the spirit of the anti-capitalist movement of May 1968 for instance: André Gorz's (1985) celebration of idleness, and advocacy for the end of labour. At the same time, however, this image of tribal life revealed the gap between communism as a living practice and communism as a construction of middle-class urbanites and intellectuals.

In fact, is it not paradoxical that the cosmonaut – travelling through blackness and towards the end of history in weightless and abstract trajectories – found himself trapped, a few pages later, in the white heat, small-scale economies and material harshness of life in the desert?

The image of the cosmonaut resonated with the spirit of the time. In 1968, the painter Tambellini discussing the colour black with Piet Mondrian, Ad Reinhardt and Cecil Taylor compares abstract art to the experience of outer space of the Soviet cosmonaut Yuri Gagarin – the first man in space:

Here again is a primitive man, a caveman, but he's the caveman of the space era. I see him as the most important man. Its's immaterial who he is: it's immaterial what his name is. But that's what our children are going to be. It's what the future is going to be. He's got to get rid of this whole concept of black picture or of black anything as a physical object. He is got to realize that he is black right now.[47]

For Tambellini the cosmonaut is a metaphor for the power of art to dematerialize life, free the imagination from patriarchal, racist and capitalist entanglements, and embrace humanity's own darkness. Tambellini gives shape to this vision in his painting *We Are the Primitives of a New Era* (1961) in which a black concentric force creates its own centre of gravity in an otherwise white cosmos, marked in a forensic black Courier typeface: 'We are the primitives of a new era'.

Likewise, artist Adrian Piper describes abstraction as a flight, an act of freedom, a radical political erasure:

> [A]bstraction is a flight. It is freedom from the immediate spatiotemporal constraints of the moment; freedom to plan the future, recall the past, comprehend the present from a reflective perspective that incorporates the three; freedom from the possible boundaries of concrete subjectivities, freedom to imagine the possible and transport oneself into it; freedom to survey the real as a resource for embodying the possible. ('Flying', 1987)

Piper turns abstraction into a statement of black emancipation in her *Everything* series, consisting of black-and-white photographs of people of colour whose faces have been erased, their defaced bodies framed by the typewritten sentence: 'Everything will be taken away'.[48]

That movement of social abstraction which started among a small circle of painters and cosmonauts in the late 1960s, those first symptoms of late capitalism – the discovery of the self in the black cosmos, the primitive desert at the end of time, the cosmic infinity of the simple line – would hit the ground of planet earth much later, only in the 1980s, when the first makeshift lunar rockets, space-travelling machines and diaries of dissident cosmonauts were found in derelict flats and working-class buildings in Moscow shortly before the fall of communism.

This cosmic post-socialist diaspora was captured in 1985 by Russian artist Ilya Kabakov in his reconstruction of the apartment of a man who flew into space on 14 April 1982. The apartment is in a poor communal building in Moscow. From the neighbours we know that the lodger in this room was lonely and that he was a builder and lived very poorly, without any furniture, using the communal kitchen only to boil tea. We know that he had a grand theory – that the universe was permeated by huge sheets of energy which lead up somewhere. We know that in all probability this astronaut, sealed in plastic sacks, used the makeshift catapult he built in his room to gain initial velocity and hook up with one of these gigantic upward streams of energy, which he called petals.

We know that the voyage of the Russian proletariat away from socialist realism and into the abstract spaces of capitalism was also a hard fall back into a new dark era of primitive economy, based on market oligarchy, bartering and corporate Mafia – the 'second-hand time' poetically documented by Svetlana Alexievich (2016). Indeed, what the Russian cosmonaut left behind was the onset of the global economic crisis, the oil shock, colonial independence and the intensification of Third World power, the decline of Keynesian (welfare) capitalism and Taylorism and the deregulation of capital and labour, which kick-started neoliberalism and the beginning of the end of history in the 1990s.

Below I argue that the reorganization of capitalism in the early 1970s was accelerated, if not triggered, by two artistic and cultural trends, both prefigured in the issue of *Time* magazine mentioned above. The first artistic trend continued the cosmonaut's journey towards abstraction, but, veering away from the spiritual detachment of Mondrian, Kandinski and Barnett, its gesture was one of over-identification with capitalism, as in the celebration of the allure of commodities in Robert Morris's mirrored cubes, and Jeff Koons's rabbit mirrors (the former prefiguring the immaterial value of art's expanded field; the latter its materialization in the luxury commodity form), or in the cybernetics utopias and authorless productive algorithms of Arte Programmata, an early materialization of the poetry of finance. Indeed, the abstractionism of the neo-avant-garde – Abstract Expressionism, Minimalism and Pop Art – pushing the boundaries of perception to the edge of nothingness[49] framed the cultural logic of late capitalism as a new vision of Western democracy.

The second artistic trend moved away from lunar abstraction and followed the hunters and gatherers instead, retreating from the state, the museum and the capitalist market and operating nomadically, in camper vans, in the metro, in the streets or in self-organized spaces. Here the counterhegemonic gesture of the avant-garde operated at the level of organizations and institutions rather than at the formal level, although the struggle continued to be about forms of living.

The 1970s marked the global proliferation of artist-run spaces – Printed Matter and Franklin Furnace in New York; Zona in Florence; Western Front in Vancouver; Art Metropole in Toronto; La Mamelle and MOCA in San Francisco and Artpool in Budapest, to name but a few. 'Dropped-out' artists set up self-determined, autonomous and underground organizations operating horizontally and collectively, refusing the capitalist logic of profit and sharing resources and labour. Just as factories ought to be run by workers and universities by students, it was claimed that art organizations should be run by artists. These early forms of artistic commons saw themselves as autonomous and located *outside* capitalism (that is, outside both the market and the state), but due to their rigid boundaries, they turned into claustrophobic, regimented and dysfunctional middle-class enclaves.

These organizations refused the socialist collective model, basing themselves instead on the cooperativist model that existed in the global South or in the Eastern European block. But, paradoxically, these non-profit organizations and cooperatives ended up being run like flexible capitalist firms, the equivalent of today's Silicon Valley start-ups.

The second artistic gesture of retreat from the state and the market was relational art. Like Situationism and Fluxus in the 1960s, relational art operated in the sphere of social relations and was anti-institutional. But there were important differences. Theorized by curator Nicolas Bourriaud (1998), relational aesthetics refused the grand narratives of marginality, class struggle and direct action, including anti-racism, feminism and environmentalism, which the French curator considered as 'the most die-hard forms of conservatism'. Instead, relational art sought to build transient and site-specific communities and day-to-day micro utopias in kitchens, airport lounges and playgrounds. The value of relational art emerged from impermanent gestures of reciprocity and conviviality located at the margins of capitalism – in the 'social interstices' and fleeting economies of barter, autarchy and gift-giving.

With their idioms of participation, autonomy, horizontality, teamwork, reciprocity and diffused authorship, both artists-run spaces and relational art reflected, even prefigured, the new spirit of capitalism – the financialization and dematerialization of the economy, the productivity of the 'general intellect' (a form of biopolitical capital associated with post-industrial economies) and the neoliberal phase of capitalism schizophrenically combining repressive state institutions and horizontal, fluid and precarious forms of sociability.

But let us explore in more detail the organizational shift taking place in art and the economy in the 1980s. Made possible by global capital and labour deregulation, phenomenal IT advances and the brutal curbing of labour rights, the proliferation of small-scale and flexible organizations reflected capital's response to the crisis of Fordism, state-led monopoly capitalism, anti-colonial struggles, and the raise of Third World power. Both in managerial and radical political circles, clan- and team-based, collective, horizontal, charismatic, even spiritual ways of running organizations replaced the vertical, hierarchical, individualistic and legal-rational authority of 'big states' and corporations. The philosophical critique of the rationalism, positivism and mono-dimensionality of capitalism levelled by the likes of Marcuse and Fromm gave way to a new bio-capitalist regime that made human subjectivity, creativity, spiritualism and egalitarianism productive.

Take, for instance, Ernst Schumacher's book *Small Is Beautiful: A Study of Economics as If People Mattered* written at the height of the oil crisis in 1973. Schumacher was the chief statistician of the British Control Commission and the National Coal Board – a company with 800,000 employees. *Small Is Beautiful* is a scathing critique of Western corporate capitalism based on an ecological, Buddhist and primitivist view of the economy, in which small-scale organizations, barter, DIY craftsmanship, veganism and forest gardening become the new benchmark of a new 'humane capitalism' (does it sound familiar?). This odd convergence of neoliberalism and Zen Buddhism is based on the following false primitivist assumptions: (1) the collective is more important than the individual; (2) horizontal is better than vertical; (3) small scale is better than large scale; (4) the local is better than the global; (5) simple tools, technology and skills are more egalitarian than complex technology; (6) the social can be separated from and opposed to the market; (7) the informal economy is a separate and more egalitarian realm than the formal economy; (8) communities are better than states; (9) non-work enhances artistic creativity; and (10) solidarity, autonomy, participation and democracy are a-historical and transcultural 'values' rather than sets of negotiated practices.

This 'small is beautiful' philosophy, emerging from the terminal crisis of Fordism and of Western supremacy, found fertile ground in the anarcho-primitivism of the middle classes. The main point of reference was anarchist philosopher Peter Kropotkin, whose theories of mutual aid and communal socialism, inspired by the Paris Commune of the 1870s, were antagonistic to those expressed by Marx in *The Capital*. Marx considered urbanization and mass industrialization as necessary stages to socialism, whereas Kropotkin supported small-scale production, integration between industry and agriculture, and self-organized workers-run firms. In addition, Kropotkin saw in the egalitarian social organization of non-Western societies a prefigurative model of how contemporary socialism could work, whereas for Marx these societies, having escaped industrial proletarianization and alienation, lacked the full consciousness of the proletarian masses and were stuck in a 'childlike' and unconscious kind of communism.

Also, in the 1970s there was a revival of primitivist and survivalist theories in social science. Tribalism, nomadism and hunter-gathering were presented as the alternatives to the mass production and conspicuous consumption of capitalism. Chicago anthropologist Marshall Sahlins (1972) famously argued that the hunters and gatherers of the Kalahari desert were the 'original affluent society'; anthropologist Pierre Clastres (1974) cast indigenous warfare as the structural base of egalitarianism among Amazonian tribes; Viveiros de Castro (1982) unveiled the magic, poetic and sophisticated perspectivist ontology of Amerindian societies, and feminist economists proposed a new notion of ecofeminism based on subsistence economies.[50]

It was on the abstract arc of Zen Buddhism and of the lean, nomadic and objectless livelihood of the hunters and gatherers that the reorganization of flexible capitalism was moulded upon, not only in organizational terms but also in its capitalization on poetry, mysticism and religion, as the new forms of immaterial labour. This celebration of tribalism, irrationalism and deep ecology also fed the primitivist imagination of neo-fascist cults and organizations.

This rejection of mainstream capitalist institutions and the fetishization of small-scale and primitive communities led to the so-called ethnographic turn in art and to the new figure of the artist as ethnographer – a variant on Walter Benjamin's artist as producer. Here the assumption is that 'the real' is 'the other', that this 'other' is located elsewhere and that the artist has privileged access to it. Unlike 'the other' of the Benjaminian modernist artist that is, the industrial proletariat, 'the other' of the artist as ethnographer is the subaltern, the indigenous, the ethnic or the white working class – racialized versions of the old proletariat. The ethnographic turn also assumes that, unlike this genuine 'other', we 'the Westerners' are the fake ones: the lost ones, the disenchanted, the ideologically brainwashed. As the art world becomes increasingly absorbed in the capitalist spectacle and forms of hyper-mediated reality, the primitive world offers a promise of access to primordial, 'unmediated' and authentic cultural forms, casting cultural authenticity as the new currency of the art world and of immaterial capitalism.

The second trend emerging from such an escape from capitalism was institutional critique. Cultural workers began to argue that the art institutions employing them were bourgeois governmental state apparatuses and sought to develop non-institutionalized and unmediated spaces for art. The philosophical root of institutional critique is 'immediatism': that is, the belief that human organizations can exist without institutionalization, in a state of flow – in an unmediated state. Conceptualized by anarchist philosopher Hakim Bey[51] (1994), immediatism understands human history as a progressive movement of institutionalization achieved through some form of human medium – such as language, writing and agriculture – leading to increasingly centralized and hierarchical social structures such as families, parties and states.

In fact, immediatism ignores the fact that every human and non-human organization is self-referential (autopoietic) and partially closed: that is, it operates according to sets of internal rules of survival and cooperation and these rules are not merely functional but also affective. It is the degree of such closure that distinguishes non-capitalist from capitalist societies. The former societies are self-organized, but also fluid and partially open. They prevent institutional closures by openly acknowledging the unconscious tensions and contradictions generated by these closures (such as patrilinearity in the case of *Naven*) and deal with them through shared cosmologies and often violent and terrifying rituals and re-enactments that generate collective responses and adjustments in relation to these closures. This ongoing performance of the unconscious, blurring and imploding base and superstructure fosters democratic institutions and structures which are cohesive but at the same time precarious, rhizomatic, infinitively plastic and in ongoing transformation. Capitalist institutions, on the contrary, are rigid, ossified and hierarchical, reflecting the systematic repression of the unconscious. Thus, the institutional critique's aim of abolishing (art) institutions is deeply Eurocentric. Andrea Fraser put it succinctly: '[W]e are the institution.'[52] The best we can do, as artists or as commoners, is to be aware of our institutionalization and set up public and collective rituals or conversations that systematically deconstruct it.

Thus, the commons and self-organizations that emerged in the late 1970s cast themselves as 'outside' the art market, the social-democratic museum and the reactionary colonialism of the old canon. They wanted to become heterotopias – extra-institutional and unmediated; that is, outside humanity. But in fetishizing the small scale and the (anti)institutional, this kind of art activism uncritically reproduced the anarcho-primitivism of the 1970s and its Eurocentric imagination. At best, such artistic movement inspired the middle-class retreat from society – experiments of immediatism, urban nomadism, poetic terrorism, communitarianism – but, more importantly, it led to a new phase of institutional consolidation of capitalism – horizontal, self-organized and ritualistic. These visions of 'communal luxury', these fantastical projections of primitive socialism are still alive in our social imagination. Their power to move us and pre-enact truly existing socialism is still with us. Let us not discard them yet.

Second movement: Confronting post-Fordism (1990s–2000s)

In this second movement, the cosmonaut realized that he had been fooled – that the moon and the desert are part of the same optical illusion, that there is no outside to capitalism and that he had reached the end of history.

In the 1970s, artists' organizations were proposing a new form of artisanal production in opposition to industrial production and mass commodification. Under post-Fordism, production and the real economy had disappeared (that is, moved to the global South) and capitalist value was created from circulation, consumption and speculation. The enemy was not mass production or the deadly rationality of corporate life, but the general intellect: that is, a new invisible immaterial capital, which had exited the factory and colonized all aspects of life.

Besides, in the 1980s, relational art framed its social engagement in terms of ethics, whereas the political art of the late 1990s and the 2000s was overtly anti-capitalist.

Political art in the age of post-Fordism took three forms. One was over-identification with capital's new commodity form (liquid, immaterial and derivative) and the logic of finance. Post-production, sampling, DJ-ing and collaging shifted the focus of artistic valorization from production to circulation. Also, just as Fred Wilson mined the museum in the early 1990s, a new breed of left-wing accelerationist guerrilla artists 'mined the net' in projects of electronic disturbance, digital currency, parasitical finance, chemical warfare and a new aesthetics of mis-recognition and dis-identification derived from the techniques of filtering, scrambling and encrypting of hacked drone videos, facial profiles and artificial neural networks. The hope was that, just as pre-modern forms of mining and capital extraction triggered slave revolts and postcolonial struggles, mining the net would produce new forms of biopolitical resistance by the *cyberproletariat*.[53]

Over-identification with capitalist biopolitics took place also in the field of performance art. Following Andrea Fraser's suggestion that 'we are the institutions', bodies became site of artistic experimentation and anti-capitalist struggle. Abstraction was now performed on the artists' very bodies. This followed the legacy of the performance and feminist art in the 1970s. But those performances of the 1970s challenged the anaesthetic regime of modernity by emphasizing bodily pain, self-disruption, erotic pleasure and the abject (think Schneemann, Yoko Ono and Abramovich); whereas the more recent anti-capitalist bodily abstractions were acts of depersonalization, corporatization and institutionalization of personhood. People became institutions or institutional conduits, working for institutions or like institutions or mock institutions like the *Yes Men*, whose corporate solution to the problem of slavery's global management was an inflatable golden body suit with a gigantic phallus. Additional challenges to the sexual logic of late capitalism are the depersonalization, self-commodification and biopolitical contestation of the artist's body in the forms of transgendering and pharmacological self-transmutations through synthetic drugs, sexual fluids and hormones.

The second gesture of artistic confrontation with post-Fordism was the recasting of artistic labour as reproductive labour by feminist artists, at a time when both kinds of labour were being heavily commodified with the expansion of the service economy. Here the precursors were Mary Kelly and Mierle Laderman Ukeles whose practices emphasized the affinity between artistic and reproductive labour. In Kelly's *Post-partum Document* patriarchy is deconstructed at the point of reproduction – that is, at the level of the intimate, intersubjective and sensuous collaboration between mother and child, and through the painstaking 'feminine' labour of archiving, collecting and transcribing the traces of such immaterial and fleeting relationships.

Some artists embraced the genre of 'occupational realism' (Bryan-Wilson, 2012), becoming workers, mainly in the service industry. For instance, since 1977, artists Mierle Laderman Ukeles has spent her residency at the New York Sanitation Department performing the tasks of cleaning, recycling and looking after the urban infrastructure, and calling these maintenance and service tasks as 'reproductive labour'. Deconstructing naturalizing approaches to female reproductive labour as well as its capitalist classification as unproductive, Laderman Ukeles framed 'maintenance art' in the broader sense of caring for and looking after non-human artefacts in the same way as motherhood is a form of maintenance of human beings and critically contrasted her reproductive artistic labour to the productivity which underpins art and work under capitalism. Besides, unlike the uncritical beautification of the public by some socially engaged or community-based artists, Laderman Ukeles's maintenance art valorized the liminal zone where the public meets the abject and the dirty.

More recently, inspired by the legacy of feminism, art-activism and occupational art[54] – from the artists' union in the 1930s to the Guerrilla Girls – the collective WAGE (Working Artist and the Greater Economy) advocated the regulated payment of artists' fees in the non-profit sector based on a work certification produced by the collective itself. Here, the historical Wages for Housework Campaign initiated by the International Feminist collective in Italy in 1972 acquired new relevance, as profits in the media and art sectors mainly rely on the unpaid labour of women and young people. But the activities of WAGE beg two questions. First, fair wages for artworkers (the commodification of artistic labour) may reproduce rather than challenge the commodity form, if anything because in a post-capitalist context, fair compensations should be at least partially de-monetized. Second, sociologically speaking, it is not clear whether unpaid cultural labourers really are a new kind of lumpenproletariat – in the world of Greg Sholette (2010) 'the dark matter' of the art world – or whether they are just a small (but growing) impoverished section of the 'creative (middle) classes' described by cultural impresario Richard Florida more than twenty years ago, who continue to be economically and socially much better off than the exploited unpaid service workers who make up the majority of the workforce of post-industrial capitalism. If this latter is the case, the revaluation of unpaid cultural labour lacks the material ground to foster a broader restructuring of labour under capitalism.

The third gesture confronting post-Fordism is participatory art, a more politicized version of relational aesthetics. Unlike the latter, participatory art critically reflects on the power relations between artists, audiences and collaborators and seeks to break these through forms of co-production, reciprocal exchange, collective decision-making and delegated performance. In the United States participatory art followed the legacy of the civil rights movement especially black and feminist activist self-help processes, group discussions and community work (I am thinking of the work of Suzanne Lacy). Its main goal was to develop some form of participatory democracy at a time when national politics was dominated by the extreme neoliberalism of the Reagan era. Joseph Beuys's idea that performance was some form of 'living sculpture' was still there. But the artists' concerns were political rather than aesthetic and dictated by their self-perception as 'public servants' (Jackson, 2011), civil activists and even NGO workers (Rogoff, 2016).

The turn from ethics to politics in participatory art followed the worldwide urban mobilizations and revolutions which started with the Arab Spring and the anti-austerity movements in Greece and Spain and spread to the epicentres of capitalism with Occupy New York City and London. The involvement of artists in the 'movements of the square' was commonly described as 'strike-art' or 'post-occupy art' (McKee, 2016). Artists turned into activists and organizers, deconstructing the very art system and reinventing it in the form of direct action. Art was seen as political prefiguration, a laboratory for the imagination and a form of 'instituting otherwise'. Indeed, the artists involved in Occupy described it as a new 'artistic mode of revolution' (Rosler, 2012) and a counter-hegemonic occupation and reappropriation of life based on the very artists' skills – the same creativity, self-determination, horizontalism and anti-professionalism which had been co-opted by capital in its latest reorganization, but which could now be harnessed to de-functionalize and de-militarize life, making it non-productive.

An important strand of participatory art was the so-called pedagogical turn. Artists filled the void opened by the ruthless privatization, censorship or outright state repression of higher education to become independent educators or curators of mock academies and para-fictional schools. The merit of the pedagogical turn in art was to bypass the 'public programme racket' controlled by corporate museums and based on astronimical speakers' fees, elitist academic glamour and the 'scholar envy' of some star curators. The best pedagogical projects took the form of silent universities, informal conversations, underground gatherings or survivalist happenings in the midst of civil wars, deep economic crises and state repression.

But the main driver of this pedagogical turn was the market. On the one hand, the anti-institutional and post-disciplinary approach of autonomous and para-universities justified the full-blown closure or underfunding of critical disciplines even in well-established universities. On the other, informal selection based on word of mouth and spontaneous social clustering led these autonomous schools to reproduce privilege by recruiting mainly cosmopolitan elites – note the irony of free schools for the rich – despite their DIY ethos and the exotic charm of their makeshift locations: urban squats, artists' lofts and pop-up spaces in New York City, Berlin or Beirut.

As Occupy waned, art activists pondered how to shift back from life to art again. Some radical museology experts and impresarios set up gigantic activist fairs and world summits, much in the style of the twentieth-century industrial exhibitions, or curated expensive socially engaged artwork cashing on attention, controversy and 'social resonance'. Think of the controversy surrounding Cara Walker's *Sphinx* – an immense sugar-coated sculpture of a black female sugar worker whose voluptuous bosom and breasts ended up framing white visitors' selfies, generating much outrage from the black community.

A more recent strand of participatory art embraced a new so-called fourth-wave of institutional critique,[55] more politicized and less self-referential than the third one, based on institutional upscaling – becoming political parties, global assemblies of parties or occupying museum branches – and embracing the materialist language of the historical avant-garde. Gone are the public, the artists, their skills and autonomy. In are the makers, the users, the goals and the achievements. Gone is the bourgeois distinction between use value and exchange value, beauty and utility, and art and life. Art becomes life again – albeit in a derivative and minor version. Duchamp's urinal is put back in the toilets of the Queen Museum.

For instance, the manifesto of Asociación Arte Útil (AAU) by Tania Brugueira[56] echoes the urgency, time-specificity and pragmatic activism of the Latin American conceptualist avant-garde in the 1980s – *Tucuman Arde* in Argentina and Boal's invisible theatre in Brazil. These concrete anti-dictatorship actions and collective research interventions opened up a counter-hegemonic space – neither the state nor the market – which reflected the political urgencies and the conditions of production of the world periphery under dictatorship; whereas the targets and goals of AAU are suspiciously similar to those of the neoliberal museum, echoing its anti-theoretical and utilitarian jargon, and based on the derivative authorship and charisma of individual artists. Capitalism as usual.

Indeed, these artistic gestures of re-institutionalization, re-materialization and re-verticalization were desperate attempts by Western artists to resist late capitalism's biopolitics of creativity and irrationalism, through the nostalgic recuperation of the public realm promoted by the welfare capitalism of the 1970s, with postures that mimicked bureaucratic, verticalist, brutalist, state-led, public and modernist forms of art and life. Artists morphed into neo-modernist organic intellectuals – the bureaucrat, the party cadre, the engineer, even the economist – and started to address the public with economic graphs, forensic reports and climatological algorithms in dreary lecture performances, or doing boring administrative work in the museum's back offices. Such fetishization and melancholic recuperation of bureaucratic Keynesianism – including its corporatist appendages of the party, the union and the organic intellectual/cultural critic – fell flat, as the failure of Corbynism indicates, vis-à-vis the massive corporate reorganization of states and economies worldwide. While public services and local authorities are being violently reorganized and repressed from above, the parodical and neutered mimicking of corporate power, bureaucratic collectivism and techno-accelerationism by artists and intellectuals 'from below', if anything, reinforced the cynicism of the general public.

Some artist activists belonging to the so-called fourth wave of institutional critique set up agonistic conversations, transversal dialogues and para-collaborations with mainstream art institutions, including boycotts, occupations and negative media campaigns, which they described as 'productive withdrawals', 'institutional liberation' or 'affirmative solidarity'. Take, for instance, the Gulf Labor Campaign (GLC),[57] an artist campaign against the oppressive labour conditions in the construction site of the Abu Dhabi branch of the Guggenheim Museum. The political strategy of GLC was to combine social research on the exploitative labour conditions of south Asian migrant workers, networking within the art system, and forms of direct action inspired by the aesthetic of the historical avant-garde – such as the 'Marinettian' bursting into the Peggy Guggenheim Foundation in Venice on a speedboat, the unveiling of Malevich's black square in the middle of London's Tate Modern or the Brechtian projection of anti-capitalist slogans onto the Guggenheim building in New York City. Initially inspired by moral outrage and anti-capitalist ethics, boycotts became ritualistic performances accruing the spectacular value of art and the market prestige of the artist-as-striker.

In the era of 'radical museology', museums and biennials seemed able to represent and contain the agonistic contradictions of radical democracy, starting processes of mutual contamination with social movements or supporting the artistic mode of revolution taking place outside them. The transversal dialogue between art institutions and activist organizations worked best when a balance between the rigid and commodified structures of the former and the fluid energy and constituent power of the latter was achieved through some physical and social distance – most notably in the collaboration between museums and occupied social centres such as the one between Reina Sofia and occupied spaces in Madrid, or the MACBA in Barcelona,[58] or the Athens Biennale and solidarity organizations in Athens.

But in this exchange between activists and institutions, something got lost. Art occupations that mimicked the occupations of capitalism seemed to be disempowering rather than empowering. Some art activists started to see themselves through the cynical eyes of the master, as mercenaries, freelancers, parasites or quasi-institutions. Direct actions turned into 'negative freedom' (Steyerl, 2013). The cynicism, capitalist realism and moral indignation of some art activists seemed to reflect the latest capital reorganization, in which urban commons, instead of supporting 'rebel cities' (Harvey, 2012) and cross-sectional forms of neo-municipalism, nurtured capitalist value and exclusionary process of gentrification and urban speculation – turning urban commons into urban enclosures.

Today, this fourth wave of institutional critique[59] in which the city is both the locus and the means of political struggle is being suppressed by a new capitalist reorganization based on accumulation by dispossession, land-grabbing and the militarization of urban policing. Urban commons are being closed down and replaced with segregated enclaves sustained by homophobia, racism and paranoia.

With direct actions and activist art being violently repressed by increasing authoritarian municipalities, participatory art retreated back inside the neoliberal museums, where it is now heavily curated and continues to respond to the capitalist logic of maximizing audience numbers through a mixture of toned-down socially engaged public programmes and hedonistic and post-ideological rituals of free time and leisure, such as performative gift-giving or collective hang-outs in artificial beaches, Lego playgrounds and airport lounges.

The museification of participatory art is increasingly overtly business-like, with neoliberal museums acting as incubators or 'hubs' of socially engaged art organizations, offering marketing, communication and internal development services in exchange for ground rent and free programme. From the artist as service provider to the artist as service customer. Likewise, Brugueira's Asociación Arte Útil (AAU) is a standardized and franchised public outreach tool in mainstream European museums.

As the anti-capitalism of artists and cultural workers is either being overtly repressed by right-wing municipalities or co-opted into new forms of artist-led capitalist realism, it is important to ask what went wrong. First, as I argued above, the artist activists emerging from post-Occupy art, including some feminist groups whose valorization of reproductive labour is an important anti-capitalist tenet, failed to connect to the underpaid and precarious service workers, mostly women, ethnic and black, and other marginal social categories. In fact, these artists/activists, consciously or not, fed a new kind of municipal capitalism, in which the performance of criticality, civic activism, urban occupations and even institutional liberations went to increase urban rents and activism, rather than being emancipatory artistic practice, and constituted a new form of alienated labour.

Besides, like relational art, participatory art was deeply flawed by the way it assumed social equality between artists and participants so that, in outsourcing their performances to the public, they reproduced existing class relations and alienated labour and disguised their rent extraction as egalitarianism and collective creativity. At best, participatory art created agonistic spaces in which the impossibility of participation and the commodification of artistic labour were emphasized. For instance, the Spanish artist Santiago Serra paraded a group of homeless people in a private gallery holding banners saying: 'I am paid 5$ but the artist may be a millionaire' to denounce the intrinsic capitalistic nature of art-making. Yet what was there to be liked by an impoverished working class in seeing itself reflected in the life-condition of homeless non-participants? In other words, the artistic middle class, even when heavily indebted by university fees and mortgages, failed to reflect on its privileged status and connect to the urban proletariat that had been rendered invisible by the extreme slummification and privatization of cities, in which it played a central role.

Second, the assumption that the precarious Western *cognitariat* (including the dark matter of the art world) is representative of the world at large proved to be highly Eurocentric. In the world peripheries, including the peripheries of the European centres, post-industrial labour is only a small part of the economy, which consists more often than not in heterogeneous and dystopic mixes of Fordism, informal and subsistence economies, indentured labour, high-tech hubs and service platforms invisibly connected by the global flows of capital. In conclusion, the failure of 'post-occupy' artists and the dark matter is linked to their deep ethnocentrism.

Again, Fraser is relevant here. The first radical act in art is to recognize its privileged economic status and entanglement with capitalism – a form of colonization of life which is driven by the global North at the expenses of the global South. So the central movement towards deconstructing capitalism and breaking the walls of the neoliberal museums is that of decolonization.

Third movement: Appropriating the SOUTH (2013 onwards)

The year 2013 marks the dramatic entry of Black Lives Matter (BLM) onto the world stage with the sit-in in Time Square after the acquittal of George Zimmermann for the murder of Trayvon Martin and the national wave of protests after the killing of Darren Wilson in Ferguson which led to the declaration of a state of emergency in the city in 2014.

BLM captured the world's imagination with its direct mode of address to institutionalized racism in the United States, its powerful symbols (the hoodie) and performative 'die-ins', 'hands up don't shoot' and 'I can't breathe' actions. Although the history of black activism in the art has a long legacy that dates back at least to the black and women's liberation movements in the 1960s – the Artists for Black art Liberation and Ad Hoc Women's Art Committee in the United States and the Black British Arts Movement in the UK – the phenomenon of decolonizing art is much more recent, especially in its intersection with multiple anti-capitalist strands, such as anti-gentrification and black liberation struggles, Free Palestine, indigenous activism and global labour movements. For instance, the 'Decolonize This Place' campaign organized in 2018 against the Brooklyn museum targeted the museum's hiring of a white woman as curator of its extensive African art collection and the gentrification of the area and framed these local struggles in relation to the worldwide struggles by indigenous and Palestinian people.

I argue that this current movement against capital, that of decolonization, also marks a new stage of capital reorganization based on the co-optation of the South. Capital's appropriation of the South, through co-optation or violence, is both ancient and new. On the one hand, this latest appropriation continues past modes of colonial violence, ranging from direct annihilation and ethnographic 'museification' to the intimate recuperations by 'artists as ethnographers' in the 1980s when, triggered by the emergence of critical theories and postcolonial studies in mainstream academia, the white middle class developed postcolonial guilt and nostalgic longings for the dispersed racial and postcolonial 'other'.

In the UK, the target of the postcolonial critique of the early 1980s was not imperialism but the normative, bureaucratic and rationalist logic of the state under the Labour Party, which had betrayed the socialist ideal and turned the white masses (both the middle class and the working class) into a consumerist, hedonist and nationalist, if not racist, social subject. The *oevre* of Stuart Hall attempted precisely to counter such left-wing Keynesian capitalism and identify concrete ways in which postcolonial culture could resuscitate Western Marxism.

But the contemporary identitarian politics differs from the militant multiculturalism of Britain in the 1980s and continues to be driven by cultural appropriations and profits in the global North. Having turned the global South from a developing subject into a fully fledged economic one, Western international financial infrastructures have forcibly financialized poor households and urban slums through national programmes of credit extension, public-private partnerships and social redistribution – typically in the form of conditional cash transfers targeting specifically women, who are thus forcibly turned into neoliberal subjects.[60]

Here, the fantasy is that 'the South' (often subsumed under the vague categories of indigeneity, autochthony, virgin land and violent frontiers) is a 'natural' archetype of new forms of ecological consciousness, solidarity between humans and non-humans, post-global and territorialized livelihoods, and post-ideological communitarianism. According to the accelerationist version of this fantasy, the South is 'naturally' post-Fordist, postmodern and futurist, because it never went through the first 'modern' stage of industrialization and technological development, but 'jumped ahead' directly into an ecologically advanced and hyper-technological postmodernity. The late industrializers become the first high-tech movers in the imagined form of Afro, Gulf or Sino futurist kingdoms – how different this narrative is from the Marxist Brazilian sociologist Cico de Oliveira's description of Brazil as a 'duckbilled platypus' due to its mixture of industrial underdevelopment and hyper-development in the low-value service industry.[61] Or at the opposite extreme of technological determinism, the South is conceived as the mysterious pre-capitalist space of subjectivities and economies marked by opacity, informality, smuggling, improvisation and under-commons.

Indeed, Western curators realized that museums in the North needed to 'learn from the South' in order to survive the corporate turn. They started to exoticize and commodify art organizations in the global South, calling them extra-institutional rather than anti-institutional, grassroots, participatory, post-political, non-representational, prefigurative and operating outside the horizon of Western democracies – neither in the market nor in the state but 'in the street'.[62] It was noted that the biggest slums in the world – Delhi, Mumbai, Jakarta, Rio – were developing radical urban movements claiming their right to the city and that these urban movements emerged as community-based experiments in which artists, researchers, activists and migrants came together in hybrid institutions or 'quasi-institutions'.

The first movement of appropriation of the South entailed the geographical relocation of curators, biennials and curatorial ideas to the South, which generated hopes of democratization and economic development but in fact created very little local employment and often triggered violent reactions by local conservative forces. For instance, the 13th Istanbul Biennial was unable to open itself to the social movements that had occupied Gezi Park, despite its public programme being overtly political and centred on an anti-gentrification agenda which, on the one hand, reinforced the anti-Western stance of some municipal parties and, on the other, jarred with the history of the city, which, instead of the Western dichotomy of public/private spaces, had a tradition of urban commons that went back to the thirteenth-century city gardens.[63]

In order to 'learn from the South', museums have gone as far as relocating there such as d14 *Learning from Athens* – taking with them their heavy apparatuses of civilization and infrastructure-building including state diplomats, brand consultants, financial advisors and cultural experts (more on d14 below). We have come full circle: from the colonial ethnographic museums of early capitalism to the iterant neocolonial cultural factory of late capitalism. In fact, it can be argued that the movement of cultural imperialism initiated in early 2000s, based on the expansion of Western museums abroad and 'global museum diplomacy' (Grincheva, 2019) – think of the relocation of the Guggenheim Museum, the Lourdes and British Museum to Abu Dhabi or the branching out of the State Hermitage Museum to Barcelona, LA and Paris – pre-enacted and prefigured the current reorganization of capital, along imperialist, nationalist and identitarian lines, by neoconservative forces.

This imperialist cultural appropriation of the South is evident in the way Western museums reproduce 'in vitro' Southern epistemologies and ontologies based on slippery translations between indigenous knowledge and visual art or the reframing, reappropriation, reparation and repackaging of ethnographic archives and colonial artefacts as postcolonial artworks by diasporic and indigenous artists. In parallel to the cultural appropriation by Western museums, there is a growing market appreciation for 'postcolonial art' mirrored in the meteoric rise of the selling prices of indigenous sculptures, figurative paintings of black subjects by black artists (supposedly countering the colonial gaze), craft-based and textile art, and postcolonial visual aesthetics. The more this art acquires market value, the more curators and critics label it as black or indigenous radical politics. Even the sensuous and relational artwork of Clark and Oiticica are held captive in Western galleries and museums, against which they were originally conceived.

Most evidently, the latest appropriation of the South by the North takes place under the slogan 'decolonizing nature'. Here, postcolonial and ecological narratives converge under the anti-political Anthropocene agenda, which considers all human beings, including those Westerners at the receiving end of capitalism, to be historical agents of environmental destruction, but salvages the South by associating it with the post-human and with nature – the old nature-culture colonial divide redux. Consider, for instance, how Latin American indigeneism is often represented in terms of timeless ecological wisdom, or the Zapatistas movement as a *purely* ecological project, or the Sami culture of the Arctic as the archetypical embodiment of post-human solidarity.

We know about *Capitalocene* that ecological disruption is a product of capitalism and colonialism and that ecological activism is central to any post-capitalist project. But the idea that indigenous people are intrinsically more ecologically minded than Western people is a-historical and essentializing, as if indigenous and small-scale societies existed in a social and historical vacuum and never practised deforestation, over-hunting or slavery (of course, these practices emerged as a result of contact with capitalism). Let us not forget that the essentialization and naturalization of the other – the native, the indigenous, the woman or the slave – as 'natural beings' have been central to capitalism since its early inception. The cultural and political process that needs to be implemented is much more complex – not one of rediscovery and salvage but, rather, of micro translations, re-enactments, remembering and rediscovering. In order to stop the 'pimping of life by colonial capitalism' (Rolnik, 2017), resistance must be articulated both at the micro and macro levels.

Moreover, 'decolonization' is a slippery term, especially when it is formulated from the global centres. And is it not ironical that gestures of decolonization and cultural recognition by indigenous, diasporic and postcolonial artists end up being appropriated, commodified and displayed inside the neocolonial Western museum?

I am not talking about the obvious cases, such as Dana Shutz's *Open Casket* (2016), a visceral and voyeuristic painting of the battered body of Emmett Till, or Sam Durant's *Scaffold* (2012), an architectural reconstruction of the Mankato gallows, where thirty-eight Dakota men were executed in 1862, displayed in a blockbuster sculpture exhibition. I am talking about the repackaging of black and indigenous politics and ontology for public consumption by Western white audiences: for instance, the incorporation of the archives and artefacts of Black Lives Matter in the permanent collections of the New York City Museum and the National Museum of African American History and Culture (NMAAHC) in Washington, DC, or the appropriation of black and Wiradjuri aesthetics and its recontextualization 'from the edges (*nirin*) to the centre' in the latest Sydney Biennial.

Besides, can black politics be assimilated to anti-decolonization struggles, ignoring the specific form of commodification of existence experienced under racial slavery? And what can we say about the contemporary figure of the refugee – without a nation, an identity or even a master to return to? Does not this new exilic condition replicate the logic of the transatlantic trade within the political economy of contemporary capitalism, based on the synchronization of free movement of people and finance for the profit of transnational capital and the immobilization and social alienation of humans in emergency shelters, militarized camps, prisons and urban ghettos? And if cries for decolonization and anti-racism are regularly showcased at exhibition openings, why are the xenophobia, racism and nationalism of the populist right against migrants not being challenged by the left in the art world? If it is true that the cosmopolitan and internationalist point of view of migrants embodies the universalism of early revolutionary art (Groys, 2017), why are contemporary artists buying into the territorialized and identitarian version of culture that is being sponsored by neo-conservative states in Europe and the United States?

At the time of writing, the 58th Venice Bienniale directed by Ralph Rugoff displays in the prestigious Arsenale site the latest artwork by maverick Icelandic-Swiss artist Christoph Büchel's *Barca Nostra* (Our Boat). On this very boat between seven and eleven hundred people, the majority from Africa died when it sank between Libya and the Italian island of Lampedusa on 18 April 2015. The artist's press release, echoing the language of the Duchampian avant-garde, states: '[T]he project changes the status of the shipwreck from an object of court evidence to an artefact, cultural good and significant symbol of our "interesting times". In response to such a chilling display, there has been no major petition, boycott or open letter to the biennale by artists, activists or civil society at large. Why was there no call for decolonization this time? A famous art critic, a champion of socially engaged art, argued that the boat was more evidence more of incompetence from the Italian state in dealing with the immigration issue than of the miscalculation of the curator or the artist.

Recently, voices and interferences coming from the cosmos have been reported. Perhaps this is the voice of the Russian cosmonaut who flew into space from his apartment and is telling us from afar that there is life after death, infinite time inside biological time, solidarity between humans and non-humans, and spaces of resistance and transcendence within capitalism. For the Russian Cosmists – a spiritualist avant-garde movement which emerged in parallel to the Futurists – the 'common task' of the avant-garde museum is to bring abstraction, spiritualism and the cosmic back to earth, grounding the transcendental into everyday life and developing advanced technologies to regenerate life, combining present, past and future, and facilitating exchanges across generations. Perhaps the emergence of Russian Cosmism and of Afro, Asian and other ethnic accelerationist futures is the other side of 'capitalist realism', that is, the cynical acceptance that present-day capitalism is our only future – a future which is also increasingly post-human. But, on the other hand, these noises coming from the cosmos may mark a new sensuous attunement to those fleeting and abstract voices that have been whispering at the margins of Europe since the beginning of capitalism.

Indeed, we are witnessing the reappropriation of abstraction or 'abstractionist aesthetics'[64] by black radical artists: for example, Cara Walker's dark silhouettes casting a reflexive distance on the violence of slavery; Sondra Perry's digital animated skin floating like a sea between the colours white and Chroma Key blue (the CGI version of black); Cameron Rowland's minimalist display of objects entangled with the histories of capitalism and slavery; Theaster Gates's reappropriation of the black fetish in the form of glass lantern slides; and Kerry James Marshall's rewriting of the white abstract canon. For instance, in *Two Invisible Men Naked* (1985) – a variation on Rodchenko's Black on Black compositions – a black body emerges from the dark background as haunting living matter, while in *De* Style (1993) – a monumental ten-feet-tall by ten-feet-wide painting – abstraction instead of a formal principle is a chromatic force animating the black subjects and reframing Mondrian's abstract grids in the everyday life of an African American barbershop.

Or take Adam Pendleton's *Black Dada Manifesto* which asks:

[I]s there a role of abstraction in the abolition of alienated labour? This phrase – the abolition of alienated labour – is European in origin but would seem already to better describe the arc of North Atlantic history than that of the Continent. Or – and this is the point – the words *abolition, alienated*, and *labour* have a unique and indisputable record in the history of slavery. I begin by asking after the role of abstraction in the process of abolition. One way of asking this question is to distinguish between two modes of abstraction. The first is the experience of abstraction as a force, which happens when the body is subject to violence by virtue of its ostensible coincidence with one's identity. The belly of the slave ship, sexual violence and the fourteen-hour day on the assembly line are all examples of this kind of abstraction. Abstraction is a force whenever and wherever the subject is misrecognized as an object. We know that this misrecognition has taken place by the refusal or resistance – to use Fred Moten's language – of these subjects to their utilization as objects. At first these refusals appear simply as anomalies but with time they demand to be accounted for. It is the service of this demand for recognition that the second experience of abstraction arrives: the practice of abstraction, or abstraction as a relationship. This is the experience described by Adrian Piper in her essay 'Flying'. For it is precisely by practicing abstraction – by poetry or painting or whatever – that the subject confirms itself as other-than-object. We call this project of confirmation a revolution.

(Pendleton, 2017)

The expansion of colonial capitalism is limitless and is based on the naturalization of the other – in the various historical forms of 'the slave', 'the female', 'the lumpen', the 'alien', 'the environment', 'the hyper-object' – and the limitless extraction of mineral and labouring energies from these non-human others (the connection between mineral extraction and labour extraction was first made by the Scottish physician Andrew Ure whose geological treatise *New System of Geology* (1829) and his more famous book on scientific labour organization *The Philosophy of Manufactures* (1835) became epistemological building blocks of early capitalism). Such a naturalized, objectified, feminized and racialized 'other' – opposed to the male cultural and industrious 'us' – constitutes both the living source of and the limit to capital and the thresholds where feminist and black anti-capitalist struggles meet the struggles for decolonizing nature.

In the face of global ecological collapse, politically engaged artists have developed multi-scalar, multimodal and multisensorial forms of documentation, research interventions and critical epistemologies based not on identification or representation but on long-term modes of coexistence, dwelling and contemplation. Take the collaboration between anthropologist Elizabeth Povinelli and the Australian Aboriginal filmmaking collective *Karrabing,* whose experimental aesthetics and collaborative process create a space of commoning of indigenous knowledge and ontology that challenges the Western 'geo-ontological' distinction between life and non-life and recasts Western categories such as solidarity, precariousness and antagonism within the materiality of everyday life – as *tailings, embankments* and *strainings*; or Amar Kanwar's poetic visual renditions of the conflict between capitalist and non-capitalist political ecologies; or the longitudinal visualization of the global geography of land extraction under neoliberalism in Uwe Martin's *White Gold* (2007: 14) and its advocacy of 'the seeds commons'.

But the abstraction of capital is limitless. Perhaps the Russian Cosmists had anticipated capital's move to colonize the cosmos. Indeed, nation-states and corporations are mining and extracting core natural resources – water, minerals and solar energy – on the moon in anticipation of future planetary catastrophe and planning further expansion into the universe. Neocolonialism unbound.

So the central questions remain. What constitutes the limit to capital? What are the external boundaries of its arc of abstraction? Is it possible to put transcendence, abstraction and imagination in the service of the commons? Perhaps the convergence between life and transcendence can take place only with the end of the aesthetics realm. Indeed, as Western ethnographic museums are facing the possibility of their own extinction in the form of restitution of looted indigenous artefacts (which they insist in calling 'art'), contemporary art museums should contemplate the return of artworks to their makers and their communities so that they can be properly buried, as non-capitalist custom dictates. But it is up to the artistic community to take up this struggle. Indeed, according to Kazimir Malevich the task of the revolutionary avant-garde was, first of all, to burn all existing artworks, since such artworks, and their makers, were already dead.

What would be the artists' contribution to a critique of the political economy of colonial capitalism? Not in the de-commodification of labour (as per the historical avant-garde) or in its recommodification (as per the WAGE group). Not in the political liberation of the colonies (for instance, by setting up artistic projects that reconstruct stateless parliaments in the global South like artist Jonas Staal) or in their re-commodification (for instance, by teaching Congolese plantation workers to become neoliberal workers as for the artist Renzo Martens). The role of the Western precarious artists and wage workers is to listen and learn from the colonised, including Congolese plantation workers and African leaders, how to create solidarity, communal economies and egalitarian organizations in the midst of economic deprivation, state violence and wageless lives. To convey to us the message that beyond the frozen and fragmented commodity form, there is a world of relations in constant movement.

Conclusion: Part I

As individuals, how do we take position vis-à-vis an environment made of images, sounds and gestures that, travelling through different human and non-human mediums, touch us and enfold us not only visually, but with all the senses? How do we reach a steady equilibrium and go beyond the Western schizophrenic oscillation between critical distance and engagement, abstraction and absorption, encapsulated in the Adornian double bind of art and capitalism?

In this first part of the book I have argued that the 'artistic mode of production' – based on the capture, commodification and circulation of images (mental or embodied in physical media); individualized notions of human agency and skills; externalized and simplified epistemologies of doing, giving and receiving; and ontologies of unrelatedness between humans, objects and environments – is the technology of enchantment[65] used by colonial capitalism to beautify, naturalize and legitimize the new system of slavery and environmental destruction transplanted from the colonies into the old world, in the form of enclosure of the countryside and enslavement of labourers in modern factories, which led to 'the great capitalist transformation' described by sociologist Karl Polanyi (1944), which is still ongoing.

I have supported such a claim by describing the historical relationships between art and political economy and highlighting how the avant-garde's speculative actions are constantly co-opted by new forms of capitalism, the former providing the prefigurative 'shell' out of which the latter emerges. Specifically, I have argued that artistic movements and gestures of abstraction, decontextualization and critique of capitalism lay new ground for new valorizations and concretizations by capital and that capitalism works through a speculative economy of attention based on images, projections and choreographed actions, which are *artfully* disguised as life but that, in fact, are simplified, flattened, standardized and commodified versions of it, overdetermined by the logic of capital.

The central question is: how can art contribute to the making of commons? What kind of skills and knowledge, which ontologies of human and non-human relatedness and which social relations of production and circulation can unlock and decolonize capital's enclosures, mobilize life, 'concretizing' forms, practices and ontologies of commons and re-embedding economy into society? How does non-alienated and communist art look like?

In the next section, I discuss some of my practices at the intersection of art, anthropology and activism, through which I have researched and worked towards the collective imagining and co-production of commons. Specifically, I discuss my three projects of art/commons: making the film *Steel Lives*, directing the Athens Biennale and setting up the think tank Institute of Radical Imagination (IRI).

These projects are aimed at developing a post-capitalist imaginary in the realms of respectively, aesthetics, social relations and epistemology. They entailed different forms of involvement and approaches to the commons – authorial and ocular in *Steel Lives*; institutional and performative in the Athens Biennale, and epistemological and relational in *IRI*. Each of them entailed a personal transformation towards deeper and wider collaborations, in which the issue of friendship and comradeship is increasingly central. So the text starts as an autoethnography and ends as a relational mosaic of ideas and knowledge emerging from the collective work of IRI. This second part can also be read as a list of failed personal experiments, but experiments which nonetheless left deep emotional and intellectual traces both in my life and in the lives of others. Thus, for me, it was in the contemplation and acceptance of failure that the value of art emerged.

Part II

(AUTO)ETHNOGRAPHY OF COMMON PRACTICES

1

BEYOND THE CINEMATIC MODE OF PRODUCTION: FILM LABOUR, MANUAL LABOUR AND INTELLECTUAL LABOUR IN THE MAKING OF 'STEEL LIVES', SHEFFIELD

Sam Yazzie was the oldest medicine man in the community. We explained to him our project to teach young Navajos to make movies. After some thought Sam turned to Worth and asked: 'will making movies do the sheep any harm?' Worth was happy to explain that as far as he knew no harm would befall the sheep if movies were made in the community. Sam thought for a few seconds and looking straight at Worth asked, 'Will it do them any good?' Worth was forced to reply that as far as he knew it wouldn't do the sheep any good. Sam looked at us both and said, 'Then why make movies?' (Worth and Adair, 1969)

Yazzie was a Navajo elder whom anthropologists Sol Worth and John Adair met in Palm Springs (Arizona) in 1966 while developing a media project with the local Navajo community. Whenever I think about setting up a new film project I go back to Yazzie's line and ask myself: What is the point of filming? What kind of social relations will the film trigger? What economies will it generate? How will the film's subjects benefit from it? Where will the images produced go, and what consequences will their circulation outside the context of their making have?

Film critic Jonathan Beller describes capitalism as a 'cinematic mode of production' (2006) which relies on visual media to generate docile capitalist subjects. Specifically, modernist cinema mass-produced a standardized working-class audience, just as Taylorism mass-produced standardized commodities. It captured the viewers' attention and moulded their minds to the commodity form. It was the Russian revolutionary filmmaker Sergei Eisenstein who first understood the power of cinema in crafting the revolutionary consciousness of the proletariat and that industrial cinema, like economic industrialization, was central if the Soviet Union was to catch up with the capitalist West. Eisenstein's epic mass re-enactments, multi-perspectivist framings, intellectual montage and grotesque depictions of the bourgeoisie were meant to reproduce, in filmic form, the Bolshevik revolution, as envisaged by Lenin. Under the new regime of post-industrial capitalism, it is the gallery rather than the cinema that 'puts the soul of the working-class to work'. By making the film *Steel Lives* I wanted to experiment with cinema's potential to multiply and diversify the working-class experience and point of view and, at the same time, reflect on the nature of the labour of filmmaking.

My film *Steel Lives* is mostly set in a Victorian tool workshop in Sheffield where I worked as an apprentice forger between 1999 and 2000. When I first entered the place, I felt as if I had stepped into a Dickensian sweatshop. All the press hammers, forges, and turning and grinding machines dated back to the nineteenth century, when they were powered by the nearby river. Because of the unusual density of the machines on the shop floor, half of which were inactive, I first thought that it was a second-hand machine shop. But why were the workers using them? Then a gigantic man, pulling on a rope a rusted box filled with rusted steel bars, invited me in and introduced me to 'the guys'. I left the shop floor fourteen months later, an unskilled forger with plenty of vivid memories and local attachments, and very confused about how to turn such personal experience into an academic project.

Indeed, my engagement with filmmaking came from having to deal with the radical openness of my fieldwork experience, which is always a negotiation between theory, political beliefs and personal circumstances. For twenty years, I have been researching the processes of state violence, social exclusion and urban segregation generated by capitalist forms of living in the context of the historically and geographically shifting relationships between global centres and global peripheries.

For sixteen months between 1999 and 2000, I lived in a deprived working-class neighbourhood of Sheffield, among boarded-up pubs, derelict factories and Roma campsites. There, I worked in two local steel factories: a small engineering workshop with twenty non-unionized and underpaid workers (British, Pakistanis and Eastern Europeans) and an integrated steel plant with 200 workers, mostly unionized. In *The Capital* Marx describes the Sheffield steel artisans as backward, individualists and Luddites. He particularly disliked these micro capitalists because they blocked the accelerations and contradictions of capital, which would eventually lead to the collapse of bourgeois society and the transition to communism.

In my fieldwork, I wanted to know what strategies of survival the working class in Sheffield had developed in the face of the radical deindustrialization and privatization of their city, initiated by Conservative Prime Minister Margaret Thatcher and continued under Tony Blair's New Labour, and its momentous reconversion into a post-industrial economy. One year into my fieldwork the integrated steel mill was closed down, despite being technologically advanced and economically profitable. The small tool workshop, on the other hand, continued to thrive and make a profit. Evidently, the post-industrial economy had not eliminated the steel industry but fragmented it into myriad small, unhealthy, hazardous and exploitative 'pre-capitalist' sweatshops like the one I had worked in, managed by ex-workers-turned-capitalists.

After my research in Sheffield, between 2008 and 2018, I conducted fieldwork in Volta Redonda, a Brazilian steel town built in the middle of a depleted coffee valley in the state of Rio de Janeiro, by the dictator Getúlio Vargas in 1946. There, I lived in a favela for one year and researched in the *Companhia Siderúrgica Nacional* (CSN), the biggest mineral and industrial complex in Latin America and one of the world's biggest polluters.[1] During fieldwork, I experienced how black and working-class communities from favelas and urban squats deal with daily economic dispossession and environmental degradation produced by the CSN.

With this new fieldwork in Brazil, I wanted to compare how the working-class communities of Sheffield and Volta Redonda – two world peripheries – experienced and struggled against the dehumanizing forces of capitalism. Going beyond experiential and cultural differences – the smells, colours and voices of a new place – I wanted to highlight the universality of the everyday struggles, the common vocabularies and the enduring solidarities of people who lead precarious lives.

But what can one's fieldwork say or do about capitalism, the relationships between core and peripheries or the future of labour struggles? How does one relate the experience of fieldwork to the structural articulation of capitalism in space and time? With what temporal delay do global and national political and economic events (crises, *coups*, inflation hikes, electoral successes and radical privatizations) impact on everyday life and, in turn, what is the cumulative effect of local actions on the broader context?

Indeed, although my fieldworks are motivated by the attempt to understand the causes of structural inequalities, and the impulse to act upon them, the politics of fieldwork consists of unspoken, hardly visible, affective micro-interactions whose scale and consequences are often unpredictable. Anthropological fieldwork requires a radical openness – a constant suspension of beliefs, analytical displacement and relational attunement. More than a methodology, it is a poetic and relational praxis – in the sense discussed by Glissant – which escapes the 'timely' political interventions of contemporary activism and socially engaged art.

In *Steel Lives* I wanted to capture the spirit of that time, suspended between Thatcherism and New Labour, when a new imaginary of classless, individualist and post-industrial society was erasing previous forms of working-class history, solidarity and livelihood and, at the same time, resurrecting Victorian forms of work and labour relations.

Instead of representing a homogeneous political subject – the working class – as an outsider/observer, I wanted the filmmaking process to catalyse, bring into the open and socialize the contradictions, power imbalances and structural violence implicated in the working-class lives I had witnessed. As manual labour was being made redundant by the invisible forces of finance, I wanted the camera to trigger a process of co-production of a common class position by subjects with very different skills and personal backgrounds. In other words, I wanted the camera to trigger new social relations of production around a process of collective self-representation, rather than documenting a section of the otherwise disappearing working class.

Also, I wanted the film to encourage a marginal section of the working class to critically reflect on the performativity of labour – that is, on how human gestures come to acquire economic value and be classified as 'productive labour' through a mixture of private accumulation and public, collective and often unconscious performances, negotiations and struggles. Specifically, I wanted them to reflect on why they considered their gestures of activating rusted Victorian machines to produce old-fashioned tools on a semi-derelict shop floor as 'work' and why these gestures were remunerated with wages that (nearly) sustained their livelihood. I also wanted to see if they felt threatened by the so-called the working-class decline that was being trumpeted by mainstream media.

The spectacle of labour and working-class cinema in the UK[2]

There is a long tradition of working-class representation in British cinema that dates back to the early documentary movement of John Grierson in the 1930s. Grierson and his school mixed the experimental use of sound, light and editing with direct observation – a genre that Grierson described as 'poetic realism' and later became the trademark of British 'social realism'.

Early documentary films were publicly commissioned and had an overt social agenda – for instance, improving working-class housing in East London or fostering co-operative relations between workers and management in the National Coal Board. The second generation of British social realist cinema is represented by the Free Cinema Movement funded by Karol Reisz and Lindsey Anderson in the 1960s, the so-called British New Wave. These middle-class communist filmmakers developed a new register of working-class representation that mixed direct observation and a personal storytelling that endorsed the point of view of women, black and the unemployed. Their often tragic stories depicted the clash between a rebellious and sexually liberated youth and the older petty bourgeois working-class generation, in which the gritty northern industrial landscape embodied the feeling of anger, melancholy and ruination for the lost working-class utopia.

Experimental and militant cinema reached its apex with the explosion of the community video movement and of independent filmmaking in the 1970s – Cinema Action, the London Filmmakers' Co-op, the Sheffield Film Co-op, the Black Audio and Video Collective and Sankofa – whereby black, female and young activists set up film collectives for both labour campaigns and self-representation. The tension between class and identity within independent cinema was not always easy to hold in balance. Take the powerful documentary *Nightcleaners* (1975) about women who clean office blocks at night. The film was made by the Berwick Street Collective, a group of young activists and artists, to rally support from the labour movement for the cleaners' strike. Its reflexive, experimental techniques were well received by middle-class intellectuals and film critics, but labour activists considered the film 'untruthful', too personal and over-intellectual.

Indeed, paradoxically, it was Thatcher's deregulation of the national TV industry that led to the funding of the independent private broadcaster *Channel Four* which allowed a new generation of women and black independent filmmakers to articulate powerful critiques against the racism and patriarchy of the white bourgeoisie – including sections of the Labour Party.

Their representation of the British working class was infused with a new sense of hope, openness and radicality associated with the multiculturalism of 'The New Left'.

Eventually, the onset of commercial television, the migration of art films into galleries and of film theory into film departments led to the consolidation of a national film industry, branded by 'social realism'. In it the British working class was represented as national cultural subject rather than a political formation. Unlike the militant multiculturalism of Stuart Hall, this was the culture of money and the media industry that spun the wheels of the financial economy – the 'cool' Britannia of Tony Blair, the Britpop and the Young British Artists (YBAs); these latter were artists/self-motivated entrepreneurs from a working-class background who, endorsing the Third Way, took the distances from both the Conservative power elites and the 'uncool' working class of the previous generations. Profiteering from the commodification of working-class identity, left-wing directors brooded on 'left-wing melancholia' (Brown, 1999).

Take, for instance, Ken Loach's film *Kes* (1969) in which a tormented working-class boy momentarily escapes the brutality of family and school life in a small mining town in Yorkshire by developing a friendship with a falcon, from whom he learns to view the world from a distance, be resilient and connect with the half-industrial, half-natural landscape that haunts the film. *Kes*'s detached observations of the brutality of everyday working-class life, combined with the empathic micro exploration of the intimate solidarity developed among two captives (the boy and the bird) in a traditional working-class community, prefigures, in *beautified* form, the end of industry and the loneliness, isolation and alienation of future working-class generations.

During my fieldwork, the expansion of the cinema industry and the collapse of the steel industry went hand in hand. While profitable steel companies were closed down or downsized by venture capitalists, huge EU structural funds went into the development of the Sheffield Film Festival, the Showroom cinema complex, art galleries and luxury industrial lofts on the sites of abandoned Victorian steel factories. While my friends battled against the management nearly every day, the spectacle of working-class decline, defeat and unemployment was being played out in local cinemas, with stories that historicized a reality that was still unfolding. The convergence between working-class images and working-class lives becomes evident to me when some unemployed steelworker friends of mine 'tried their luck' by auditioning for Ken Loach's latest film *The Navigators* (2001), which tells the stories of five railway workers made redundant after the privatization of British Rail in 1995.

Loach's film on the social consequences of industrial privatizations clearly resonated with what was going on in Sheffield, which was still suffering the catastrophic effects of the privatization of the steel industry. But by describing events that had taken place just six years earlier, it historicized working-class struggles that were still unfolding and made the triumph of neoliberalism seem not only inevitable, but already present. While the genre of social realism boosted the profits of the British cinema industry, the British working class saw itself entrapped and abstracted in the parallel fictional reality of the cinema screen. Maybe it is just the immense beauty and empathy that Loach is able to evoke from simple working-class stories that pull the viewer into a state of passive speculation. Had *The Navigators* followed the path of advocacy rather than of realism and beauty, it would have achieved a different effect among my friends, perhaps prompting them to wanting to tell their stories in their own voices.

Yazzie's question remains. How do workers benefit from filming labour? In fact, it has been argued that films on labour always take the point of view of capital, in the form of middle-class voyeurism, a managerial gaze or state propaganda and that workers are seldom able or willing to tell their stories.

Indeed, the story of cinema starts with workers leaving the factory. The Lumiére Brothers' *Workers Leaving the Lumière Factory in Lyon* (*La sortie des sines Lumière à Lyon*, 1895) by the brothers Louis and Auguste Lumière, 45 seconds long, shows the approximately 100 workers at a factory for photographic goods in Lyon-Montplaisir leaving through two gates and exiting the frame to both sides. But why does the story of cinema begin with the end of work? Is it because, as it has been suggested, it is impossible to represent work from the perspective of labour but only from the point of view of capital, because the revolutionary horizon of the working class coincides with the end of work?[3] Or is it the compulsive reproduction of images of workers leaving the factory in Western cinema a reflection of the impossibility of representing the agency of labour due to its dispersed, immaterial and fragmented nature under post-Fordism?[4]

One day I went to the Sheffield Industrial Museum with one of my co-workers and found an exact replica of the small tool shopfloor where we worked every day, scattered with mannequins of Victorian workers standing by the self-animated steam presses and hammers (the only living worker, dressed up in Victorian working gear, turned out to be the museum guard). This museification of working-class life was even more hurtful and cruel than the filmic depiction. Was our real workshop the hallucinatory space of post-industrial capitalism, where gestures of labour are merely symbolic and totally abstracted from use-value? And was this fictional workplace the new site of productive labour?

Thus, while I was in Sheffield, the narrative of working-class decline and the socialist realist aesthetics based on observational techniques (that is, long takes, non-professional actors and real settings) were the commodity form and the grammar of the new post-industrial capital – a force that was turning deindustrialization and working-class struggles into 'industrial heritage', in the forms of cinema, gentrification and real-estate development. So my film also wanted to reflect on working-class representation as the new spirit of capitalism.

Relations of production, economies of film and modes of circulation

Steel Lives was made with the financial support of a British producer with a professional background in editing who at the time was running a media-training project in the Indian steel town of Bhilai, facing a similar process of deindustrialization to that of Sheffield. Steve, the director of production (DOP) in *Steel Lives*, was also the DOP in the Indian media project. From a working-class background, Steve was one of the founders of a Sheffield media-training cooperative for unemployed youth. The gaffer and the sound recordists were trainees in the cooperative from which we also rented the lighting, sound and video equipment. Apart from Steve, the crew and the editor were semi-professional. The overall budget, including the fees and the rental of equipment, was around £10,000. The film was shot in just over five weeks and edited in two weeks.

The crew, the editor and the DOP got involved in such a low-budget film because they shared with me a critical stance towards how the New Labour Party of Tony Blair was continuing Margaret Thatcher's policy of deindustrialization, while casting itself as working-class saviour. At that time, the governmental media machine would consistently paint this process of deindustrialization and economic reconversion as inevitable, and even desirable, depicting a rosy future of totally automated, financialized and hyper-consumerist society. We all empathized with the point of view of the steelworkers who were facing incredibly harsh working conditions and a future without work. We all considered *Steel Lives* as a counter-information project showing that the steel industry had not disappeared and continued to be profitable based on deregulation, marginalization and precarization of its labour. But despite our common intentions, our different class backgrounds clearly stood in the way of us smoothly working together so that in the end the filming process tended to reinforce existing class relations in terms of authorship and divisions of labour.

For instance, while the DOP and the sound technicians were struggling with extreme light and sound conditions, I was preoccupied with capturing the details of the steel production process, and these different priorities coalesced around perceived class positions. I was put off by the 'artists'' preoccupation with aesthetics which got in the way of documenting an important political process. In turn, the DOP and the technicians considered me a middle-class scholar with no practical understanding of filmmaking (or of steelmaking for that matter) who was uncritically and romantically endorsing the point of view of 'the working class'. Like the steelworkers we were filming, they came from the working class too. But they considered the former reactionary, patriarchal and even racist. The steelworkers, in turn, had no respect for these artists.

With the steelworkers I had more than a year to negotiate my class position, whereas with the film crew the negotiation took place during the very process of filming. I had assumed that the DOP, the gaffer and the sound technicians would act as my peers, underestimating how, in fact, I expected them to execute the tasks I set, acting like a manager delegating the execution of work to wage workers. Unintentionally, I was reproducing the hierarchy of the film industry and its class divisions. Because the continuous conflicts and discussions were slowing down the film process, we restructured it entirely, rotating tasks where possible and having long post-production sessions every evening in which decisions were taken collectively and based on consensus. Besides, because of their personal investment in the film, the crew and DOP agreed to be paid just a nominal fee, below the industry's standard rates. At the time, there was little discussion about a fair wage for art workers in the not-for-profit sector. For the younger working-class generations, refusing to be paid or being outside the wage economy was considered a form of political resistance against the patriarchal and materialistic mindset of their parents' generation.

The aesthetics of *Steel Lives* reflects the egalitarian structure of the labour process, our joint commitment to a low-budget and DIY ethics – to find things out together, socialize the process and pool resources – and our defiant attitude of wanting to narrate a story about the working class that was neither romantic nor cynical, as in mainstream media representations, but showed the grounded and resilient point of view of the steelworkers, a social category that was believed to have disappeared long ago.

In visual anthropology, the awareness that images are relational, durational and socially embedded requires an ethnical commitment to make sure that their circulation outside their social milieu does not endanger those social relations which they carry with them. Today, when different truths are fabricated through the collaging, decontextualization and post-production of images freely circulating in the limitless expanse of national and global media infrastructures, this ethical commitment is all the more important. Indeed, the political life of films does not end at the moment of production. It continues in the processes of distribution and circulation. One advantage of making a hybrid film form, between observational documentary, political advocacy and experimental film, is that it circulates across different platforms. *Steel Lives* was screened at the Sheffield Film Festival; the Socialist Film Co-op in London; the Beirut Gallery in Cairo; Tate Britain and Gasworks Gallery in London; a local Communist Party branch in Brazil; a Metalworkers' Trade Union branch in India; the Trade Union Congress (TUC) in London and in academic screenings, seminars and political meetings.

In each of these venues the screening of the film was never an end in itself. Rather, it was always entangled in political debates and social gatherings connected to the working-class lives depicted. The protagonists of *Steel Lives* attended its screening at the Sheffield Film Festival together with a delegation of Indian steelworkers. After the screening, they took part in a charged Q&A in which they challenged local and national MPs about the demise of the steel industry and told them about their survival struggles, their anxieties and hopes for the future.

Antinomies of realism: Indigenous aesthetics/communist aesthetics and militant cinema

In the 1970s, social realist film was under attack from both feminist and black film collectives for its voyeuristic distance, rooted in unequal class relations between the filmmaker (often male, white and middle class) and the subjects (often 'the poor', 'the marginal' or 'the working class'); their victimizing approach; their lack of intersectional narratives; and their excessively materialistic and productivist focus on work, poverty and inequality. At the same time, the Third Cinema movement in the global South radicalized cinema, using it as tool of political mobilization against military regimes and colonial powers. Refusing the imperialist forms of the commercial Hollywood films (First Cinema) and of the European authorial cinema (Second Cinema), 'Third Cinema' devised democratic and participatory film processes, a popular and non-elitist visual grammar, grassroots forms of production and distribution, and a powerful realist style that reflected 'allegorically' the condition of underdevelopment in the global South (Solanas and Getino, 1997; Xavier, 1993).

In addition, visual anthropologists argued that Western cinema's strictly visual aesthetics and linear forms of storytelling differed from the densely rich, multisensory and multimodal imaginary and aesthetics of non-Western cultures. Their media projects among indigenous communities in the global South opened new uses for cinema which went beyond the mere aesthetics and function of the documentary. Take, for instance, the media projects of anthropologists Cavadini and Strachan's *Two Laws* (1982), in which the law of Western capitalism and Aboriginal epistemology confront each other in their different aesthetics (the former impoverished, mono-logical and linear, the latter complex, layered and multisensory) after a process of long-term collaboration with the indigenous community, including the filmmakers' advocacy against land repossession by the government. Or consider Terence Turner's media project among the Kayapo of the Brazilian Amazon (1989), in which the videocamera performs the three functions of repository of oral history; weapon of intertribal politics and sophisticated media campaign against the development of the Altamira hydroelectric dam by the Brazilian government, and means to re-enact the Kayapo's ideal of beauty (as repetition) through camera framing and editing. Or, more recently, consider Elizabeth Povinelli's *Karrabing* film collective, for whom the film is a medium of translation, co-production and retrieval of practical and ancestral knowledge, a way of dwelling and doing together, lost first with colonial occupation and then with the forced integration within the Australian nation state.

Inspired by the video ethnographies of work by artist Darcy Lange,[5] with *Steel Lives*, I wanted to combine the political urgency of Third Cinema and the ethnographic approach of indigenous media. I wanted to experiment with the politics of filmmaking, explore non-Western ways of telling and interrogate the double nature of cinema, of it being both commodity and life form. I wanted to make the tension between these polarities present and transparent and to create an imaginary space of both capitalist critique and active construction of a post-capitalist imaginary. I wanted to tell a story that did not reach the spectator already completed but, instead, pulled him or her into a dialogical, polyvocal and multilayered space of resonance in which all the diverse affective, imaginative and material facets of working-class identity would come alive and coexist in the fragile space in-between the autobiographical, the fictional and the historical.

I also wanted to go beyond the spectacularization of industrial decline, the abstract and distant documentation of working-class life, or the reproduction of alienated labour in the form of film process. I asked myself: 'What does a communist aesthetic look like?'; 'Can my film unveil and change the class relations in which I myself and my subjects are entangled?'; 'Can it function as catalyst for social re-composition, commoning, and co-production of a holistic, non-alienated and historical materialist working-class imaginary?'; 'Does the dichotomy between Western and non-Western "ways of seeing" hold true?' And 'Can the holistic, sensory, transcultural, dialogical and durational aesthetics of non-Western societies be replicated under capitalism in order to imagine and prefigure the political horizon of communism?'

Moreover, following the Navajo precept I asked myself: 'Whose knowledge am I presenting?'; 'What kind of social relations at the point of production am I engaging with and activating?'; 'What kind of work process, and what economies, am I setting up?' and 'What kind of circulation and consumption am I generating for the film?'

I started to film in the small workshop following a suggestion by Trevor, a skilled worker/artisan whose task was to reproduce missing or damaged mechanical parts following the ancient craft of casting moulds in the sand. During break times, I would often try to understand in conversations how my co-workers subjectively and affectively experienced labour. Skilled workers in the smelting and forming ('hot') department struggled to describe their work, skills and knowledge because these are sensory, bodily and implicit – in the words of Trevor, 'work cannot be spoken of but only performed' – and follow repeated abstract patterns of colour, touch and smell. In the finishing ('cold') part of the shop floor, however, workers spoke about their work with precise measures of monetary bonuses, costumers' specifications or market prices. One day, Trevor brought a camera on to the shop floor and suggested I film them while working.

When I mentioned my idea of setting up a film project that represented the point of view of labour, workers of the cold department were sceptical. Jim immediately rebuked me: 'Films on labour are always made from the point of view of someone who is not a worker.'

Trevor disagreed with Jim, saying that it depended on who controlled the production process. 'If workers are in control', he said, 'then the film will represent their point of view.' Jim objected: 'If workers were in control, there would be no factory.' Skilled workers were proud of their work and willing to restage it for the camera, whereas the workers of the cold department thought that the film would slow down production and lower their bonuses.

But clearly, their discussion about labour representation was more than a reflection on the labour process. It was also a collective conversation on the possible future beyond capitalism, which the older workers conceptualized in productivist terms, as workers' control over the production process, and the younger workers of the cold department, in terms of 'liberation from work'. With my film I wanted to question and overcome this class polarization on the shop floor.

Having worked for more than one year on the shop floor myself, I knew exactly the best locations for the camera to have a clear overview of the workflow. Indeed at least initially, the camera created an unintended managerial gaze effect. The workers increased their production pace and cut down jokes, gossip and small acts of resistance – sabotages, slowdowns and petty theft.

First, I shot each production task separately. Then I shot them again, this time creating linking shots to the rest of the production process, which gave a feeling of how the workers' tasks were interconnected and interdependent. The former shots included sensuous close-ups of the electric-blue coolant liquid dripping on the workers' hands, the graffiti and writings on the machines, and small particles of dust floating in the sunlight. The latter were static mid-shots of the workers taken from a distance.

At the core of the filmmaking process were editing sessions with the workers, when they were asked to suggest the edits that best reflected their contribution to the whole production process. Skilled workers preferred the objective observational mode based on long takes and a minimum of editing, whereas the workers in the cold department preferred a more subjective representation of the labour process based on a quick editing pace, different camera angles, sensory close-ups and images showing their social interactions – having fun and talking by the machines.

In fact, the workers' preferred representations of their labour were quite different from the way they spoke about it. The skilled workers described it in holistic, multisensory and poetic terms, whereas the unskilled workers in quantitative and monetary terms. Also, skilled workers saw labour value as embodied in single, autonomous and virtuoso gestures, which explained their preference for unedited shots of individual tasks. For unskilled workers, on the other hand, the value of labour was relational, and they were keen to express such relationality through intercutting and superimposing different phases of the labour process.

Eventually, the editing sessions became a public forum about the value of their labour in which the workers' different perceptions and experiences were expressed and considered and 'agonistically' confronted each other. Despite their materialistic narratives, unskilled workers were egalitarian and collectivist, whereas skilled workers were sectionalist, individualistic and hierarchical. These conversations also triggered a more general reflection on the strange nature of that capitalist workshop and of the workers' role in it. Was such a sweatshop filled with Victorian machines really a capitalist workshop? Why was the owner never around? Who ran the business? Was it really a business? Why did they put up with working there?

It turned out that most workers, the migrants as well as the local, led difficult and precarious lives and yet money was not their primary motivation to work. Their salaries were well below the minimum wage and just above the unemployment benefit income. They mostly enjoyed the social relations in the workplace, the comradeship and the sense of solidarity that came from being still in employment despite the crisis in the steel industry. They all strongly opposed the model of urban regeneration that was being forced upon Sheffield by New Labour MPs and the EU, and they would rather be unemployed or on benefit than working in the local cultural and art sectors.

Steel Lives gives voice to different class positions (miners, women, migrants, steelworkers, tool makers, union representatives and the film crew) emphasizing their differences, uniqueness and tensions while also showing the invisible and affective threads that bind them together. It reflects and encompasses these different perceptions of work and labour value but also attempts to go beyond fragmentation, by showing above all a unified front of struggle and cohesion in their willingness to co-produce a collective point of view held by labour. It attempts to reconstruct a communist aesthetics based on the workers' efforts to create a common visual narrative of labour as organic totality, with the same revolutionary engagement that Lukács (1930) attributed to realist literature.

But I was not so much interested in realism as a pure ontological class position embodied in a specific aesthetic form. Rather, I was interested in realism as 'a methodology' revealing the internal tensions, contradictions and articulations between the two affective, political and epistemological regimes of identification (absorption) and critique (abstraction).[6]

In the film, the steelworkers never talk formal politics. Their political register is micro, informal and affective – based on jokes, hints and pragmatic utterances. The workshop is animated by a minor, sensory and embodied politics based on small interactions, fragile and fleeting positionalities and corporeal feelings, captured in the floating speckles of dust, the sonic reverberations and the undercurrents of draughts and heat splitting the shop floor into different microclimates and different entry points into the hallucinatory world of capitalism. In such micro and sensory observational space objects, machines and humans are organically interconnected, and humans are so entangled and absorbed in their work that they consider any direct commentary on work, including 'taking position' vis-à-vis the boss, 'tautological', 'alienating' or 'artificial'.

I often break such absorptive and intimate mode with my strong voice-over emphasizing the hazardous working conditions or the exploitative wages and endorsing the point of view of labour against the bosses (in heavily Italian-accented English), which creates an alienation effect by openly begging the question of why the images and/ or the subjects represented do not speak for themselves. Indeed, my voice is specifically intended to distinguish from the workers' relational and subjective experience of labour, the different class position of the filmmaker who is framing and holding that representation in place. That is to say: the viewer's empathic identification with the working-class subject is disturbed by the 'alienation effect' created by my authorial commentary, representing the point of view of a foreign observer.

The workers' absorption is itself one of the subjects of film, which is dreamy and surreal at times, mirroring the workers' surreal experience of labouring every day on such a Victorian shop floor. It shows that while at work, they drifted out into parallel thoughts and dreams – of playing snooker, fishing, or rambling with friends and family. They considered these dreams and imagination creeping into the workplace as minor forms of resistance against the boredom upon which the capitalist discipline is built. Yet it could be equally argued that daydreams and mental wanderings are precisely the raw material for capital's abduction of the agency of the workers.

Steel Lives ends with a close-up of a reflection of a derelict Victorian workshop floating on the surface of the river Don. Wildflowers and litter are scattered along the riverbank and a small red poppy stands out from a hybrid landscape of wires and grass. My voice-over asks: 'Is this what the economists call immaterial economy? Is this the future? And if so, what will come next?'

By ending its gaze on that surreal landscape – half industrial wasteland, half wild nature – the film is both a critique of capital's abstractions (especially historical narratives of decline, progress, modernity and backwardness) and a document of the deep scars it leaves on the landscape, in the form of industrial ruins, waste and ghostly remnants of labour – a smelter's glove, a broken tool, a personalized mug.

This is where I deal with the politics of time and memory, addressing the 'pensive spectator' (Mulvey, 2005) and endorsing 'left-wing melancholia' in a programmatic, rather than reactionary fashion.[7] The landscape, faces and machines depicted in *Steel Lives* are allegories of a 'pre-modern' capitalism – non-Fordist, independent, skilled and family-based – which was believed to have disappeared a long time ago. In fact, in the film we witness how the superfast and high-tech post-industrial capitalism resurrected slow and low-tech forms of Victorian artisanship, machine production and semi-indentured labour. Thus, it opens a space of both nostalgia for the disappearance of skilled labour and critique of the degenerated simulacrum of it, produced by capitalism. I consider this abstract and concrete space, where history confronts the ghosts of the present, as political.

The most meaningful experience on the film shoot came when we filmed the steelworkers walking through boarded-up pubs, highways and industrial ruins to reach their familiar pubs on a Saturday night. These walks were liberating and empowering because they showed that despite the forced relocations, the top-down economic conversions, and state repression in the form of disciplinary 'workfarism' or direct police aggression, working-class life was still standing. They showed how the workers' reappropriated movement as a form of resistance against capital.

Going back to Yazzie's statement about Western art: what Adair and Worth must have learnt from the Navajo films is that their aesthetics cannot be detached from their ontology or from their ways of sharing and generating knowledge. In 1966, Adair and Worth set up a media project to teach to a community of six hundred Navajo Indian in Palm Springs, Arizona, to make and edit films. Initially the anthropologists were surprised that most students' films depicted the act of walking and that, indeed, some were entirely about walking. Then, they realized that for the Navajos, walking is a foundational event, unlike in the

West where it is just a way of getting somewhere. This reflects Navajos' ontology which sees the universe as animated and in motion. Even neutral categories emerge from the motion of the universe. For instance, architecture is described as frozen music. Navajo myths and stories, too, focus on the act of walking and lack a linear plot and a closed ending.

By focusing on the act of walking, Navajo films strive to appropriate the movement of the cosmos. As in Navajo myths, this movement is not linear or smooth. The Navajo films in question are edited in jumps, cuts and spirals and with people coming out of nowhere. Unlike the smooth and naturalistic editing style of Western commercial cinema, which hides cuts, temporal disjunctures and differences, Navajo filmmaking emphasizes precisely the cuts, ruptures and gaps that interrupt human movement and make room for the transcendental. The Navajos' incorporation of uneven, illogical and jarring movement in their aesthetics, resembling the philosophies of imperfect or Third Cinema, not only challenges the linear logic of conventional storytelling. It is also a way of marking the cosmological space from which the human horizon emerges and acquires value.

Besides, the Navajos' insistence on representing the act of walking is also a gesture of walking away and taking a distance from Western way of making images, which, they believed, captured and stole the souls of the living. Thus, their films cropped human faces out or avoided their close-ups, shooting heads only from behind, because the filmmakers did not want the soul of the actors, whom they chose from among their kin, to be taken away by the camera. When animals were shot, they would ask permission to 'borrow' their image from their owners.

The Western artistic avant-garde was aware of the dehumanizing power of cinema and often used the camera to 'de-face' and de-construct the bourgeois person, as a broader critique of capitalism. Recall how Eisenstein used close-ups of faces to turn humans into political stereotypes ('the bourgeois', 'the scab' or 'the proletarian') or even animals/totems – a technique he learned from revolutionary theatre – or the way filmmaker Jean Epstein turns human faces into mysterious photogenetic landscapes. It has been argued that the freezing of people and objects by the Western cinematic avant-garde was a way of reaffirming movement, by virtue of its absence. But did such abduction of human agency by images really empower the working-class public?

The Navajos' claim that images disempower humans, deprive them of creativity – or soul – and force them into perpetual immobility resonates with the claim I have made in the first part of this book: that Western cinema reproduces the commodity form.

The Navajos' opposition to the commodification of images is aligned with Marx's and Lukács's theories of reification, described above. Brazilian philosopher Jean Tible describes the cosmopolitical ontologies and practices of commoning of the Yanomami people in the Amazon rainforest, which challenge the ideology of scarcity and competition of Western capitalism and prefigure an alternative world of excess and beauty, as instances of 'savage Marxism'.

I believe Yazzie's question remains: What did Adair and Worth's media project do for the Navajo community? At best, it can be said that it gave the Navajo community a means of self-representation, that is, of ontological reflection and re-enactment, albeit in a reduced and partial form, as negation of the Western commodity image. But it can also be argued that the project imperialistically imposed a Western alienating and commercial visual technology on to the multisensory and multimodal Navajo universe. In the end, making *Steel Lives* made me aware of the limitations of the film medium – even when it is participative and socially engaged – in relation to the possibility of prefiguring and implementing post-capitalist aesthetics and social relations. With their rigid narrative frames, singular authorial point of view, violent visual distance and predatory economies of production and circulation films reify life, in the sense discussed by Lukács (1968), in that they present a disconnected, alienated, fragmented and contingent world and co-opt into the commodity form, as the Navajos knew only too well, the social relations implicated in the film process.

2

BEYOND INSTITUTIONAL CRITIQUE:
INSTITUTING OTHERWISE WITH
ATHENS BIENNALE

After making *Steel Lives* I started looking for a practice that disposed not only of the artwork and of its technical apparatus of framing, but also of the individual, autonomous and private agency of the artist through which the public supposedly acquires self-consciousness. The realization of the possibilities of curating came when I attended a training course on Augusto Boal's 'invisible theatre' at the Centro do Teatro do Oprimido (CTO) in Rio de Janeiro. Unlike Boal's Theatre of the Oppressed, in which a main choreographer (*curinga*) leads an open process of negotiation of the story between actors and the public, invisible theatre is a process initiated by actors, which remains invisible and progressively involves the public, and radically upsets social conventions. The first invisible theatre performance took place in a busy restaurant in Buenos Aires. At the end of the meal an actor-customer told the waiter that he could not pay the bill and instead offered his labour. He asked the waiter how much he would be paid to take the rubbish out. Then, helped by other actors disguised as customers, he asked the real customers in the restaurant how they would remunerate different forms of labour. Eventually, these customers were asked to contribute to the bill.

Invisible theatre was developed by Boal while he was in exile in Argentina as a way of dealing with censorship and repression by the military junta. It was a form of organizing and articulating dissent that escaped the gaze of the authorities because it blurred the boundaries between public and private upon which states normally operate. Indeed, in Latin America there is a long tradition of time-specific, collective and performative political interventions, such as those by the Colectivo Acciones de Arte in Chile, the Brazilian collective 3Nós3 or the project Tucumán Arde in Argentina, in which artist and sociologist Roberto Jacoby collaborated with social scientists, the CGT trade union and the residents of the city of Tucuman in producing counter-information, highlighting the poverty and starvation caused by the closure of the local sugar mills and farms by the military regime, which was being covered up by the bourgeois media. I was intrigued by the hybrid nature of the Tucumán Arde project – part sociological workers' inquiry, part performance – and by how such performative, non-representational and politically engaged art defied the conventional Eurocentric boundaries between art, knowledge-production and activism.[1] Also, these conceptual experiments pointed to a different way of curating akin to the way I normally set up my ethnographic fieldworks – that is to say, as dialogical, sensory, multimodal, corporeal and open-ended collaborations and co-productions with 'the other' in which new practices of living and dwelling and new forms of resistance emerge in the 'threshold space' where the individual and the public merge into each other.

The chance to be involved in curating came when I was invited to be the programme and artistic director of Athens Biennale in 2015. The invitation came from Poka-Yo and Xenia Kalpatsoglou, directors of the Athens Biennale, after Poka-Yio and I met at an international symposium on art and politics. In his speech at the symposium, Poka-Yio described the relentless occupation of Athens by a new kind of poverty tourism fuelled by the economic crisis. Northern kids joined the autonomists' squats in Exarchia Square; up-and-coming artists and curators set up socially engaged art projects offering welfare services (such as migrant support, education and youth media training) that the collapsed Greek state was unable to provide, turning these services into Beuysian 'social sculptures'. Austerity politics was the hot topic of conversation even on the sandy beaches of the Greek islands.

Likewise, Poka-Yio and I were sceptical of the heavy political language – of decolonization, commoning and anarchism – spoken in that exclusive art venue which was largely funded by a wealthy capitalist and increasingly xenophobic Northern European state. Sneaking out from the symposium, over hot dogs and chips, we puzzled together: what would a really politically engaged art institution – one supported neither by the state nor by the private sector – look like? We came to the realization that in Athens the conditions were ripe to try out such an experiment.

Past 'post-occupy art'

Since its opening in 2005, the Athens Biennale had been a subversive and experimental art institution critically reflexive of both mainstream art and politics and of the new narratives that were being imposed upon Greece by Europe's centres as the nation was being co-opted into the euphoric 1990s movements of global finance. *Agora*, the name of Athens Biennale's (AB) 2013 edition, was set in the empty building of the former Athens stock exchange and captured the sense of urgency and effervescence of that moment of capitalism in crisis and of popular rebellion against austerity that coalesced in Syntagma Square in May 2011. The legend has it that it was the horizontal, bottom-up and participative format of *Agora* that inspired Adam Szymczyk to move the next iteration of the contemporary art exhibition documenta 14 from Kassel to Athens and collaborate with the Athens Biennale.

In 2013, 44 per cent of the population had an annual income below the poverty line (7,180 euros per year), unemployment was at nearly 30 per cent, and the state was shutting down health clinics, primary and secondary schools and support structures for refugees. Poor neighbourhoods were without electricity or water. By then, the Syntagma movement had reorganized itself into horizontal neighbourhood assemblies and solidarity networks providing health care, education and food in self-organized solidarity clinics, schools and food markets. Exchanges of services between these urban commons were based on time-banks, a bartering system for services, where people exchange services for labour-time–based credits, rather than money, which effectively demonetized, socialized and 'de-grew' the economy, bringing it under citizens' control. There were also several successful industrial workers' occupations, for instance, of the Vio.Me factory in Thessaloniki.

In addition, responding to the radical cuts to the arts and culture sectors, cultural workers occupied the Embros theatre, the national television network ERT, the national newspaper *Eleftherotypia*, and bookshops, print shops and libraries. Film, art and architectural collectives sprung up everywhere. *Agora* was a call for the public to come together and collaborate at such moment of economic crisis and social solidarity. It did so through a subversive format, which shifted authorship from the artist and the curator to the public itself, and set up discursive, performative, grassroots and research-based dialogues between art professionals and people from different disciplines.

The wave of occupations and socialization of the art and cultural sectors in Athens reflected the worldwide radicalization of cultural workers and the global mobilizations of the 2010s in which they had a central role – for example in the Gezi Park uprising, the 15-M in Spain, the Maidan in Kiev, the *movimento Beni Comuni* in Italy, and in Occupy

Wall Street and Occupy London. From these urban mobilizations new municipal platforms emerged in Spain, Greece and Italy, led by grassroots cultural and civic organizations, scholars, artists' collectives and intellectuals, and upsetting the normal course of parliamentary politics. Art historian Yates McKee defines this transmutation of art into forms of direct actions, political organizing and urban occupation taking place outside the normal bounds of art as 'strike art' or the 'post-occupy condition'.[2]

From the movements of the Square a new Gramscian, Lacanian and postcolonial left emerged (*Syriza* in Greece and *Podemos* in Spain), veering away from the Marxist notion of class struggle and emphasizing instead the centrality of cultural struggles for gaining popular support. Its leaders advocated an anti-hegemonic politics, which discoursively articulated different and often antagonistic class positions in the horizontal institutional formats of civic platforms and 'assemblies of assemblies' instead of the vertical and homogeneous party. These political platforms emerged from basic economic struggles (house repossessions or the high cost of transport). Moreover, they were 'populist' in the sense that their political imaginary rested on the figure of 'the people' – instead of the capitalist individual or the Marxist class – and their cohesion came from their common opposition to 'the powerful elites', rather than from a shared class consciousness. Art and cultural organizations were central in crafting common political imaginaries and socializing cultural skills for these new municipal platforms. For instance, Teatro Valle Beni Comuni in Rome was one of the first occupied spaces in Europe to set up a (short-lived) agreement of co-management with the municipality.

Similarly, under the direction of Manuel Borja Villel, the MACBA became a node of aggregation for social centres, neighbourhood associations and occupied spaces revolving around the platform Barcelona en Comú, which subsequently won control of the municipality. For example, in 2001 MACBA supported the national campaign against the World Bank coordinated by the art collective *Fiambrera Obrera* and organized international symposia and events around this issue with international activist groups such as Reclaiming the Streets, the Yes Men and Indymedia. The museum also operated 'under the radar' through its public programme based in *Espai Obert*, an autonomous social centre, working with the collective Las Agencias – made up of neighbourhood associations, feminist and ecological groups, squats, social centres, NGOs, university assemblies and local residents – in the Raval neighbourhood in a space the museum had made available free to the collective. Las Agencias organized anti-corporate actions (such as *economia de casino*), counter-information campaigns (such as *dinero gratis*) and anti-gentrification demonstrations in the Raval, which was undergoing a process of clean-up and gentrification.[3]

MACBA embodied the so-called radical museology paradigm (Bishop, 2013), in which public contemporary art museums started to act like anti-capitalist movements, refusing commodified art forms and engaging directly with an expanded and emancipated public in post-representational, discursive and radical pedagogical practices. There were problems with 'radical museology' – the institutionalization of institutional critique, the emergence of forms of authored activism and the co-optation of urban commons by increasingly corporatized museums. Nonetheless, 'radical museums' were able to push forward progressive, if not anti-capitalist, platforms in some municipalities.

The radicalization of cultural workers and museums was due to their strong bargaining power linked to the exponential growth of the cultural, art and media industries worldwide. Tourism, art and culture are the central motors of the Western post-industrial economies, structurally coupled with finance, around which new invisible urban factories and sweatshops are being established and a new cultural proletariat is emerging. Progressive municipalities understood that to prevent the wholesale privatization of cities by an increasingly aggressive and monopolistic *rentierist* block, they had to empower museums and cultural workers and give them the resources to socialize, co-manage and de-commodify the cultural sector. But while for municipalities this was a short-term and oppositional measure to fend off the private sector, for the commoners the aim was to render these new socialized urban spaces sustainable, and while generating new forms of public value or *commonfare*,[4] avoid being incorporated inside the state, the private sector or the public museums that sponsored them.

The movement of the Square emerged also from the renewal of the feminist movement and of alternative and queer political subjectivities associated with new forms of public gathering and people's assemblies, which challenged and deconstructed the male, individualist and heterosexual bourgeois imaginary and advocated the right to appear against the exclusionary biopolitics of capitalism. In Athens, the occupations of Green Park in 2015 and of Navarino Park were led by a young generation of women artists with a background in performance, film studies and architecture, who considered these occupations to be practices of spatial justice and grassroots democracy based on new ways of inhabiting and activating the city. Besides, under the direction of geographer Stavros Stravrides, the faculty of architecture of the National Technical University of Athens (NTUA) had become a hub for radical new experiments in urban commoning and collaborations between teaching staff, students and social centres.

In 2015 when I took the reins of the biennale, the situation had radically changed since the time of *Agora*. The Greek government, led by Syriza, had been brought to its knees by the European troika[5] and forced to agree on its bailout – which the Greek people had just rejected in a dramatic national referendum. The urban organizations from the art sector and outside it, which had emerged from the anti-austerity movement and practised some forms of cooperativism, commons, self-organization and participatory democracy, were barely surviving. The state and national capital had collapsed so that there was no public or private institution to resist or critique. In Athens, the public contemporary art museum EMST had been shut down for years, and independent art initiatives – including fringe festivals, socially engaged and even anti-capitalist projects – were kept alive by the two major Greek private art institutions: NEON and Onassis. Even grassroots initiatives by the Solidarity4All movement in support of migrants, solidarity schools and autonomous film collectives were adopting the private legal form of NGOs and non-for-profit organizations in order to attract private capital. Art and activism in Athens had passed the post-occupy condition.

Considering this history of appropriation of grassroots art and activism by the private sector, I did not want the biennale to incorporate existing urban commons (the urban hub model discussed above) or be in agonistic dialogue with them (the radical museological model). Instead, I wanted the biennale *to become* a commons, producing and sustaining forms of non-alienated art and life and bringing into coexistence heterogeneous, fluid and dispersed economies and subjectivities.

OMONIA (unity): Instituting the collective subject

The chosen title of the biennial edition OMONIA AB5toAB6 (*OMONIA* means 'harmony' or 'unity' in Greek) reflected our chosen location in OMONIA Square – an urban heterotopia where migrants, homeless people, street vendors, office workers, retailers, professionals and tourists come together every day – and signalled our ambition to connect to the fluid, diverse and dispersed political and cultural ecology of the city, acting as a social threshold and a connective tissue between museums, civic organizations, occupied spaces, the independent art scene and an expanded public.

OMONIA AB5toAB6 was located in the magnificent four-storey Bageion Hotel built in 1890 by architect Ernst Ziller, which was in a state of disrepair when we first entered it and which the biennale team cleaned, fixed and fitted with bathrooms and solar panels. The central area of the building has a vast glass roof, which casts a spectacular light down into it. In 1930 the Bageion Hotel was the spiritual refuge of a bohemian community of communist and gay poets, intellectuals and writers like Napoleon Lapathiotis, Mitsos Papanikolaou and Tellos Agras, who met in the hotel's cafe on the lower ground floor. In choosing the Bageion Hotel, we wanted also to valorize this Greek modernist architectural and literary legacy, underrepresented in the European art historical canon. The entrance to the Bageion was permanently hidden by a row of street-market stalls and was difficult to locate. On a voluntary basis the AB team offered free guided tours of the building, mostly to Athenian residents and occasionally to tourists. The ground floor was used for films installations; the first floor for temporary exhibitions and projects; the second floor for the resident groups; the central ballroom for workshops and symposia; and on the third floor there was a fifty-seat cinema.

My first objective was to invert the Fordist logic of art biennials, based, first, on mass-producing artworks and then marketing and distributing them to the public. In order to achieve this, we first reached out to our intended public with the clear proposal of jointly developing an urban commons. Then, we hosted some of these groups in the Bageion developing common vocabularies and practices with them in support of their projects. Third, we organized international 'summits' at which we invited the public and some selected experts (rather than the usual academic stars) to co-produce knowledge about commons and post-capitalism. Finally, we commissioned work by those established international and Greek artists who were committed to work towards the construction of a commons. In this model the relationship with the 'emancipated public' came first and the commissioning of the artwork came last.

In addition, instead of working towards the final climaxing opening in 2017, we established a two-year-long process bridging AB5 and AB6. We intended for AB to become a permanent cultural and artistic laboratory to last well beyond 2017.

In September 2015, after two months of research and mapping of social centres and urban commons, I met about thirty grassroots groups divided into four categories: (1) *cooperatives*, including worker-run factories, independent publishers, a self-managed newspaper and television company, and a rural cooperative; (2) *urban commons*, including occupied theatres, filmmaking and feminist collectives, squats for the homeless and radical pedagogy collectives; (3) *hackers*: cryptocurrency collectives; P2Plabs and urban wireless networks; and (4) the Solidarity4All network, including social and health clinics, schools for refugees and migrants, social kitchens and anti-fascist groups.

After the meeting thirteen organizations agreed to be permanently resident in the Bageion. Some were well-established Greek art collectives (such as Campus Novel, 3137, Depression Era and Urban Dig) or established curators such as Iliana Fokanidis from State of Concept, the first non-profit gallery in Greece, who at the time was running an important project of free consultations to artists. Others were activist organizations such as the radical pedagogy group Avtonomi Akademia or the Residents of Mets Initiative, an ecological group based in the Met area. Some groups were sceptical about joining the biennale. Others supported the proposal as external collaborators. Having mapped the existing expertise, we developed initial conversations with commons that had important technical skills and local knowledge – for instance, on de-growth, de-monetized economies, wireless communities, co-housing and sustainable architecture.

In the opening speech of AB5to6 OMONIA on 17 November, entitled *Introducing a Laboratory for Production Post-2011*, I argued that the biennale's main ambition was to learn from the existing urban movements in Athens how to become a cultural commons and, in turn, involve them in the co-management of the institution. In particular, I emphasized how urban commons

- are committed to collective, process-based and open-ended ways of working;
- are aware of the performative dimension of politics and the play of emotions, desires and affects in material life;
- experiment with new institutional forms that cut across the state and the market; self-determination and institutionalization; autonomy and the collective;
- struggle against the privatization of the state and provide free welfare, food and education using culture both as a common resource and as a space of democratic participation.

I highlighted three dimensions of collaboration and dialogue with the movement of the commons, which also formed the biennale's three main conceptual vectors: (1) *Alternative Economy* focused on how to implement permanently and in a sustainable way the four post-capitalist economic institutions of alternative currencies, cooperativism, urban welfare or *'commonfare'*, and commons; (2) *Rethinking Institutions* looked at alternatives to the existing corporate/ Fordist model of running biennales and explored specific strategies of cultural commoning and forms of 'instituting otherwise'; (3) *the Performative in the Political*, taking as a starting point the feminist notion of performativity developed by critical theorist Judith Butler, explored the intersection between modes of public assembly and forms of political subjectivity, particularly in terms of intersectionality and the convergence between anti-capitalist and postcolonial politics. This session asked: 'In what ways does the coming together in communal and assembly-based institutional settings such as that of AB contribute to imagining post-capitalist and non-Eurocentric forms of political subjectivity and agency?'

I wanted to explore the performative potential of durational art events such as biennales to produce 'inoperative communities', sharing sensuous, corporeal, dialogical, practical and multimodal forms of living and dwelling in commons. Besides, the notion of political performativity referred to the idea of curating as a politically militant and non-Eurocentric form of knowledge production. I was interested in how the tradition of workers' inquiries and action research could be brought into conversation with artistic practices, such as in the paradigmatic case of *Tucuman Arde* in order to explore the very conditions of production of the biennale – the local economies, the class relations and the broader structural forces of Greece's dependent development vis-à-vis the EU – taking the point of view of those precarious and anti-systemic social groups that are normally marginal to the art world.

The opening symposium ('Summit') was divided into three sessions corresponding to the three main conceptual strands of OMONIA – *Alternative Economies* (divided into four panels: labour, cooperativism, commons and alternative currencies), *Rethinking Institutions*, and the *Performative in the Political* and included scholars, curators, activists, members from workers-run companies and cooperatives, and artists directly engaging with these thematic strands.[6]

On the following day, we invited into the Bageion forty-five groups of workers-run companies, cooperatives, solidarity spaces, urban commons, social centres and solidarity organizations and asked them how the theoretical issues debated on the previous day related to their activist experience and invited them to make a list of recommendations for action – in terms of both art production and urban commoning in Athens – to be undertaken by the biennale in the next two years. After four hours of group discussion we started a general assembly in which we sketched out the main lines of collaboration between AB and commons, social centres and art organizations and some ideas for the OMONIA public programme in the next two years (see Appendix One).

The general assembly was heated and emotional. First, there was the issue of the economy. Would the biennale support these commoning projects directly in cash, in kind or through artistic interventions? How would the biennale pay its workers? Would it pay the artists in residence? Then, there was the political framework of the commons, which some felt was Eurocentric and ignored the local political context. Moreover, occupations and commons had already been appropriated and commodified by the art world (for instance, in the 7th Berlin Biennale), and there was a sense that our general assembly was more a performative staging of direct action than a truly democratic and consensus-based event. Lastly, there was a palpable resistance by some curators and private art organizations to my choice of having an 'artless Biennale' – as the press described it after the opening[7] – as this bypassed the normal circuit of capitalist value creation and pimping.

The participating public, a mix of international and Greek artists, activists, curators, art dealers and collectors, was jammed into the majestic neoclassical ballroom of the Bageion, reflected in two giant rococo mirrors as they sat in a circle. No doubt the gathering had a theatrical and ritualistic flavour. But there was a feeling that a new political subjectivity was coming together – diverse, polyphonic and committed to a long-term and collective dialogue. In the conversation, social centres suggested that OMONIA AB5 to 6 could function as a transitional institutional space accommodating a new coalition of subjects across the art and activist worlds, but without the ambition to become a stable configuration. Indeed, given the context of deep political and economic crisis at the time, OMONIA was perceived as transient and transitional from the very beginning. This was a challenge for AB, as it is precisely the combination of fungibility, repeatability and short-term profitability of biennales – the opposite of the de-commodified, localized and durational format we were proposing – that attracts private institutions and the international public.

On the evening of the general assembly, as squatters, activist groups and 'artivists'[8] came together to discuss occupations and actions, intellectuals and scholars discussed about post-capitalism and collectors, art historians and curators assessed the curatorial value of OMONIA – all under the vigilant and voracious eyes of the press – I appreciated the immense power of art in triggering specific social relations and intended behaviours. But was that first meeting a real first step towards creating a commons? Or was it just a performance? This question haunted me. I knew that it is precisely on such spaces of uncertainty and social prefiguration that the artistic mode of speculation thrives. But how to stabilize and concretize those fleeting unfolding social relations which had been triggered by the speculative energy of the art opening?

During the ten days of the first iteration ('Synapse') there was a huge self-mobilization of the artists in the Bageion. Curator Iliana Fokianadi opened an office for one-to-one art consultancies; activist Julia Strauss organized six lectures for the Avtonomi Akadimia's winter sessions; film director Takis Spetsiotis read out poems by Napoleon Lapathiotis; Valentina Karga gave a performative lecture on the value of immaterial labour in art; Anastasia Douka made colourful chair covers for the cinema at the Bageion as part of her screening of Marco Bellocchio's 'I Pugni in Tasca' (Fists in the Pocket); architect Fanis Kafantaris organized a group walk through the unoccupied empty buildings in OMONIA Square; the Met group organized a workshop on sustainable practices, starting from a Wi-Fi, water and electricity self-sustainability project in Bageion; the collective Depression Era discussed their 'tourism' project, connecting the predatory economy of tourism in Greece to the broader structural forces of war, economic dispossession and mass migration; and Ivor Stodolsky and Marita Muukkonen from Perpetuum Mobile (PM) gave a lecture on artists-led humanitarian interventions, presenting their collaboration with AB on the project Artists at Risk (AR), an international residency for artists, curators, critics and scholars who were targets of politically motivated threat and persecution across the world.

AB's relationship with the twelve groups hosted in the Bageion was a mixture of collaboration, negotiation and horizontal 'agonism'.[9] AB gave each of them the symbolic fee of €500 for an initial six-month-long collaboration – including on research and fundraising. With Kalpaktsoglou I had developed durational and one-to-one conversations with each group, with the aim of finding a common understanding of the conceptual framework of OMONIA, facilitating their artistic practices in relation to it, and developing joint funding applications.

These relationships were central to our vision of OMONIA. Some collectives, such as Depression Era and 3137, used the Bageion as a performative base, not for residence. Other artists such as Giorgia Sagri and Margherita Tsomou were tremendously supportive of the biennale as a political/institutional project but did not participate in it as artists. Some collectives considered the Bageion a space to occupy for their own ends, hosting parallel activities and political meetings below the official radar of OMONIA with the aim of turning Bageion into a counter-institutional space developing a critical and agonistic view of AB.

The movement of self-organization by local artists became evident especially after the international summits, when the international art crowd disappeared. Its absence was palpable in the trendy streets and cafes of Exarchia. But the week-long programmes self-organized by the resident groups in the Bageion after the international events were filled by a different, local crowd from across the artistic spectrum. For instance, in addition to the programme put together by the artists residents for Sinapse2, various independent art platforms ran non-mainstream projects in the Bageion – a queer, gay and transgender performance festival; a programme of Arab films censored by the state; and several experimental theatre productions.

That the independent art sector was establishing a stable operative base in the Bageion, mostly outside the mainstream events, was an achievement for AB, especially Kalpatsoglou and me; we had been working hard towards establishing a stable relationship with these independent art organizations, with the aim of enabling them to become the driving force of the biennale. The Athenian independent art sector, with its molecular and dispersed creativity, capacity for self-organization, sustainable low growth and resilience in times of crisis, constituted the perfect economic/ecological paradigm of life in post-capitalist conditions. It also embodied the urban cultural commons, as described by David Harvey (2012). But I was aware that such independent art space was being targeted by private capital precisely for its sustainability and productivity, a sign of which was Szymczyk's decision to open d14 in Athens.

With Kalpatsoglou we organized Acts of Involvement, a discussion with seven well-known independent Greek initiatives on how the political and economic climate of the time affected their practices. There was scepticism among the younger generations of artists towards the political framework of the biennale, especially the notion of the commons. Against this framework, they described themselves as entrepreneurial, individualist, free-riders, and even selfish. They considered the whole idea of the gift economy part of the 'cruel optimism' of late capitalism – an exhortation to put up with it which, in fact, reproduced existing structures of inequality. They did not like institutions, especially state institutions, and feared becoming institutionalized – although one artist claimed to miss 'not having any institution to be against'.

Yet, despite these self-descriptions, their practices were deeply relational, durational and non-commercial. They had set up gallery spaces in their homes or in squatted buildings and regularly involved each other in long-term conversations, collective writings and rotating curatorial sessions within their inner circle and occasionally involving their international networks. They avoided the official art circuit and worked through personal relations, word of mouth and informal communications. They experimented with different media – predominantly painting, but also collective writing and readings. Two artists had set up international residencies: one in an up-and-coming area of Athens and another in an Ionian island. They survived through a mixture of support from private art institutions, fundraising and mutual help. Some were involved in the struggles to unionize the art sector and for the artists' rights to pensions.

A good example of the relational politics of the independent art sector in Athens was the residency space Ὕλη[matter]HYLE opened by performance artist Georgia Sagri in her small one-bedroom flat near OMONIA Square. Sagri is well known for the way she has actualized the tradition of feminist performance and Fluxus in the context of late capitalism and from the point of view of Greece, intended as a periphery of EU. Her cruel and durational public performances addressed directly and uncompromisingly capitalism's biopolitics – the way capital becomes inscribed on to the female body itself, affecting social habits and identities. In the piece *Polytechnic* – made in 1999, when she was twenty – Sagri stood semi-naked inside a vitrine for seven hours in the middle of the mass commemoration of the uprising against the military in November 1973. In the film of the performance, which we showed together with her other work at the Athens Biennale, the glass cage containing Sagri's body is seen ripping at the seams the dense sea of red flags otherwise effortlessly flowing past the Athens Polytechnic. The impenetrability and vulnerability of Sagri's body addressed an alternative kind of counter-biopolitics to the homogeneous self-directed and linear movement of the masses. In the performance *The Invisible Ones* (2008), Sagri acted out the process of being repeatedly struck by an invisible blow, falling and rising to the sound of the strike for three hours, staging a kind of possession ritual against the invisible forces of the market, which is hard to witness.

Yet the contemplative atmosphere of Sagri's flat triggered a different and more constructive dynamic, inviting the guests into an unknown social space – neither private nor public but 'semiprivate' – and asking them to engage with mechanisms of disactivating capital's biopolitics. I was touched by a glass jar at the entrance, politely asking for donations to pay the electricity bills. In Sagri's small bedroom, David Harvey and David Graeber had famously discussed communism surrounded by an electrified international art crowd. Sagri argued that the Athenian art scene was deeply marked by such mixture of work and personal life and that, in the absence of consolidated art markets and audiences, intimate conversations and social interactions among friends, constituted both a form of aesthetic practice and a social process of mutual care and healing within the artists' community.

The practical philosophy of these independent art organizations also reflected the spirit of OMONIA. Events, discussions, shows and gatherings inside the Bageion were spontaneous and self-organized, advertised through word of mouth, supported by micro-budgets and involving people who knew each other. Despite the scepticism shown by part of the local art community towards the idea of turning the Athens Biennale into a commons, the space of the Bageion was beginning to function like a commons because outside the summits, its programme and activities were informal, spontaneous and self-organized with only logistical support from the biennale team – Marilena Batali, Vanessa Melissourgaki and Nefeli Myrodia – whose professionalism in adapting to flexible and changing schedules was impressive. The Bageion was always full of people constructing sets, performing, discussing and listening to each other. These relationships in the building shaped the general mood and practices of OMONIA.

As well as developing social relations in commons with local artist groups, we involved in the process of commoning more established international artists. Our main sponsor was the NEON Foundation, which gave us 40,000 euros towards art production with no conditions attached. We used this money to commission artworks from Suzanne Lacy, Theaster Gates, Sophia Dona, Dexter Sinister and the twelve groups based in the Bageion.

Despite going along with the commercial logic that asks biennales to produce new work, the kinds of relationships and projects we supported were deeply performative and politically engaged.

Suzanne Lacy's work was emblematic of the kind of art AB wanted to support – durational, grassroots and activist. I had been inspired by Lacy's recent project, Between the Door and the Street, a conversation about gender, race, ethnicity and class the American artist had with over 400 women activists in New York City over the course of five months and which ended up in a performative public conversation on sixty stoops in Brooklyn.

Lacy travelled to Athens to meet activists from the anti-house repossession groups and social centres operating with homelessness and migrants. She involved in the initial conversation Nobel Prize–winning economist Joseph Stiglitz, former Chief Economist and Senior Vice President of the World Bank in the 1990s, who had become the leading voice of the anti-globalization movement – including of OWS, whose political slogan, 'We are the 1%', was taken from an article Stiglitz wrote for *Vanity Fair*.

At the time of AB, Stiglitz was leading the international outcry against the European Troika over its dealing with Greece's debt. Casting the Eurozone as a profiteering scheme run by Germany, Stiglitz inspired the 'Grexit' plan proposed by Syriza's main economist, Costas Lapavistas which was supported across the Greek political spectrum, including the radical left, social movements and urban commons. At that time, the biennale was connected to local hackers and activists who were frantically working underground to develop an anti-capitalist crypto currency in preparation for the disbanding of the euro. I supported 'Grexit', as in my opinion it would have reconnected the left-wing faction of Syriza that had remained in the Tsipras government to the vast network of social centres and civic organizations that had initially supported it, especially the Solidarity 4 All coalition, which since 2011 had been building a vast non-monetary network of free exchange – of social services, food and even 'natural' commons such as electricity and water – to which the new currency could have attached itself to.

Lacy envisaged her project to be a durational conversation between herself, Stiglitz and some heavily indebted families, on austerity in Greece in the final form of a live performance, video or publication with Stiglitz talking about the dire social consequences of the crisis.

AB's other main production was with Sophia Dona, a Greek architect working at the intersection of art and urbanism and a member of the Athenian Green Park collective. Dona proposed the cohabitation project AKINITO (landed property), a collaboration with architects, lawyers, urban planners, economists and some European housing project initiatives. The basic premise of the project was that the Greek model of co-ownership of large buildings by single extended families represented a Mediterranean model of co-governance – based on a mixture of conflicts, negotiations and anti-market regulations – similar to the anti-gentrification and cohabitation strategies used by housing project initiatives in Leipzig and Zurich, where Dona had previously worked. Her project was set up to explore how to hybridize the anti-gentrification and co-housing strategies developed in northern Europe, which somehow ended up being depersonalized and overcentralized, with the family-based and personalistic Mediterranean model. I thought that the AKINITO project furthered in a clever way some important cultural differences through which forms of commoning and socialization are imagined in Europe – the German model being premised upon the idea of homogeneous political communities, the southern model on the fractious affectivity experienced within close-knit families, but both being equally dysfunctional.

The project started with a symposium in the Begeion with anthropologists, geographers, architects and one of the leaders of the 116 existing 'housing syndicates' in Germany, Marcel Seehuber. A workshop followed the symposium, focused on the legal, organizational and economic practicalities of setting up a housing project in Athens. Artist and architect Marjetica Potrč talked of participatory design in community-based projects; Seehuber described in detail the functioning of German housing syndicates; and a Greek housing activist proposed a P2P tool to socialize the Airbnb network in Athens – which, together with the huge number of empty buildings, heavily distorted the local housing market – and to turn such a network into a non-profit-sharing platform.

At the end of the workshop, a member of the public approached us suggesting we try out the AKINITO housing model on the empty estate she owned in the city centre. After a conversation with Dona, we agreed to explore the co-habitation model for AB, starting by exploring a legal framework for co-ownership of the building with art groups and urban commons as a first step towards AB's post-capitalist transformation. In fact, the German model combined three central post-capitalist elements: (1) the de-commodification of the housing market through collective ownership; (2) reciprocal exchanges of 'solidarity money' and labour across the nodes of the syndicate; and (3) democratic self-governance. Regarding this last point, the buildings of the housing syndicates are co-managed by the residents' associations – composed of residents co-owners – and the syndicates – composed of the members of all associations.

In conclusion, instituting the commons as a collective subject was difficult, especially because the majority of independent art organizations and urban commons, which in our mind constituted the core of such a collective subject, wanted to remain autonomous from any formal institutional engagement, including with AB.

In 2015, the ecology of art organizations in Athens reflected the wider neoliberal institutional landscape polarized between a small number of powerful private institutions (in the Greek case the family-owned private foundations NEON and Onassis) and a vast number of small independent art organizations, start-ups and urban commons – the immense wealth of the former supporting the profitless operations of the latter and often relying on their cheap labour. The independent art sector regularly received funding from these private foundations as well as being self-sustaining through its own sharing network; therefore they did not want to be involved in a long-term and labour intensive collaboration with AB.

Their refusal was partly due to their scepticism over OMONIA's focus on commoning – an understandable scepticism given how the word 'common' had been uncritically appropriated by the cultural sector first, in the 1980s, and more recently under the banner of relational art. Likewise, urban commons preferred to be sponsored by the same private foundations for their politically engaged projects, rather than engage with AB.

But there were also encouraging signs. Some independent art organizations made their stable base in the Bageion; others regularly involved AB in their activities. Likewise, we had developed a dialogue with some urban commons, but these relationships followed the slow and uneven temporality of solidarity in times of survival.

I was aware that AB could not be turned into a commons, by simply making it autonomous from private capital or simply creating a self-enclosed artistic community. Rather, commons emerge from building relationships of trust and reciprocity; learning to work, make and dwell together; and valorizing differences, all of which require time, more time than any biennial can offer. Besides, in order for a collective institutional subject to emerge, it was necessary to put in place a solid ecological and economic infrastructure for sustaining the commons.

The contested political economy of art: Between commons and rentier capitalism

As well as socializing the building of the Athens Biennale, through a co-ownership scheme, I was determined to socialize its labour, through the implementation of some cryptocurrency project. I imagined that this double form of socialization, of property and of labour, would lay the ground for a sustainable and participatory economy for AB, bypassing the exploitative economy and alienating labour processes in the art and cultural sectors. We started by looking into alternative economies right after the general assembly on 19 November with Emanuele Braga (from the collective Macao), Andrea Fumagalli and members of the Spanish financial cooperative platform FairCoop which also included the FairCoin cryptocurrency. With his collective Macao and through international collaborations, Braga had been experimenting with cryptocurrencies and parasitical finance for some time, seeking to implement in practice, the models of the *moneta del commune* (the currency of the commons) developed by heterodox economists.[10] Unlike other cryptocurrencies, which are essentially a form of capitalist money independent from state control, the model proposed by Braga and Fumagalli links the use of digital currency to the creation of alternative labour-value circuits. For instance, from a commoning point of view, it can be argued that the reproductive labour of cleaning the toilets of the Bageion or demanding translation work should be paid more than curatorial or artistic labour.

Moreover, some alternative currencies, such as FairCoins, are guaranteed by ethical banks and, therefore, easily convertible into euros. The common currency system would have allowed the Athens Biennale to account for and remunerate all its employees, including volunteers and interns. Lastly, because cryptocurrencies rely on a collectively agreed value system, they also automatically set up a model of collective governance. That is to say, they open the decision-making process regarding labour remuneration to the currency-holders, unlike capitalist money which is anonymous and impersonal.

To explore the use of FairCoins in OMONIA I met its creator Enric Duran, the famous Catalan financial activist who back in 2005 borrowed 424,000 euros from thirty-nine different financial entities, which he had no intention of repaying, to fund various anti-capitalist projects. Duran was a celebrity in the art world because through his Troika Fiscal Disobedience Consultancy (TFDC) he was beating the financial system on its own turf, creating shell companies and parasitical currencies to support social movements and grassroots cooperatives including FairCoop, which was present at OMONIA's general assembly.

The meeting with Duran was short. He asked me to invest a minimum of 15,000 euros in FairCoins. Then he left abruptly, apparently because he was being chased by some undercover intelligence agent. Given his track record of defaulted payments, I gently turned down the offer – the money he asked for was nearly half of AB's budget. Also, Duran's impersonal and detached business attitude made me fear that FairCoin was just another form of capitalist money used by anti-capitalists to bankroll the 'art' system – in this specific instance, the Athens Biennale.

Instead of investing in an existing international cryptocurrency, I felt that the Athens Biennale needed to develop its own currency, compatible with its economic structure and with the local economic landscape. We invited art critic Kuba Szreder,[11] who had set up several projects for mapping the economies of the art sector, to map the economy of AB starting with a workshop in the Bageion. Szreder used Gibson-Graham's feminist, queer and discoursive approach, asking the workshop participants to classify their experiences first in the art industry and then of AB, along the three dimensions of entrepreneurship (non-capitalist, capitalist, state capitalism), transactions (market, gift and quasi-markets) and labour (unpaid, waged and paid in kind). Participants found it difficult to classify artistic labour according to these objective criteria as their experience of it was uniquely emotional and personal. It was precisely this speculative gap between subjectivity and surplus value – thrived upon by the art world – that we wanted to capture with the workshop. But we struggled to come up with a final model. With Szreder I agreed that we would initiate a project of mapping the economies of the Athens Biennale as a first step towards the constitution of an AB currency.

The issue of OMONIA's economy was complex. We started with no money, apart from the sums Poka Yio and Kalpatsoglou had received from the prestigious ECF Princess Margrit Award which they decided to split with AB's two collaborators (one working full-time and one half-time), thus covering their wages until 2016. I had agreed with Kalpatsoglou and Poka-Yio that I should not be paid or receive any fee or monetary compensation because I knew that AB did not have the money, and I continued to receive a salary from Goldsmiths, where I worked full-time. An ex-Goldsmiths MA anthropology student worked for AB for six months, supported by an Erasmus scholarship under my mentorship. When I took over, the biennale operated through a mixture of waged and unwaged economy, private entrepreneurship and minority governance by the directors. This structure was very different from that of a commons.

I mentioned above the structural coupling between small-scale organizations and private monopolies in the art sector. Since its inception, the Athens Biennale had managed to operate in between these two institutional poles. The scale of its operations was the same as that of big organizations, but it was achieved by allotting several productive tasks to external service providers or to the artists themselves – pretty much like the prototypical model of flexible production in which the main firm internalizes only the brand and externalizes all the other productive and non-productive activities to small-scale suppliers. In the context of economic crisis and social emergency, this model worked well, as the Athens Biennale had become a 'cultural catalyst' able to attract, and multiply around its brand, the existing circuits of reciprocity and solidarity within the art community – which was willing to self-organize, pool labour and waive off fees in solidarity – and to capitalize on such bottom-up process of value creation.

But this dynamic had pulled AB into the same logic of continuous growth and short-term speculation of big museums and smaller organizations which was unsustainable for it. With OMONIA, I was keen to reverse this trend – from capitalizing on the value created by the dispersed art community to co-creating it with it, and following a long-term, relational and spatially grounded logic. It was clear to me that to counter the de-territorialization associated with the management of the Athens Biennale as a global brand, a counter-process of re-territorialization was needed. Moreover AB, with its fluid, flexible and scalable structure, could operate anywhere between these two institutional extremes and combine very different institutional logics – that of commons, confederation of commons, party, activist organization, museum, policy-making body, transnational institute, an artists' run space or a small collective.

A few months into OMONIA, the biennale was becoming entangled with different value circuits: the non-market economy and socialized ecology of solidarity groups and urban commons; the molecular network of 'start-up' art organizations (entrepreneurial, flexible and profit-orientated); the transnational market circuit of private funders, curators and artists (who nonetheless agreed to operate according to the logic of reciprocity and gift-giving, with token fees well below their 'normal market value'); and an international public keen to connect to non-professionalized art organizations and social centres in Athens.

But it was difficult to match our relational, multimodal and spatially embedded institutional structure to the economy with which we were involved. We did not want to follow the radical museological model: internalizing activism, education and research and having the state sponsoring our critical thinking. Neither did we want to externalize criticality onto the community, speculating on the general intellect of the commons and unwaged labour. I wanted AB to function as an 'institutional threshold' both *outside* the capitalist state and *inside* the new socialized public sphere which the state had abandoned. In fact, urban commons, solidarity organizations and radical art collectives in Athens were aware that not only 'the public' but also 'the commons' were being occupied by private capital – solidarity spaces were becoming private NGOs; socially engaged and even 'radical' art projects were sponsored by private collectors – and that they needed to set up some transversal co-management and collaboration with the state and the municipality of Athens in order to halt the occupation of the art and cultural sectors by private capital.

To avoid becoming a private enclosure rather than a commons – or, at the other extreme, a speculative factory of collective labour – OMONIA needed the support of the local government if it was to be sustainable. The Minister of Culture Aristides Baltas was deeply sympathetic to the OMONIA project, but after he was embroiled in the Jan Fabre controversy (caused by the fact that Fabre, as newly nominated director of the Athens and Epidaurus Festival, put together a programme with nearly all Belgian artists) and was nearly forced to resign, he was unable to actively support OMONIA.

The municipality was in a better position to collaborate with the Athens Biennale. In 2013, the deputy mayor Amalia Zeppou, a LSE-trained social anthropologist, had led the project SynAthina, a comprehensive mapping of 300 social centres, solidarity groups and grassroots civic organizations in Athens, which led the mayor Giorgios Kaminis to win the prestigious Bloomberg Mayors Challenge award – a philanthropic scheme set up by the New York City ex-mayor Michael Bloomberg to tackle urban problems and regenerate inner-city communities. Zeppou had also mapped all the empty buildings in Athens and pushed through a regulation that facilitated their use for social projects by the private sector.

We proceeded cautiously with the municipality, as Kaminis was unpopular among civic organizations and the Solidarity4All movement, because he was pushing through a major urban redevelopment of the city centre, which threatened to displace poor families and small shops. There was a palpable fear that both the mapping and the new regulation for accessing empty buildings marked a new offensive of private capital against existing solidarity spaces and urban commons.

One year into OMONIA, the municipality gave AB a small space in Varvakeios Market Square located by the general food market, which was also earmarked for regeneration. A few metres from our space were the SynAthina offices, run by a curator hired by the municipality and hosting various solidarity groups – for example, a hairdresser's for the homeless, a social kitchen and a language school for migrants. These groups were run as 'economically sustainable' businesses rather than demonetized and post-capitalist spaces, and this turning of reproductive labour and social welfare into 'professional services' threatened to undermine both the modus operandi and the formal structure of solidarity organizations. In the negotiation with the municipality we asked to be involved in the public consultation on the regeneration scheme it was running with local commercial groups. We suggested that AB could act as a public observer of this regeneration process liaising with all the social constituencies implicated in it. The municipality accepted this suggestion.

In conclusion, in terms of economic model, the economy of biennales is based on the appropriation of de-territorialized and brand-based cultural rents by a small managerial group, which then redistributes part of it to international and, to a minor extent, local artists, whose benefit is often immaterial – that is to say, based on publicity, attention and media coverage. But OMONIA wanted to reject this paradigm and develop the kind of sustainable economy practised by urban commons and the independent art sector, which I call the model of 'art de-growth'.

During my directorship I experienced how the 'brand-centred' and foreign-led speculative economy of art tended to pull AB towards the upscaling and de-territorialization of its operations, social network and audiences. In the past, the Athens Biennale had used its 'brand' to activate social and economic forces well beyond its reach, even by the loose standards of the economy of art. But this speculative surplus relied on the political energy unleashed by Syntagma Square, which had long since vanished as the economic crisis unfolded. As a consequence, the 'brand' trapped the institution into an operating level that by far exceeded its assets and staffing and, therefore, made it dangerously dependent on the capricious tastes and volatile finances of the international art community and the EU funding machine.

With OMONIA, I tried to reverse this trend by down-scaling, re-territorializing and re-embedding the economy within the models of sharing, co-production and co-management adopted by the independent art sector and urban commons. As a result, AB was beginning to develop de-commodified and socialized modes of work and distribution and had also started to reflect on how to map and conceptualize such a post-capitalist economy in order to socialize it further.

But the tension between commons-based and brand-based economies of art was constant, especially due to the constant pull towards the latter exercised by traditional art brokers (sponsors, curators, art historians and private galleries) and by the media, whose pressing need to generate capitalist spectacle was both frustrated by the artless nature of OMONIA (or so it seemed to them) and magnified by the presence of documenta 14 in Athens.

Postcolonialism versus neocolonialism: Commoning the South?

From the start of OMONIA, the issue of colonialism would regularly come up in relation to the presence of documenta 14 in Athens. Our proposition of 'learning from the commons' resonated with the framework of documenta 14th entitled 'Learning from Athens', which, under the directorship of Adam Szymczyk, had relocated to Athens with the aim of hosting the documenta 14th show in both Athens and Kassel in 2017. With this title, the curatorial team wanted to cast the post-democratic and crisis-ridden condition of Greece as an allegory for the global South, in dialectical tension with Europe's colonial North, of which Germany, at the time the most hostile member of the European Troika in the negotiations with Greece, constituted the core.

Szymczyk's curatorial framework, reflecting Greece's historical and contemporary colonial dependence on Germany, was a brave move which ruffled many feathers in Kassel.[12] But as things progressed, the 'Learning from Athens' framework showed its cracks.

First, there were only eleven Greek artists out of a total of 212, the majority of whom were invited very late in the process and had only four months of production time. In addition, despite his commitment to collaborate with the Athens Biennale, Szymczyk offered no formal curatorial role to Poka-Yio or Kalpatsoglou and made it clear that they would not be on documenta 14 payroll. Moreover, with an astronomical budget earmarked for Kassel, documenta 14 had very little resources to allocate to Athens, so it had to do more fundraising there, draining resources from local private institutions and donors which were fundamental to the survival of small art organizations including AB. Also, in an infamous interview with German Cultural Radio, Szymczyk said:

> We were, however, not that interested in the artistic scene of Athens, but rather in the city as a living organism. And this goes beyond contemporary art. Athens is not alone; it stands for other places in the world. Lagos. Guatemala City.[13]

This framework objectified and commodified Athens into an anonymous marker of the global South. The former Greek Minister of Finance Yanis Varoufakis compared documenta 14 to 'rich Americans taking a tour in a poor African country'. A group of Greek anthropologists set up a two-years-long ethnographic research project Learning from documenta 14 which critically described the deleterious artistic, economic and psychological impact of documenta 14 on Athens.[14]

But despite the neocolonial sound of documenta 14's postcolonial framework, I believe that Szymczyk truly intended to provide economic and logistical support to the artistic community in Athens and that he was prevented from doing so by the documenta board in Kassel. Indeed, there were several conversations between d14 and the Athens Biennale, in which Szymczyk made substantial proposals for collaboration. But participation in the curatorial team of d14 was a deal breaker for Poka Yio and Xenia Kalpatsoglou. This was a lost opportunity for both institutions.

Since the very beginning I had imagined that documenta 14 and AB could work together in a complementary fashion: sharing resources that they each lacked of, subverting together the rules of the game of biennials and, at the same time, proposing a new institutional format – multiscalar, both local and transnational and vertical and decentralized, and bringing together discursive iterations and co-productions informed by the specific historical conjuncture and broader ongoing anti-colonial and anti-capitalist struggles in Greece and in other 'souths'. Without being able to reach out to the dispersed and horizontal 'living organism' it wanted to capture, and which AB could have provided, 'Learning from Athens' became an empty Third-Worldist statement which alienated both the Greek and the international art community.

When Paul Preciado, later in the game, took over the public programme of documenta 14 and set it in the Museum of Dictatorship – once the headquarters of the EAT/ESA (the junta dictatorship from 1967 to 1974) where countless Greek guerrilla fighters were tortured and killed – things got worse. In an interview with the press, Preciado said that he wanted to use the historical framework of the dictatorship as exemplary of the lack of democracy in contemporary Greece and of the broader failure of representative and participatory democracy in Europe. His 'parliament of bodies', in which forty-five participants were invited to 'exercise freedom with the building', was a call to come up with other ways of doing politics together.

Following the usual capitalist process of speculation and abstraction by the art world, Greece's history of dictatorship was decontextualized, abstracted in time and space, 'collaged' with the history of Latin American dictatorship – with the intellectual support of the usual high-profile intellectuals whose modular thinking is made to fit different, often divergent and scholarly dubious art propositions – and then recontextualized in contemporary Greece, in the form of terror caused by the rise of neo-Nazi party Golden Dawn and obtuse Greek nationalism, as in Daniel García Andújar's book, *A Lexicon of Dictatorship*. There was no reference to ongoing struggles of the social movements for participatory democracy and against Golden Dawn, and no reference to Greece's struggles against the EU, which were still unfolding. Art tuned the local situation into a living and frozen abstraction, with no connection whatsoever with the unfolding reality.

Likewise, despite several invited guests who were (ex)Marxist, the documenta 14 culturalist framework underestimated the class dimension of right-wing populism in Greece and reproduced a reified and romantic Third-Worldist view of subalternity without engaging with the precarity of life in Athens at that specific time. This clashed with AB's focus on class intersectionality, which polarized the public debates taking place in the two venues. This polarization took the form of zero-sum struggles – between the local focus of AB and the international one of documenta 14, or between the supposedly patriarchal orthodox Marxism of the former and the supposedly queer, feminist and postmodern decolonizing perspective of the latter. The Greek public got bored very quickly with these high-caste intellectual struggles.

Athens Biennale made a different postcolonial statement from documenta 14. We argued that new post-capitalist forms of life were emerging in Athens from the rubble of the latest violent capitalist crisis unleashed by Europe's North and that these life forms were not just instances of Darwinist survival or bare life. Instead, urban commons, social centres and independent art organizations were spaces of luxury, enjoyment and self-expression. We argued that the commons – a social space and a practice for living which had been historically marginalized and persecuted by the capitalist centres – was the form we had chosen for the biennale.

The growing tension and unease of the Greek cultural and artistic community regarding documenta 14's presence in Athens prompted AB to organize a second Synapse (iteration) as a postcolonial reflection on the role of art biennials, in relation both to the broader ongoing institutional critique debate and to the wider regional role played by Greece, as threshold between the global South and the global North and between Europe and Asia.

With this second Synapse co-organised by art writer Stephanie Bailey AB wanted to take its distance from documenta 14's culturalist framing of the global South (and, by default, Greece) as 'a state of mind'[15] and focus instead on the long-term structural relationships of imperialism, cultural othering, essentialization and racism between global centres and global peripheries which render the South a state of necessity and dependency, in addition to being 'a state of mind'.

It could, however, have been argued that the materialistic framework of OMONIA was neocolonial too. Indeed, I had been deeply troubled by some conversations I had with Greek and Mediterranean activists and artists, which caused me to fear that by focusing on the institution of the commons, I might be imposing an Eurocentric and materialistic framework on to the 'different cultural context' – as they called it – of the South. Some argued that the notions of 'commons', 'Occupy art', 'public art', 'anti-capitalism', 'anti-gentrification'; 'art/activism', 'structural violence', or 'artistic labour' made little sense in the context of collapsed states, peripheral capitalism, political repression and civil war in which Europe's South and the Mediterranean area found themselves.

With this second iteration, co-organized with art writer Stephanie Bailey we wanted to engage in an act of self-criticism on the Eurocentric epistemology that had dominated the first Synapse. Moreover, reflecting on documenta 14's endorsement of the point of view of the South, we wanted to reiterate Spivak's question: 'can the subaltern speak?', and think about how two international and middle-class institutions such as documenta 14 and AB could truly resonate with the voices of subaltern constituencies, instead of speaking 'for them' or 'through them'. Spivak agreed to discuss this issue at the Bageion Hotel later in October.

Rather than aligning ourselves with a generic South, we wanted to stress the geopolitical proximity between Greece and the Middle East and North Africa (MENA) region, where Neocolonialism and transnational capitalism emerged in the form of extractivism, super-rich urban enclaves, indentured labour and migrant ghettos. Arab artists Sophia Al Maria and Fatima Al-Qadiri have developed the notion of 'Gulf-Futurism' – a phantasmatic space where the hyper-consumption, technocratic bureaucracy and corporate automation of financial capitalism clashed with nomadic, post-human, informal and subterranean forces of counter-insurgent Islamic guerrillas and splinter kingdoms. In conjuring up the ghost of a Mediterranean/Eurasian 'black Atlantic' threatening the very core of European civilization through a mixture of terrorism, petrodollars and state violence, these artists captured the experience of living in Greece, which was also plagued by an increasingly aggressive foreign extractivist capital, Islamophobia and state violence.

We were also keen to engage with the political language developed by a new generation of Arab women artists such as Larissa Sansour, Ala Younis, Monira Al Qadri and Marwa Arsanios and the relatively recent strand of art criticism focused on the MENA region developed by art critic Anthony Downey and the Ibraaz research group (to which Bailey also belonged to). With Stephanie Bailey we involved in the conversation the group associated with the *Naked Punch Review* (Guardiola Rivera, Qalandar Bux Memon and Simon Critchley) whose Fanonian and Third-Worldist line was infused with Lacanian and Derridean philosophy, non-Western popular culture and poetry. The Dadaist parties and lecture performances of this cosmopolitan group of artists and scholars had infused the postcolonial scene with an irreverent and joyous spirit, which fitted well with the communal spirit of OMONIA. With the editors we agreed to establish *Naked Punch* in the Begeion Hotel throughout the duration of OMONIA so that the discussions taking place in Athens could be more widely disseminated and commented upon.

Lastly, with this second iteration we wanted to renew our intention to continue the occupation of the Bageion Hotel and the institutional transformation of Athens Biennale into a commons. But this transformation was fraught with many challenges and contradictions. For instance, some social centres were critical of the fact that a part of Synapsis 2 was sponsored by the Onassis Foundation, whose artistic director, Katia Arfara, had developed the Onassis Fast Forward Festival (FFF) that year around the notion of 'the border' in the MENA region – in relation to civil wars, forced migration and transnational capitalism – through collaboration with Middle Eastern artists, scholars and curators.

The symposium Rethinking Institutional Critique – a View from the South, took place on 15 and 16 April at the Bageion Hotel and included several international and Greek curators, artists and scholars as speakers. It asked: What is the point of replicating the mainstream Western format of biennales in the Greek context of deep economic and political crisis and dispersed and fragmented artistic and political subjectivities?

The postcolonial reframing of institutional critique varied across generations. Some curators focused on the struggle between art organizations and authoritarian states. Viktor Misiano, for instance, compared the post-Syntagma context in which AB was taking place to the momentous social and economic post-socialist transformation in Russia in the 1990s. Abandoned by the state, artist collectives developed radical anti-institutional relational practices, heavily performative and public (in Misiano's opinion much more political than Western relational aesthetics) and informed by a new critical engagement with Marxism. But the consolidation of a new authoritarian state under Putin destroyed this critical space and led artists to develop post-relational critical art *from within* the state. It was in this post-authoritarian context that Misiano was involved in the First Moscow Biennale of Contemporary Art in 2005, with a strong curatorial statement that led to his removal from the curatorial team.

The second, even more radical, wave of state repression came after 2011–12, with Putin's controversial election to a third term as president. After the declaration of war on contemporary art by Putin's Ministry of Culture, the art community was forced to operate underground, beneath the radar of the state, separated from the increasingly compromised and corrupted public sphere (Vilensky, 2019) and engaged in the creation of counter-publics linked by friendship and group solidarity.

Misiano argued that considering the variety of extra-institutional political and artistic subjectivities emerging after Syntagma (similar to the contemporary post-socialist Russian context), Athens did not need a biennial institution. For a start, AB would not be able to escape the commercial logic and narrow Western epistemology of contemporary biennials. In fact, on the whole, Greek private galleries and well-established artists disliked the non-commercial, open-ended and durational framework I proposed, because it bypassed the speculative circuits of capital (indeed, from the perspective of the commons, artwork is not separable from the social relations that produce it and the physical space in which it is produced; hence it is not alienable or commodifiable). Besides, according to Misiano, the artwork exhibited must be coherent with the epistemological framework set-up. In the case of AB, 'what is the form of art of the commons?' He argued that the notion of commons as a social project and that of commons as an artwork were incompatible. Lastly, for Misiano the function of contemporary museums is to construct a vision of the past, not of the future: art institutions are sites of historical memory, not of political intervention.

Like Misiano, artist and curator Ala Younis stressed the agency of individual artists in developing alternative and dissident 'canons' outside official state narratives and even becoming 'quasi-institutions' with long-lasting political legacies. In her own projects, Younis collects oral histories and archival material to create counter-narratives that disrupt the linear ideologies of modernity, democracy and progress supported by authoritarian states in the Arab region. The activists Vasil Cherepanyn from the Visual Culture Research Centre (VCRC) in Kiev described the newly founded biennial 'school of Kyiv' in the post-Maidan context as a bricolaged institution whose function was to mark and consolidate the emerging cultural field and the new political subjectivities coalescing against the authoritarian state. Lastly, Marwa Arsanios discussed how her feminist institution 98 Weeks, based in Beirut, challenged state censorships by staging conversations between Western Marxism-feminism and Middle Eastern philosophy and poetry, based on new institutional formats, including women's reading groups (ranging from the study of transsexuality by Iranian scholar Najmabadi to excerpts from Kathy Acker's *Algeria*), storytelling workshops and direct urban interventions.

Looking back, the sense of personal agency and political empowerment of these artists and curators reflected the short-lived democratic opening in the MENA and post-socialist regions in the aftermath of the Arab Spring, which were subsequently repressed by reconsolidated authoritarian states.

A second group of speakers took a psychoanalytic approach, describing how the institution of biennales in the global South triggers strong desires, fantasies and affects regarding the 'other', the 'foreign' and the 'subaltern', therefore mobilizing energies and economies that ultimately benefit the South.

Cultural critic Qalandar Bux Menon gave a Fanonian reading of such decolonized space of othering. Neocolonial and transnational 'racial' capitalism forces the South to exist in two ontological zones at the same time – as beings and as non-beings. This double consciousness throws the subaltern subject into a state of hopelessness. But art offers an entry point into zones of non-being, the struggle for self-representation and the failure of humans to engage with the Lacanian Real. In this sense, a decolonized biennial is one that deals with the possibility of its own failure.

Likewise, the French critic Nicolas Bourriaud argued that as Greece was being pushed to the brink of bankruptcy by the European Troika, AB came more and more to embody the contemporary condition of the global periphery, thus, mobilizing strong desires and affects around solidarity, comradeship and gift economies. Subverting Hal Foster's paradigm of the artist as ethnographer,[16] Bourriaud argued that international biennials turn the local public into ethnographers who try to understand the cultural baggage that foreign artists and curators carry with them. I found this idea thought-provoking. Thinking of William Morris's *News from Nowhere*, I imagined how a mainstream artist must have felt suddenly waking up in an unknown communist society, hungry, begging for money and exposed to the voyeuristic gaze of passers-by, and being told that money had been abolished long time ago and that now people created art for pleasure. But it was difficult to imagine that communist land as Athens, where in fact foreign curators and artists act like colonialists rather than outsiders.

A third strand focused on institutional change instead of critique. Vasif Kortun veered away from 'the curatorial' and described how he used a post-curatorial and multidisciplinary approach to set up SALT in Istanbul. Criticizing the Western 'industrial exhibitionary complex', he strongly rooted SALT in the urban and political texture of Istanbul, combining expert research and state-of-the-art archiving technology and, following Brugueira's notion of 'useful art'[17] (*Arte Útil*), reaching out to a diverse and heterogeneous 'community of users' rather than a traditionally conceived public.

Karen Mirza and Bred Butler described the term 'participation', often used by biennales and artists as gesture towards social engagement, as a white colonial term. Against it, they advocated non-participation and institutional boycotts as new forms of political engagement for the decolonization of art and discussed their own counter-institutional project: the museum of non-participation – a fictional institution through which they experimented with a mode of self-organization based not on participation but on withdrawal.

Lastly, Binna Choi described how she was leading the transformation of CASCO into an urban commons and, together with curator Maria Lind, building a nested and expanded institutional network – including social centres, NGOs and non-arts organizations – within the Guanju Biennial which resonated with the international and cross-institutional network AB was developing.

A fourth set of contributions focused on institutional critique in terms of postcolonial critical cartography and regional politics. Curator Simon Sheikh and artist and curator Sengupta from the Raqs Media Collective stressed how Athens, by being located in the Mediterranean, was a threshold of opaque transatlantic shipping routes, Southern epistemologies and post-imperial economies. Veering away from the well-rehearsed narrative of Greece's subaltern role in Europe, they emphasized its cosmopolitanism and role of cultural and political mediator between Europe, Asia and the Arab world. As newly appointed artistic director of the Shanghai Biennale, the Raqs Media Collective was experiencing the hypermobility, continuous and uneven accelerations, fissions, escape routes and quick reconfiguration of the South. Sengupta pointed out how the history and geography of the South changed at a very rapid pace and suggested that globalization should be rethought in terms of South-driven acceleration. For instance, the Chinese company COSCO had just bought the port of Piraeus in Athens; this meant that in a not-so-distant future, the Shanghai Biennale might take place in Athens.

The emerging postcolonial field was confusing. Some narratives strongly resonated with me, for instance: Bourriaud's description of artists as foreigners. Indeed, the work of foreign curators and artists does not only abstract, reduce, extract and cancel out the local context. It also showcases the uselessness, narrow-mindedness, dysfunctionality and fragility of Western art outside its narrow geographical and political boundaries. Such vulnerability was nowhere more tangible than in the 14th Istanbul Biennial, curated by Christov-Bakargiev, which I attended while I was working on AB. The artists and their artworks were hidden away from the public sphere – for fear that they could reignite anti-Western sentiments as had happened in the past – and displayed in private basements, subterranean garages, private hotel lobbies, empty buildings and distant islands. The eerie atmosphere of uncertainty, dysfunctionality and secrecy that I experienced at the 14th Istanbul Biennial seemed an apt metaphor for the broader trend of cultural repression and artistic censorship by authoritarian states in the global South, as well as the social irrelevance of art in its progressive identification with the commodity form in the global North.

Moreover, Bux-Menon's discussion of art as a safe space for both utopian experiments and failure resonated with the way I had imagined OMONIA: as a utopian horizon of communal self-transformation but also, possibly, as a common horizon of failure.

But, with the exception of the sense of agency and practical engagement communicated in Kortun's and Choi's talks, I was puzzled by the general agreement that museums can only function as sites of historical institutionalization, phantasmatic reunions, ontological self-reflection and affective identification. I was also unconvinced by the postcolonial accelerationist framings of the South. On the one hand, they challenged the teleological, technological and victimizing framings of the South by mainstream critical theory and media narratives, but on the other hand, they strongly clashed with the intended durational and 'slow' temporality of OMONIA, and the relentless state of crisis and historical suspension Athens had been experiencing since 2011. Additionally, the romantic imagination of the South as the original 'hyper-capitalist other' mirrored, in an inverted way, the timeless revolutionary subalternity that was being cast over it by documenta 14.

To a certain extent, all these curatorial frameworks were just philosophical or cultural abstractions (although some curators consider them to be artistic intervention in their own right) intended to capture the attention of the public just for the duration of the show. But what were the material and long-term consequences of these artistic abstractions for the subjects of abstraction?

I found the argument that artists can only either do politics or make a kind of art that is reflexively and narcissistically focused on itself trapped in the Adornian double bind of capitalism. Besides, I considered the Third-Worldist and culturalist postcolonialism of some curators disingenuous because it was oblivious to ongoing structural economic, political and moral dependency between global North and global South and the global capitalist structures that sustain international biennials – from Shanghai, to Kochi, to Sydney – and the role artists have in reproducing such a spectacular economy.

Of course, we were no exception. AB too was deeply entangled with capitalism – the flights, the hotels, the taxis, the restaurants and the sponsors' money – and in fact, its economy was even more speculative than other comparable biennials, as AB functioned almost entirely with no money and based on the energy, attention and free labour that the AB 'brand' captured locally and internationally. But it was precisely because of this immense threshold space it had created – located between the gift economy and immaterial labour and between the commons and capital – that AB could make the transition into a commons.

This, I believe, is the value of biennales in the South. They emerge from the unrecognized and unremunerated contributions of people who aspire to be part of the art world, move from the periphery to the centre and escape the logic of dependent development, avoiding boring industrial work to become creative workers – the totality of these unremunerated efforts and contributions existing outside markets and museums, accruing speculative value in direct relation to poverty, inequality and social alienation, and routinely being captured by the very monopolistic patrons who are responsible for these socio-economic conditions in the first place. This speculative and unproductive labour created from the aspiring artists, art historians, cultural critics and curators who, like me, worked for a better future was *our labour* and *our commons*. It was the transformation of this invisible and fragmented labour into a commons that OMONIA was meant to set in motion. Talks about artistic labour and the parasitic economy of art had become part and parcel of the art world and the business as usual of 'socially engaged', but over-resourced, art institutions. But the commons was the very condition of existence of OMONIA – its horizon of action and, possibly, also of failure.

It was thanks to philosopher Alexei Penzin, and his discussion of the post-Soviet, or post-communist condition, that the debate opened up to an investigation of the revolutionary possibilities of art again. Penzin discussed the post-Soviet condition in relation to two hegemonic contemporary political narratives: of the postcolonial and the post-Fordist. Indeed, the post-Soviet is not quite the culturalist postcolonial space of the South, and neither it is the technologically determinist and materialist post-Fordism of the North. Yet the post-Soviet imaginary shares with the North the rampant privatization, monopolization and commodification of life by capitalism and with the South state authoritarianism, the suppression of civil liberties and the militarization of society.

According to Penzin, the post-Soviet condition represents not only the political and economic situation in Greece – its Balkans identity, and mixture of unbridled capitalism and oligarchic patrimonialism – but the global contemporary condition too. Penzin reflected on the possibility of constructing a form of institutional critique based on the 'epistemology of the Soviet' rather than on the epistemology of the South. When is an institution a collective? Does the collective negate individual subjectivation? What forms do non-state institutions take? What does a post-Soviet communist museum look like?

Penzin's contribution strongly resonated with my desire to develop a critical Marxist epistemology from the point of view of the South – in the legacy for instance of Cedric Robinson's *Black Marxism* or Cico de Oliveira's *Critica a la Razão Dualista* – which could sustain OMONIA theoretically and intellectually in its movement to socialize and occupy the capitalist space of art through non-Eurocentric and decolonized processes and imaginaries.

Listening to the final discussion in the symposium I realized that, despite all the talks about 'the other', most speakers were really talking about themselves – about their specific experience as artists, activists or curators; their specific positionality as a white or non-white – female, male or queer – person; or their specific place of birth.

I asked to myself: 'Is my proposal of turning the biennale into a commons Eurocentric, if not "neo-colonial"'? Was the political grammar I was using coming from the North? And were those who criticized it for being Eurocentric, with their cosmopolitan style, elitist education and high status, representative of the South? Or was my family background really representative of the North? (My father was born in a small town in South of Italy, just on the other side of the Ionian Sea, once a small colony of the Greek Empire – *Magna Grecia* – and which had been expunged from Italian history well into the 1950s, when it was forcibly 'developed' under the US Marshall Plan. From an impoverished middle-class family, he migrated to Milan, the birthplace of the xenophobic and neo-Fascist party Lega Lombarda, where, like all southerners, he experienced cruel discrimination, if not outright racism, by 'the locals' – an experience which deeply marked myself and my siblings.)

I felt that the postcolonial arguments being advanced were turning Spivak's admonition not to speak for the subaltern into a narcissistic, self-righteous, identitarian, nationalistic and self-reflexive cultural relativism that reproduced the neocolonial status quo and the aristocratic ideal of high art held by an enlightened cosmopolitan bourgeoisie determined to silence any attempt to develop conversations and solidarities across classes. I felt I had to go back to Gramsci's proposition that culture can be a bridge between classes and prefigure 'the outside' of capitalism and the exit route to its enclosures. I felt I had to go back to class.

So, in the conclusion of the symposium, the issue of post-capitalism returned together with some theoretical concerns of Synapse 1. We questioned: how to build 'common practices' that go against the commodity form and alienated labour in the art world? How to go beyond the dichotomy between private and public and build sustainable institutions that work in the interests of the exploited and the dispossessed? How to rethink the male, productivist and capitalist ontology of art value through the feminine labour of care, commoning and social reproduction? How to develop communist and communal art from a decolonized and non-Eurocentric perspective?

In conclusion, the relocation of documenta 14 to Athens, made under the curatorial frame of 'Learning from Athens', embodied that movement of appropriation of the South that I have discussed in the first section of this book. In this context, the upholding and valorization of cultural identity was an act of cultural appropriation and neocolonialism – not only when it was done by Western institutions on behalf of the subaltern 'other' (as in the case of d14) but also when it was done by the cosmopolitan bourgeoisie on behalf of 'their subaltern co-nationals' on the basis of an aristocratic notion of art and an exclusivist and nativist cultural relativism. In the end, the tension and opposition between documenta 14 and AB, rooted in the illusory conflict between 'foreigners' and 'locals', were a script that was being played out from within that same reified space occupied by the cosmopolitan bourgeoisie. The failure to broaden the discussion outside the autonomous and claustrophobic space of art, for instance, by trying to imagine how the global racialized view of social exclusion constructed by foreign curators and artists mapped on to the local structures of exclusion and dispossession, in terms of family relations, class articulation and urban development, aroused cynicism and resentment.

Art's structures of feeling: Capitalist realism, cinism and melodrama

After Synapse 2, OMONIA started to fall apart. The durational work of the international artists we had commissioned, and of our artists in residence, happened below the radar of the international art public and of the Greek mainstream art world, reinforcing the perception that OMONIA was an 'artless biennale'. To rectify this perception, Poka-Yio and Kalpatsoglou suggested that AB send out an international open call to creators, activists, theorists, collectives and cooperatives asking them to co-shape and contribute to the running of OMONIA. I resisted this move. We had neither the financial resources to pay more collaborators nor the human resources to implement new projects. Besides, the lexicon of collaboration and participation was discredited within the independent art world, which considered it exploitative. This was especially the case in Athens in the post-Syntagma context, when Siryza, once in power, had cut links with grassroots constituencies and disavowed their practices of participatory democracy. I was convinced that the expanded participatory framework suggested by Poka-Yio and Kalpatsoglou could be achieved only under exploitative conditions for the participants and that we ought to stick to the modus operandi and institutional structure that reflected our existing economic conditions.

In addition to this internal divergence, the socialized and open framework of OMONIA allowed for various attempts at its occupation. Some artists in residence, protesting against AB's collaboration with Onassis (which they were happy enough to use as sponsor of their own projects), boycotted some of our events. Young and ambitious curators used AB's invitations to stage public vitriolic institutional critiques against AB. As well as providing a parallel artistic engagement on the issues discussed in Synapse 2, the collaboration with Onassis was vital if AB was to pay collaborators' wages and speakers' fees, while remaining autonomous. In fact, we decided to collaborate with Onassis only on parallel events without seeking sponsorship for our main programme. I considered such collaboration a way of socializing money, negating the exploitative economy of art and using private capital to sustain the commons.

Athens Biennale was developing good relationships with social centres and commons especially with the Solidarity Schools Network (SSN), occupied spaces working with refugees, migrants and architectural collectives. But these relationships were slow to materialize into concrete projects, since the operative logic of commons is slow, collective, consensus-based and relational and much of it is invested in co-producing ways of living together which cannot be accounted for or easily operationalized into 'art projects'. Indeed, it was difficult to synchronize long-term processes of commoning with the short-term temporality and attention span of the art industry. Some centres and urban squats refused to be involved in the biennale, which they considered too institutionalized. For instance, the occupied space Green Park refused AB's invitation to collaborate and started its own performance biennial. Others got involved on their own terms.

Moreover, the issue of my foreignness both to Greece and to the art world became somehow contentious after the Jan Fabre controversy. All sorts of gossip started to circulate. It was rumoured that I had received an astronomical fee from AB; that I had had an affair with Kalpatsoglou; or that I was never in Athens – despite having relocated to Athens during my sabbatical leave and subsequently spending on average one week per month in the city. It was also rumoured that AB was on the verge of bankruptcy from the previous edition; I was told that this could have legal consequences for me as I personally secured and signed the collaborations with Onassis, NEON and the municipality. We were only six months into OMONIA and the speculative wheels of capital were spinning fast against it.

Ten days after Synapse 2, in a meeting in central Athens, Kalpatsoglou and Poka-Yio informed me that they intended to close down AB by the end of May, after the planned symposium with Onassis. I had not seen this coming.

The process that followed reflected the undemocratic nature of the art industry, in which decisions taken at the top are not shared with the people at the bottom so that they keep on working on already aborted projects until they suddenly close down. Apologists for this undemocratic style of management will respond that decisions are kept confidential in order not to deter the hypothetical investor who will save the day. But we know how this capitalist tale works. Saviours do not exist, or if they do, they save their own interests, dismembering and reselling what they bought based on the logic of profit.

But the show had to go on. On 27 March, at the Onassis Cultural Centre (OCC), we had the first day of the symposium 'Art at the borders: spatial politics and postcolonial strategies in the Middle East' with speakers including Lara Khaldi, Yazan Khalili, Tania El Khoury, Sandra Noeth, Marwan Rechmaoui, Christine Tohmé and Jalal Toufic. The symposium started with a terrific lecture by Jalal Toufic on the ontology of radical closure, a concept that Toufic had developed in his book *The Forthcoming* which applies Sufi philosophy and aesthetics to the analysis of Middle Eastern cinema. Starting from the Taoist precept that vital energy emerges from interrupted gestures, Toufic asked how the vital breath could still hold along the 750 checkpoints in the West Bank. He talked about partition walls as forms of sensory motor disconnection and cognitive breakdown akin to those that follow traumatic experiences. Yet, he argued, something emerges from this disconnection. Hallucinatory voices and visions insert themselves into the gap so that we can see the entire wall appearing. The wall is a relative closure. An entanglement in separation.

Sites of radical closure, by contrast, are sites of extreme violence, conflict and 'surpassing disasters'. They are completely separate from the surrounding environment and marked by 'unworldly, fully formed and a-historical interruptions' – for instance, the condition of the Palestinians in the West Bank and in Gaza during the siege by Israel in 1982 or Sarajevo during its siege by Bosnian Serbs. What kind of art corresponds to the traumatic condition of radical closure? Toufic's poetic lecture, in which existential discontinuity, cuts, breaks and personal trauma were translated onto aesthetic and ontological planes, resonated with the condition of relative closure in Greece especially vis-à-vis the emancipatory horizons of 2011. But it also resonated, on a personal level, with my thinking about the looming closure of OMONIA and its failure.

The next speaker was Christine Thomé, founder of the art platform Ashkal Alwan in 1994, the triennial art event Home Work Forum (HWF) in 2002 and the pedagogical Home Workspace programme in 2011 – three central institutions in the reconstruction of the art sector in Beirut after the civil war. Thomé had been just nominated artistic director of the Sharjah Biennale, due to open in 2017 in parallel with AB and documenta 14. In all of Thomé's initiatives, the relation between art practices and civic activism is central. But her pedagogical and artistic platforms are not built as institutional alternatives to neoliberalism or spaces of autonomy from the commodified art industry. Instead, these initiatives are aimed at building new public infrastructures and civic discourses in the midst of war, state collapse, censorship and forced mass migration. Thomé discussed how the Syrian civil war had reignited the conflict between Israel and Hezbollah, creating a mass exodus of Syrian refuges to Lebanon (1.5 million in 2016) and triggering capital injections by foreign NGOs and private foundations, which went into money laundering and housing speculation as well as into humanitarian reconstruction – a situation analogous to that of Athens.

According to Thomé, this new influx of foreign capital fuelled identitarian and religious narratives and obscured the fact that Lebanon is still ruled by a very small social and economic elite, making it impossible for art institutions to maintain a critical stance. Thomé had just decided to suspend the Home Work Forum, and she talked about her difficulties in keeping Ashkal Alwan going. Then she added: 'Big art institutions today do not work. Look at this empty auditorium.' I turned around. Only ten people were in the audience. She urged artists and curators to abandon big institutions and work together in small-scale, non-institutional, non-public, underground and informal ways. It was from such dispersed and informal gatherings after the civil war that the institutional reconstruction of the art world in Beirut emerged.

Despite the low turnout, the panel presented a very powerful 'Southern' critique of the institutional critique paradigm. It showed that in the context of civic unrest, collapsing states and non-existent cultural infrastructures, the aim of politically engaged artists and curators is that of building, sustaining and supporting new cultural and political institutions rather than challenging, deconstructing and abandoning the existing ones. Besides, the feeling of hope and ontological openness articulated by Toufic and Thomé clashed with the cold and cynical criticality of socially engaged artists in the global North.

The second panel of the symposium entitled 'Political economy and postcoloniality in the Mediterranean and the Middle East' took place on the following day in the Bageion Hotel; Eric Baudelaire, Amin Husain, Andrew Ross and Nato Thompson were the speakers. This panel addressed the so-called fourth wave of institutional critique that is the artists'/activists' strategy of setting up 'transversal collaborations' and agonistic relationships with museums with the aim of 'liberating' them.[18] I had asked the panellists to reflect cross-culturally on the role of art institutions, artists and cultural workers in both reproducing the transnational and neocolonial operations of capital and triggering anti-capitalist and anti-colonial struggles.

Andrew Ross talked about the Gulf Labour Coalition (GLC), the anti-sweatshop movement he funded with artist Walid Raad in 2011 to oppose the use of indentured labour by cultural institutions in the United Arab Emirates (UAE). The US academic argued that the art world is an agent of financial capitalism and that museums are 'sweatshops' entirely based on precarious and exploited labour. But instead of focusing just on the exploited labour of artists, Ross highlighted the exploited labour of the workers who build and run art institutions.

One of such art sweatshops is the Guggenheim Museum developed in the Saadiyat island in Abu Dhabi, entirely with indentured labour. The Guggenheim Museum is only one of several franchises of Western cultural institutions (including the Louvre, the British Museum and even New York University) the United Arab Emirates (UAE) is developing in the 'happy island' of Saadiyat, as part of its process of nation-building and consolidation as a global centre of offshore capitalism. In parallel to these exclusive cultural sanctuaries, luxury residential developments are being built by ruthless subcontractors who employ only migrant labourers from Southeast Asia, using the *kafala* system of indentured labour.[19]

According to Ross, labour activism in the art sector is more effective than labour activism in the services and industrial sectors, where firms can quickly close down and relocate. Unlike these sites of flexible labour, museum-sweatshops are permanent 'capital fixes' particularly vulnerable to ongoing labour action. The confrontation between GLC and the Guggenheim Museum started in 2010 after GLC sent out a call to artists to withdraw their participation in the museum, including the sale of their work, until it addressed the issue of labour standards. Initially, the museum was open to dialogue with GLC but subsequently it withdrew from the conversation. In 2013, 7,000 workers went on strike at the site of the Louvre and in the following year the GLC demanded debt settlement, living wages and the right to labour association for the workers of Guggenheim Abu Dhabi. The board of the museum turned these demands down.

On 1 May 2015, members of the Global Ultra Luxury Faction (GULF), a group within GLC, occupied the Guggenheim Museum in New York City, and on 8 May, GULF and two Italian art activist organizations occupied the building of the Peggy Guggenheim Collection in Venice for the entire day. Okwui Enzewor had invited GLC to participate in the Venice Biennale; the collective did so by discussing the report it had produced on labour conditions in the Arab Gulf and South Asia. Like the 'politically timed' interventions of the Latin American collectives I mentioned above, the GLC operated through a mixture of militant research and performative activism. Its ambition was to develop an aesthetics that reflected the political spirit of the time. Ross described the recent storming of the Peggy Guggenheim Collection by speedboat as a re-enactment of futurist aesthetics.

Amin Husain, one of the founders of GULF, described the role of the contemporary artist as one of a political organizer. GULF went beyond single-issue politics, combining struggles against 'ultra-luxury' capitalism and struggles for de-colonization. More recently, Husain and Nitasha Dhillon had funded Decolonize This Place (DTP), a group of artist activists involved in the occupations of and transversal conversations with cultural and art institutions in New York City on anti-gentrification and environmental, labour, black and anti-colonial struggles, including in the Palestinian-occupied territories.

Husain's contribution to our conversation was important because it highlighted how processes of accumulation by dispossession and of military and financial occupation, in which capitalism and the art world are reciprocally entangled, affect not only relationships between global North and global South, as Thomé had stressed, but also peripheries within the centres. For instance, the black residents in the Bronx in NYC were as much affected by the gentrification and 'whitefication' caused by 'progressive' art institutions as the migrants and squatters of Exarchia Square were by the relentless occupation by German capital, which followed the arrival of d14.

For Husain, the artist as organizer holds in balance research, activism and aesthetics. This was his aim in making the experimental film *On This Land* with Nitasha Dhillon – under the signature name 'MLT collective' – a film about life, land and liberation in occupied Palestine. With this film Dhillon and Husain wanted to revive the revolutionary aesthetics of Third Cinema by using a decentered, sensuous and multimodal method of storytelling in which the camera told of its encirclement, embeddedness and enframing within the boundaries and hierarchies established through checkpoints, barriers, military surveillance and killing.

This was also the main topic of Eric Baudelaire's intervention. I had been captivated by his lyrical investigations of political terrorism in the form of 'landscape filming' – a way of interrogating the landscape for insights into wider structures of oppression developed by Marxist film criticism in the 1970s. In his talk at the Bageion Hotel, Baudelaire was emphatic in drawing a line between his art and his activism. As an artist his role was 'to find a form to accommodate the mess' and seek a decolonized epistemology – that is, open to states of emergency, confusion and sensory ways of knowing. But in this sense, Baudelaire's art was also political, because it triggered ways of knowing quite unlike the logic of visual evidence or visual pleasure underpinning much of Western visual art. His new project on terrorism looked at the bureaucratic apparatus of social science and at the archaeology and form of knowledge generated in the classification of terrorist acts. This new project, prompted by Baudelaire's background in social science, was a powerful visual rendering of how state governmentality is produced through violent, abstract and often hallucinatory official systems of classifications and representation.

Nato Thompson concluded the session by describing his vision of the artistic avant-garde of the twenty-first century, the focus of his famous 2011 show 'Living as Form' – a nod to Harald Szeeman's landmark 1969 exhibition at Kunsthall Bern: *When Attitudes Become Form: Live in Your Head*. The show, devised by more than twenty-five curators working under Thompson's supervision, included documents of more than 100 artists' projects, nine site-specific commissions and a newly created online archive of more than 350 socially engaged actions that have taken place since the early 1990s.

Thompson argued that the aim of the contemporary avant-garde was 'to put Duchamp's urinal back into real life', and he sketched the historical legacy of today's socially engaged art: the social sculpture of Joseph Beuys, Suzanne Lacy's public art, the relational aesthetics of Nicolas Bourriaud and the participatory art of Tania Brugueira. According to the American curator, the twenty-first-century artistic avant-garde has the following traits: (1) it is non-representational (as per Burgueira's statement 'I don't want an art that *points* at things but an art that *is* the thing'); (2) it uses participatory processes; (3) it is situated in the real world; (4) it operates in the political sphere – that is, in the tradition of Brazilian playwright Augusto Boal's theatre and pedagogue Paolo Freire, it aims at the politicization of the agency of the oppressed; and (5) it uses the methodologies of public gatherings, action research, media manipulation, DIY processes and dialogical communication.

Thompson's framing of contemporary political art within the historical genealogy of socially engaged art seemed bland in the contemporary context characterized by violent processes of land-grabbing and accumulation by dispossession fuelled by homophobia, racism and worldwide working-class repression – a very different context from the Keynesian and neoliberal hegemonic regimes that shaped socially engaged art from the 1970s to the 2010s.

Nonetheless, his description of avant-garde art resonated with the way I increasingly saw my curatorial role as a process of micro, durational and relational framing of social patterns and forms of life 'in commons' and, at the same time, of engagement with the hyper-mediatized and superstructural forces through which frames and forms of art are spectacularized and made to travel. But I was interested in non-institutionalized ways of framing that escaped not only the commodity form but also the enclosures of cameras, museums and even formal public gatherings. I was intrigued by imagining how Kaprow's microprocesses and underground social gatherings, with which he experimented back in the 1960s, could be scaled up to the level of the biennale and made to circulate across different social constituencies. I was also sympathetic to Eric Baudelaire's vision of the artist dwelling in the disorder and messiness of everyday life, trying to find order in it by switching frames and lenses ever so slightly, reining in movement, if only provisionally, and generating counter systemic forms and economies of attention – grounded, rooted and relational. Besides, I was intrigued by the panellists' reasoning around issues of communist aesthetics and epistemology, which had also inspired my film *Steel Lives*, especially by the propositions for Third Cinema articulated by the MLT collective: developing modes of production and circulation aimed at opening up spaces of solidarity, co-poiesis and reciprocity between filmmakers and audiences.

But there was also something about this panel that bothered me. All of the speakers, with the exception of Baudelaire, considered themselves 'artivists' – that is, artists producing specific aesthetics through their political organizing, be it Third Cinema, Futurism or Situationism. Also, they considered their political leadership as a form of choreography of the movement of the masses, thus subscribing to Joseph Beuys's authorial approach to 'social sculptures' in the same way as less-politicized relational artists, such as Rick Lowe and Tino Seghal, did.

We saw above that the historical avant-garde appropriated the media of film and sculpture to legitimate the bourgeois ideology that artists are magicians or shamans with the power to animate the inanimate – infusing motions into objects and images – or, conversely, to make people stand still like sculptures and objects, based on some innate knowledge or skills of theirs. Of course, the whole idea of kings and managers having the power to control the movement of their subjects is not only authoritarian but also ethnocentric. In a non-capitalist and non-Western world, value is relational and does not stem from autonomous and individual gestures. On the contrary, personhood is dividual and fractal rather than individual and self-contained, and individual gestures are interruptions of movement – holes in the communal texture. The work of shamans is to make visible the continuous and unbroken temporality and the unfolding social texture out of which humanity emerges. So, in the case of Sehgal, turning people into sculptures or their actions into objects does not produce any critique of capitalism by questioning object-based value production or conjuring modes of unmediated absorption, as some critics have argued. It simply reproduces the frozen commodity form in the context of the post-Fordist museum/factory through new forms of exploitative immaterial labour and intellectual property relations, and based on a taxidermic aesthetics.

I was not sure about what kind of claim 'artivists' were making. Were they artists who used social relations as the raw material for their artworks, pretty much in the relational aesthetics tradition? Or were they activists who happened to identify with the old symbols and forms of revolutionary art? To me, their split self-perception seemed to stem more from their identification with the artificial categories of 'art' and 'politics' than from their critique of it.

When Kalpaktsoglou and Poka-Yio announced their intention to suspend AB, I made clear my intention to continue OMONIA. But I knew that the founders would pull out without AB. In the meantime, the municipality had agreed to lend us the building in the Varvakios food market square after a fractious communal meeting, and I was worried that the closure of the biennale would have political consequences for the municipal coalition that supported us. At some point I had to let the municipality, NEON and more importantly, the artists know that OMONIA was about to stop. But I had promised to Poka-Yio and Kalpaktsoglou to do so without harming the public image of the Athens Biennale.

On the evening of 28 May 2018, my last day as AB artistic director, the Athens municipal band marched through the Varvakios Market Place, stopping by the Nick Boricua Museum. This museum was part of the 'Puerto Rico' project realized by artists Alexis Fidetzis, Panos Sklavenitis and Kostis Stafylakis in order 'to address the (self)exoticization of Greece through various representations of it as a quasi-Latin American country'. Under a scorching sun, I cut the red ribbon and invited the public in. The story of Nick Boricua was written on the museum's walls close to a full-sized painted portrait of the hero. Glass cases all around showed the hero's important memorabilia – his sword and watch, a map drawn by him, and his personal letters. Born on the island of Ithaca, Boricua took part in the Greek revolution, but, disenchanted with the authoritarian stance of King Otto, in 1835 he travelled to Spain as Greek ambassador. Winning the favours of the Royal Court, he was sent to the colony of Puerto Rico (known as 'Dorado' at the time) as a colonial administrator. There, he fell in love with the native way of living and became one of the leaders of the *Grito de Lares* revolution against the Spanish Empire.

In my opening speech, a mixture of burlesque and pomp, I emphasized the symbolic importance of this early anti-colonial hero, especially his cosmopolitan and internationalist spirit. Speeches by a historian, a museum curator and the curatorial team of artists followed. At the opening party, cultural celebrities showed up. The German ambassador approached me congratulating for the excellent work I was doing for AB. After the opening, a Dada Cabaret performance with Flamenco dance, food, short speeches and Greek Rebetiko music continued throughout the night.

This clever project addressed the exoticization of Greece as 'another Latin American South' that was being perpetuated by Third-Worldist national and international narratives, including by documenta 14, and at the same time, reflected on the peculiarity of Greek politics, which the artists described as 'a mixture of revolutionary cosmopolitanism and revolutionary insularity'. As the camp performance of transgender flamenco dancers unfolded in the packed square by the food market, I reflected that revolutionary insularity was perhaps not just a Greek feature but characterized the global contemporary situation where cosmopolitan financial capitalism was mutating into a new insular, nationalist and autarkic regime of accumulation of dispossession. The queer celebration of the romantic but inconsistent Southern hero Nick Boricua threw me into a melancholic mourning for the bygone era of solidarities and internationalism (in which I grew up as a young member of the Italian Communist Party) and of prefiguration of a future of fake heroes, cultural appropriation and media manipulation.

As the whole edifice of OMONIA was collapsing, it was uncanny that Theaster Gates's lecture performance at the Bageion Hotel – our last event – focused on AB as a 'structure of relative closure', a term Gates had taken from Toufic's talk. I had chosen to commission Gates for OMONIA because of his experience in combining grassroots advocacy with black communities, an ethos of craftsmanship (as builder, pottery maker, *acapella* singer and city designer) and entrepreneurialism in devising sustainable urban development projects 'at the margins' by appropriating the modus operandi of corporate capitalism.

For instance, Gates's Dorchester Projects revitalized Dorchester Avenue in the dilapidated South Side of Chicago using a 'circular ecological system' – a form of self-finance based on selling artworks made from the scrap material of previous renovations. Gates now owns several buildings in the area. Each of them is a separate legal entity but is also connected to a larger social network. Archive House holds 14,000 books, the Listening Room is home to 8,000 records and the Stony Island Arts Bank – the heart of the Dorchester Projects – has artists' studios, a gallery space, rooms for performances and music and a bar. By socializing real estate, and using capital to reproduce commons, the Dorchester Projects resonated with my idea of making the Athens Biennale economically self-sustainable by grounding its operations in the local urban economy through the cohabitation project, labour commoning and participation in the solidarity networks. Yet, of course, the self-entrepreneurial nature of Gates's projects was very different from our institutional commoning.

In his poetic talk, Gates focused on the relationships between institutional structures both imaginative and material, and forms of agency. Structures of 'relative closures' – for instance solid roofs and strong foundations – protect life but also enclose and limit it. He then suggested that the Athens Biennale could be thought of as a space of relative closure, a liminal zone cutting across traditional and informal art institutions, a space of material and existential transition, and a 'minor structure which may have more importance than higher ones because of the desire it occupies'.

He argued that his projects operated along thresholds too, for instance, between art and business, fictitious and real value, production and speculation; and that he dealt with the tensions generated by these antagonistic processes through performative rituals that involved some form of doing things together – singing, making pottery or building. In the packed ballroom of the Bageion, Gates's talk magically chimed with the state of the biennale: open to infinite possibilities, yet sliding towards an end. Casting himself as a master of ceremonies, and sketching on a huge blackboard the transitional space in which AB was dwelling, Gates suggested that, in fact, curating was a process of devising rituals for human institutions and turning them into vessels, receptors, containers, repositories and carriers of human agency. Perhaps, Gates continued, AB needed 'a monastic curatorial programme based on the desire to pray and build and develop a new generation of builders'.

Gates's idea of curating as sacred ritual and collective ceremony intrigued me because this is how indigenous cultures deal with their social relations – that is, through rituals that acknowledge and sacralize the space between people, and strive to reduce it.[20] Gates's performance also reminded me that it is through collective, sensuous and performative rituals that non-Western communities act materially upon the world in order to change it – unlike the seriousness, self-importance and individualism of some Western politics or socially engaged art.

The day after Gates's lecture performance I went to the National Archaeological Museum and, passing through the section on mortuary fragments, I stopped by 'the Stele of Farewell'. In it, a dying woman, clearly in distress, was being lifted by the wrist by a relative, who was raising her other hand in a gesture of speech. To the left of the dying woman another one was looking up, lost in contemplation.

This fragment troubled me deeply. The would-be-relative was in fact, death, and her hold on the dying woman's wrist, which at first appeared gentle, was on closer inspection firm, if not violent. And was the figure on the left the real relative ignoring her beloved's pain? And what was death whispering to the dying woman? Was it the content of that conversation that was troubling her? It turned out that the farewell had taken place in OMONIA 2,300 years ago. It was an uncanny coincidence: I suddenly realized that I would soon bid farewell to Poka-Yio and Kalpaktsoglou. I felt like the dying woman.

It then occurred to me that the whole of OMONIA had been built on the fragile foundation of the structure of the tragic Greek myths, in which humans struggle against a history already established by gods and obstinately continue to do so because the system is built in such a way that they are brought to believe that they will succeed in the end, that they will seize the opportunity, changing the course of their lives for ever.

The 'arrogant' (this is how Greek gods described ambitious humans) utopia of making a biennial without money and out of a revolutionary political vision; the foreign hero who turns traitor; the friendship between Poka-Yio and Szymczyk that becomes the fight between David and Goliath; and the endless conflicts, betrayal, boycotts, parricides and fratricides inflicting deep personal wounds, breaking friendships and even families – with the mighty force of the economy in the background, which a distant European god had decided should hit Greece with untamed violence. I read the failure of AB through the lens of the catastrophic and tragic future associated with late capitalism: a darker retelling of ancient tragic human histories.

Then I realized that I wanted to have a last iteration of OMONIA, structured like a death ritual which would unveil the invisible tragic script that had been set up for me since the beginning and was hanging in the air like a 'deus ex machina'. I spoke with Theo Michael, a Greek artist living in Mexico City, whose exceptionally crafted small-scale environments depicting post-human dystopian worlds were apt allegories not only of the crumbling of OMONIA but also of what might lay ahead in Greece and Europe.

I had also been discussing with the artist duo Dexter Sinister the idea of reconstructing the Bageion Hotel as a virtual world, hosting what was left of OMONIA there: a sort of transition from the world of the living to the world of the dead; and with Suzanne Lacy I had several conversations about the catastrophic affective impact austerity had on feelings – the family break-ups, broken hearts and the end of the 'cruel optimism' (the love, the trust and the solidarity) that had fuelled AB's previous editions.

I also wanted to use the last Synapse to apologize to the public for all the energy, expectations and collective efforts I had asked of them and for trying to be a curator, which I knew nothing about. In fact, what was I thinking? There is a whole industry out there, mass-producing curators, cultural critics, museums officers, art managers, dealers, gallerists, art historians, material culture conservators, curatorial collectives, artist organizers and conceptual artists, just for this purpose. Did I think I could jump the queue? What skills did I think I was bringing to the table? As an anthropologist I had spent my last twenty years befriending unemployed, ageing manual workers, persecuted political activists, precarious working women and illegal migrants, making my home in favelas and working-class housing estates in polluted and deindustrialized towns, trying to find myself in obscure and unfamiliar corners, marvelling at small local events, and searching for the new in everyday surroundings. How did I think I could keep up with the superfast spinning wheels of contemporary art, which at the periphery spin even faster?

So I wanted to invite all the people I had hurt and disappointed to a ritual event – a banquet, a party or a city walk – to mark the end of OMONIA and also the end of certain ways of being together – in assemblies, public gathering and open conversations – where I could properly bid farewell to Xenia and Poka-Yio.

But I did not have time for that. Kalpaktsoglou and Poka-Yio let me know that OMONIA and perhaps AB were to be closed down. Shortly afterwards, in a meeting at the Bageion, two artist groups in residence let me know that as part of a broader Mediterranean coalition wanting to decolonize art biennials, they would occupy the Bageion, close down the Athens Biennale and 'kick foreigners out' – by which I understood they also meant me. 'This is our artwork,' they said.

This is when I sent my letter of resignation to Poka-Yio and Kalpaktsoglou. They asked me not to make my resignation public yet in order not to harm the reputation of AB. I did send the letter to the municipality and NEON, to whom I had personal commitments as AB artistic director. Kalpaktsoglou resigned too. With Kalpaktdoglou I later founded the Laboratory for Urban Commons (LUC) an art organization currently operating in Athens. A few days later, Poka-Yio announced that the Athens Biennale would reopen in 2017 under the vaguely postcolonial framework 'Waiting for the Barbarians' (which meant the Germans). After my resignation I refused interviews from Greek and international media who were seeking to dig into some dirt on AB. But my resignation letter was never officially released by Athens Biennale, as I had asked. As a result, nobody knew why I had resigned. I disappeared from the spectacle as quickly as I had appeared.

In a recent discussion on art and capitalism, Frederic Jameson argues that curating is like financial derivatives because it makes loose connections between artworks that are forgotten nearly immediately. Indeed, curators are derivative too. They disappear with the same rapidity as finance.

The issue of the Greek myth is not entirely a joke. The experience of OMONIA made me realize that there are some narratives and affective structures, including of dependency and oppression, that are transhistorically resilient and can break even the most obstinate will to struggle. At the end of OMONIA in 2016, the long period of popular insurgency that ran from Syntagma Square in 2011 to the capitulation of Tsipras in 2015 seemed just a short interval in the long history of Greek oppression by foreign empires punctuated by violent uprisings.

The failure of OMONIA made me also reflect on the temporality of political events, an issue that is central in my own anthropological practice. My fieldworks in Brazil and the UK were motivated by a desire to intervene in the political urgencies and great historical events of the time – the momentous rise to power of the working class in Brazil and its demise in the UK. But, in fact, during these fieldworks, I mostly dealt with the consequences, aftermaths and reverberations of these momentous structural changes which, moreover, I was encountering in mediated form – that is, through the lived experiences and stories told to me by 'others' and through my own class position.

In other words, by the time I had identified the political urgency, this was already over, because the dense texture of everyday human actions – of oppression, resistance, solidarities and confrontations – triggered by specific historical material conditions sometime in the past and producing the structural movement that was visible to me in the present had already been changed by life's restless movement. So I wondered: 'Was the failure of OMONIA the aftermath of the crisis of Syntagma Square?' – 'Or the aftermath of the Greek economic crisis?' – 'Or was it the prefiguration of the new regime of accumulation by dispossession reflected in the cynicism, negative freedoms and institutional parasitism that I had encountered in the art world?'

Indeed, the notion of 'politically time-specific' art (Bishop, 2019; and Brugueira, 2019) overlooks the continuous movements of capital, its uneven reverberations, the existential condition of being under constant attack by it, and the difficulty of synching temporally and existentially the micro, human scale of the political with its macro and structural scales. Besides, those who regularly perform the interpretative labour of envisioning the structural and the relational beyond the imminent are precisely those who are systematically denied the agency to trigger change and condemned to dwell in the present – to political irrelevance.

Moreover, the terms 'political urgency' and 'political failure' seem inappropriate vis-à-vis the current generalized regime of accumulation by dispossession and of ongoing state violence in which we make history every time anew: with the same sense of urgency and survival and knowing that the marks we make on it will probably be invisible to us and visible only sometime in the future, somewhere else and to somebody else. This is how Boal and Freire must have imagined their struggles against dictatorships – as continuous, subterranean, embodied, unaccountable and only meaningful in terms of depersonalized, distributed and socialized agency. Indeed, the myth of the individual artist's clairvoyance in prefiguring and making history is the same myth of political leadership of the now defunct Western social democracies. Only in commons can collective intelligence prefigure and pre-enact life after and outside capitalism.

Thus, the failure of OMONIA reflected the historical moment of retreat and folding back of popular forces into the structure of the Greek original myth. Or perhaps it reflected the end of collective emergencies, resistances and solidarities – which turned out to be part and parcel of the smooth working of neoliberal biopolitics – and the beginning of a new regime of normalized, individualized and totalitarian violence.

In addition, OMONIA's failure to institute a commons related to the more general problem of political organization. Leo Panitch, who was close to Syriza during the party's early rise, and who was collaborating with the AB at the time, argued that AB had the same problems as Syriza – being pressurized simultaneously by bigger institutions above and smaller organizations below. Indeed, the decline of political parties and of representative democracy reflects not only their instrumentalization by the bourgeois state, as per the narratives of the radical Left, but also the organization of social relations under contemporary capitalism – polarized between micro, dispersed, individualistic and horizontal interactions on the one hand and invisible and unconscious mass cooperation in platforms, hubs or second-order organizations on the other hand. Or, to put it another way, capitalism's cynicism fosters a sense of disidentification and dispersed agency that becomes the raw material of corporate monopolies. In this sense, the failure of OMONIA is linked to the difficulties of building a social platform and political coalition akin to a party, at a historical moment in which democracy is either deemed obsolete or reductively associated with dispersed and horizontal direct participation.

Was I wrong to set up a politically engaged framework for AB in the post-Syntagma context of 2015? More generally, had art/activism passed the 'post-occupy' condition as a consequence of the current brutal repression of popular forces and dismantling of urban commons? Was the critical distance I experienced from a section of the art community, and the occasional institutional boycotts and institutional liberations against OMONIA, ways of reclaiming the autonomy and de-commodification of art? Or were they melancholic repetitions and nostalgic recuperations of revolutionary art as a cultural form, but subsumed under the cynical and realist spirit of capitalism?

Or could the failure of OMONIA be read otherwise – as the tragedy and melodrama of the brutal annihilation of human commons, cooperation and solidarity by the unbridled forces of capital, despite the resilience and the beautiful ways of coming together, existing and dwelling that commoners devise at the point of survival?

The openly constructive and militant framework of OMONIA – its goal of 'changing reality' – clashed with the tradition of institutional critique of the Athens Biennale, which Poka-Yio and Kalpaktsoglou set up as a critical and performative appropriation of the commercial biennial art format. OMONIA was trapped within such format of the 'counter-biennale' – and its double bind of institutionalized critique, commodified activism, and criticality and cynicism in the service of capital. Trapped in this history, OMONIA had been perceived since the very start as yet another spin on activism or – even worse from the perspective of some conservative sections of the art world – as a serious attempt to go beyond capitalism.

I resolved that my next step would be to devise a militant institution for the commons from scratch.

3

INSTITUTE OF RADICAL IMAGINATION (IRI)

With the Institute of Radical Imagination (IRI), I wanted to explore further the transversal institutional collaborations between museums and social centres that had been pursued for instance by MACBA in Barcelona, Reina Sofia in Madrid, SALT in Istanbul and, to a certain extent, the Athens Biennale. All these experiments arose out of the spirit of the worldwide urban mobilization in 2011.[21]

But the recent rise of right-wing populist and neo-fascist forces, the crisis of neo-municipalism and progressive neoliberalism and the emergence of authoritarianism and illiberalism in Europe and the Mediterranean put progressive museums and cultural organizations – their transversal collaborations and socially engaged programmes – under intense public scrutiny and exposed them to accusations of squandering public money on anti-public activities.

In addition, drastic cuts in public funding to art, culture and education have polarized the ecology of art and cultural organizations between corporate museums and smaller 'start-up' organizations seeking support from new, aggressive private subjects – art foundations or NGOs – or working on the project-based logic of corporate museums, often by filling their public programmes. I have explained above that, in this polarized landscape of art and capitalism, medium-sized organizations are not only economically but also politically unsustainable as they are undermined both 'from below' by critical narratives of horizontalism, consensus, collectivism and identity politics and 'from above' by sheer monopolistic power and corporate violence.

With capitalism's capture of both unitary, one-dimensional and vertical organizational forms on the one hand, and dispersed, intersectional and horizontal institutions on the other, I thought it was necessary to imagine different ways of instituting, which took inspiration from the fluid institutional structures of some of the non-Western and non-capitalist zones I have described earlier. I was particularly intrigued by the idea that IRI could be an 'institutional threshold' – an intermediate zone between museums, urban commons and universities – with fluid forms and multi-scalar borders, marked at least initially, not so much by economic and legal boundaries as by a common culture and imagination.

The experience of AB made me realize how much 'curating activism', no matter how transparent and collective the process, ultimately reinforces the hegemonic culture of capitalism by appropriating critical gestures and turning them into stories, scripts, films, installations or choreographed performances that present the point of view of the bourgeoisie (that is, that art has an emancipatory power) as the point of view of all society. In this sense, curating is a powerful social technology of late capitalism, as Jameson has also recently argued, in which culture is both the commodity and the means of production.

But, alongside Gramsci and Castoriadis, I was also interested in experimenting with how culture and art can transcend specific economic and material conditions, develop a 'commons sense' and communities of the sensible, and empathically connect with the point of view of 'the other'. That is to say: I am interested in culture as a *political* movement away from *economically* bound locations – a shift, albeit only short-lived, from base to superstructure. Seeking connections, mending ruptures and separations, and experiencing the point of view of 'the other' – bridging economic divides and cutting across classes – culture can produce and sustain the 'outside of capital' as the horizon of the commons.[22]

More than Western culture (which is the equivalent of the Western fetishized notion of art), the issue here is one of knowledge and epistemology. What kind of knowledge supports activist lives? What constitutes a communist epistemology? What is the relationship between militant aesthetics and militant knowledge? What kind of imagination and epistemology – in images, language or simple gestures – supports life in commons?

It was this new interest in the deep interrelationships between epistemology, art and activism that led me to co-create the Institute of Radical Imagination, with a group of intellectuals, scholars, lawyers, artists, curators, cultural producers and activists, with the aim of defining and implementing zones of post-capitalism in Europe's South and the Mediterranean.

With IRI, I wanted to address the current lack of political imagination and freedom of experimentation within the art world – generated by the There Is No Alternative (TINA) ideology and manifested in the mixture of marketization and cynical criticality I have described above – and build a decolonized and communal imaginary and epistemology as a starting point for transitioning into post-capitalism and building commons. I imagined IRI as a hybrid between a travelling research centre, a refuge for intellectuals and artists at risk (and who take risks), a group of militant researchers and a policy-making body generating ideas and applied knowledge applicable to specific urgent needs on the ground – an intellectual logistical infrastructure more than a structure, operating across existing arts, academic and activist networks.

Moreover, I imagined IRI to be located in Europe's South and the Mediterranean possibly in cities where urban commons and social centres were still active after the post-2011 repression and to operate both locally and transnationally. Currently, IRI has seven nodes – Milan, Venice, Naples, Madrid, Athens, Istanbul and Cairo – and travels nomadically across these nodes but also connects with other nodes in the global South: specifically, Eastern Europe and Latin America.

Being an ex-economist who transitioned into anthropology and there developed long-term and practice-based fieldworks aimed at reframing political economy through the lenses of art practices, including through AB, I was particularly keen to come up with a specific programme of action that addressed the following core dimensions of capitalism and lines of anti-capitalist action.

Political economy

For anarchist philosopher Murray Bookchin, 'the domination of nature by man stems from the real domination of human by human' (Bookchin, 2005: 45). Capitalism's ideology of continuous growth in the context of North/South uneven development is responsible for the environmental degradation, land-grabbing and occupation of commons which today disrupts planetary life. But scholars and activists all too often Eurocentrically assume that capitalism, in its trajectory of continuous growth, has converged towards a homogeneous kind of post-industrial economy based on flexible production, immaterial labour and the productivity of the general intellect.

In the global South, for instance, in China, India and Brazil, there is no post-Fordism or 'platform capitalism'. Rather, capitalism articulates itself in heterotopic regimes of primitive accumulation – sweatshops, high-tech hubs, old-fashioned Taylorist factories and informalized, feminized and racialized labour – and forms of favelization and slummification with deep ecological impact. Such models of primitive accumulation, which started in the peripheries, are now heading back towards the centres.

The economies of late capitalism are diverse, queer and hybrid and these heterogeneous modes of production create complex class configurations. In the global South we do not find the working class or the precariat but a multitude of women, young, migrants, black, indigenous and other dispossessed citizens who survive on precarious, informal and reproductive labour. We do not find civil societies, representative democracies or states as embodiment of the public, but neocolonial elites, foreign capital and autocracies that encroach deeply on the private lives of individuals.

The transition to post-capitalism first relies on the socialization and commoning of life and this can be achieved in several ways. First, by demonetizing the economy – for instance, through parasitical finance (such as the 'Robin Hood' project), currencies of the commons (such as the Spanish FairCoin), sharing platforms and peer-to-peer exchanges that bypass the traditional functioning of the capitalist market. Secondly, by de-commodifying labour through cooperativism, subsistence economies (Mies and Shiva, 2014), reproductive commons (Federici, 2012, 2018), and informal and popular economies (Gago, 2017).

According to the OECD, currently two-thirds of the economically active population work in the informal economy. In fact, the technologically determinist assumption, made by some left-wing accelerationists, that the world is moving towards automated, information-driven and attention-based 'platform capitalism' (Srnicek, 2016), or even the idea of a global 'precariat' (Standing, 2014), underestimates the vast scale of the global informal economy, including low-skilled manual employment in the service and tourism economies and of new forms of indentured labour which, beginning in the global South, are now spreading into the centres – where art workers are a central presence in the reserve army of labour.

More research needs to be done on contemporary forms of precarious, domestic, informal and semi-rural employment for instance: looking at the 'queering' of subsistence, reproductive and informal economies in contemporary capitalism as Silvia Federici does in her analysis of women's commoning in Latin America. An important form of labour commoning is cooperative work. Cooperativism was central to anti-colonial, anti-capitalist and anti-dictatorship movements in Latin America, India and other non-aligned regions in the 1970s and 1980s. Then, in the 2000s, cooperativism became the transmission belt of neoliberal forms of development 'from below', including the popularization of finance and the financialization of poverty, pushed through by global economic institutions such as the World Bank and the IMF. In addition to rethinking the economy through the framework of the commons, it is also fundamental to develop alternatives to bourgeois law, especially notions of property that go beyond the public/private dichotomy, starting with the legalization of urban commons in Europe, as in the case of the 'liberated space' Asilo Filangieri in Naples, which I discuss below.

Citizenship

Notions of economic development and progress are intrinsically political in the way they are premised upon imaginary and fantasmatic constructions of citizenship and personhood. No commons is possible without a radical openness towards the other. New forms of gender and sexual discrimination linked to the feminization of labour and increased male unemployment are emerging. The right to appear – of lesbian, gay, queer and transgender people – is under attack.

The catastrophic impact of the European refugee crisis shows that the enclosures and 'expulsions' (Sassen, 2014) of late capitalism – based on racism, homophobia, nationalism and the coupling of appearance and privilege – are generating segregated social enclaves, urban ghettos and economies of slavery that replicate the logic of the Atlantic slave trade across multiple seas and archipelagos. What would a basic charter of citizens' rights, one which takes the extreme point of view of slaves, refugees, exiles and dispossessed migrants, look like? How can artists and cultural producers contribute to imagine an 'other' form of personhood and citizenship – equal yet unique, open and fluid? How can equality be built on plurality and the refusal 'to be a single being' (Moten, 2018a)? How can communalism avoid co-optation by neo-fascism? What do communism and anti-fascism have in common?

Space and time

The current refugee and migrant crises have highlighted the relationship between space, mobility and inequality. The main markers of colonial dispossession and dependent development in the global South have been processes of urban favelization, slummification and mass rural-to-urban migration associated with trajectories of forced industrialization and debt dependency.

Moreover, late capitalism is entangled in broader processes of nation-building and neocolonialist 'development' with catastrophic planetary economic, social and ecological impact. Yet this planetary trend of spatial inequality resists Western and ethnocentric terms of gentrification, occupation or privatization. How can the relationship between space and power be rethought from a non-ethnocentric and decolonized perspective? How can spatial justice be reformulated beyond the dichotomies of the public and the private that is in relation to the commons?

In what kind of space can the quasi-institutions and alter-institutions of capitalocene exist? Can life emerge and flourish on the threshold (Stavrides, 2016) – neither inside nor outside, but on the surface or in 'flatness' (De Landa, 2002 and Raunig, 2007) rather than in terms of verticality or horizontalism?

Finally, what is the temporal horizon of human emancipation in the form of revival of the communist project or intervention against ecological collapse? What do narratives of natural bioengineering and the Little Ice Age (Vettese, 2018) reveal about us and our primitivist striving towards a communist and egalitarian past? Will humanity be able to carve out a temporality of hope from its present state of suspension between the superfast present of capitalist accumulation and the catastrophic future of ecological destruction – in-between profit, survival and extinction? How can we act upon political urgencies without buying into the short- or long-termism of neoclassical economics – as 'middle-term' projects?

Ontologies

How can non-Eurocentric and non-capitalocentric ontologies of life and forms of solidarity, commoning and cooperation be developed, which do not conform to the redistributive ethics of late capitalism? For instance, how can zero-growth policies be conceived, without reviving the Protestant ethic and its market ideology of scarcity? How can anti-capitalocentric models of development be articulated without reproducing anti-humanist and techno-accelerationist dystopias or capitalism realism? How can a political economy of egalitarianism, care and participatory democracy be developed, grounded in decolonized epistemologies and Southern ontologies for example, in magic realism (Morton, 2017), perspectivism (Viveiros de Castro, 2009) and solidarity with non-humans?

How can an ecological consciousness attuned to the rights of Mother Earth and food self-sufficiency be fostered on the grounds of a new – non-anthropocentric – sense of humanity, rather than on anti-humanism? How can solidarity and connectedness be developed based not on religion – sacred economies, Buddhist economies or Protestantism – but on chance, spirituality, excess, openness and magic? How can distance, separation, contemplation and even asceticism and self-care be cultivated, instead of individualism, over-identification, forced dialectics and hedonism, for the constitution of the commons?

Having mapped the broad theoretical field, I then created a twenty-page-long programme (Appendix 2) focused on six post-capitalist institutions and related potential projects to be implemented by IRI. Then I made a list of those artists, researchers, activists and curators who had inspired me in the way they had addressed some of these issues, and I subsequently approached them, asking them to commit to contribute to the implementation of six post-capitalist projects, each project associated with a set of specific possible interventions, namely:

a) Digital currency/parasitical finance and sharing economy
- Pilot projects on digital currency in the arts and educational sectors
- Transnational common currency
- Post-capitalist mapping of the art economy
- European Bank of the commons
- International pilot on sharing economy
- Mapping international digital activist network
- Non-GDP-related measures of economic value.

b) De-commodification of work and labour commoning
- Mapping art labour and the economy of art
- Pilot Universal Basic Income (UBI) project
- Co-management between urban collectives and municipalities
- Mapping and valorization of informal labour in the art and other sectors
- Legal rights of workers in the service and tourist sectors
- Unionization of informal labourers
- Co-housing projects and cooperatives of urban squatters
- International networks of rural and rural-to-urban cooperatives.

c) Legalization of commons
- Legalization of commons in intellectual and industrial property rights
- Legalization of agreements between municipality (state) and occupied social centres
- Charter for cultural and artistic commons
- New charter of municipalism.

d) Rethinking citizenship
- Universal charter of migrants, the stateless and refugees
- Mapping the economy of refugees and undocumented migrants
- Urban support structures for migrants and refugees
- Study of spatial mobility and citizenship in southern Europe

- New intersectionalities of class, race and gender
- Feminist and eco-feminist networks.

e) Architecture of commons
- Socialization of the empty building in decaying urban centres across Europe
- Mapping of right-to-the-city movements in the Mediterranean
- Co-habitation agreements between municipalities and social movements
- Logistical infrastructures in the Mediterranean
- Spatial support structures and social intervention for refugees and migrants
- Political ecology and 'anti-development' projects in the Mediterranean
- Studies on privatization of urban commons such as electricity and water
- Urban mapping of commons and activities of commoning.

f) Alternative education
- This was ultimately IRI's main project, that is, to constitute itself as a militant pedagogical institution operating at the interface of universities, museums and social centres.

IRI is composed of Sara Buraya (Museo Reina Sofia), Elena Lasala, Gabriella Riccio, Margherita D'Andrea and Giuseppe Micciarelli (Asilo Filangieri), Meric Omer (SALT), Zeyno Pekünlü, Manuel Borja-Villel (Reina Sofia,), William Wells (Townhouse,), Marco Baravalle (Sa.L.E Docks), Emanuele Braga (Macao), Raúl Sánchez Cedillo, Anna Longoni and Mabel Tapia, (Reina Sofia), Dmitry Vilensky (Chto Delat), Jasmina Metwaly, Philip Rizk, Theo Prodromidis, Jesus Carrillo, Dmitry Vilensky (Chto Delat), Olga Egorova (Chto Delat), Alexey Penzin (Chto Delat), Xenia Kalpaktsoglou (LUC), and Ivet Ćurlin, Ana Dević, Nataša Ilić and Sabina Sabolović (What, How & for Whom/WHW).

Naples liberated spaces

Our first meeting took place in Naples, at Asilo Filangieri, a three-storey-high, 5,000-square-metre UNESCO-protected ex-convent located in the historical centre, owned by the municipality, and self-managed by artists and activists under the legal regime of 'bene commune' (common good). Kick-starting the meeting, Giuseppe Micciarelli, Margherita D'Andrea and Gabriella Riccio, the lawyers and activists behind the 'liberation' of Asilo, told us about its history and also gave us some background on the current movement of urban commons in Naples and Italy.

Asilo is one of the several 'former places' – former hospitals, former schools, former monasteries, former psychiatric units – to have been 'liberated' by a new civic and political subjectivity emerging in Naples and across Italy. The term 'former' implies that these places and the collectives inhabiting them are continually transforming, relational and open to different practices, uses and subjectivities. In fact, second-generation commoners such as Micciarelli, D'Andea and Riccio tend to emphasize the difference between 'liberated' and 'occupied' spaces. Liberated spaces are not used by single collectives, as are occupied spaces, but they are open to different social constituencies and uses, especially by the most vulnerable citizens towards whom the commoners of Asilo have a special commitment.

The cinema, nursery, language school for migrants, theatre, urban garden and social kitchen of Asilo are managed by autonomous groups that meet in a weekly general assembly and take decisions by consensus. In Italy, the second wave of urban occupations (liberations) was kick-started by cultural workers and artists at the time of the water referendum in 2011.[23] Asilo Filangieri was liberated in 2012, when a group of activists and cultural workers opposed the move by the municipal Ministry of Culture to transform the place into the headquarters of the UNESCO World Culture Forum in 2013 – 'a mega-event' for which the government had already earmarked €16 million.

Supported by the mayor, Luigi De Magistris, the activists resisted this proposal and made the counterproposal of transforming Asilo into an independent cultural space managed neither by subjects nominated by the state nor by private subjects or private/public partnerships but by the cultural workers themselves. Unlike the legal form of the cooperative or the workers-run firms, which operate solely in the interests of its members, and hence entail exclusive proprietary uses, the legal form of 'collective use' devised by the lawyers of Asilo includes also the citizens external to the group of occupants in the governance of the public good.

The most remarkable aspect of the liberation of Asilo is that the legal document regulating the collective use of the space was co-produced by the very artist community that inhabited it. Consequently, veering away from the usual emphasis in the legal statutes of foundations and associations on 'who' takes the decisions, the statute of Asilo focuses on 'how' decisions are taken. That is to say: the 'regulation of the collective use of beni comuni' is a legal form that emerged from the existing informal rules and practices of self-governance and commoning by the occupant community. This grassroots co-production of law shifts the authority to decide who has the right to access public goods from the state to the groups directly engaged with these goods. It also radically changes the way these goods are valorized – not solely in terms of their utility but with regard to the social relations and actions necessary to reproduce them – for instance, gardening, painting walls, teaching migrants or leading theatre workshops for women. That is to say, this new legal framework empowers those who contribute to the socialization of the public good.[24]

Yet Micciarelli, D'Andrea and Riccio make it clear that the emerging commons do not want to dispose of the state or build zones of autonomy from it; rather, they aim at rethinking the public in terms of a new articulation of popular governance.[25] In the 1990s, the Italian constitution was amended to allow forms of participatory democracy and co-management between citizens and municipalities and of horizontal and direct citizens' interventions in relation to specific urgencies. But even in the most successful cases, participatory democracy failed precisely that vulnerable strata of the population – migrants, unemployed and precarious workers – who needed it the most.

This failure was partly due to the fact that the kinds of participatory democracy and horizontal governance described in the constitutional amendment were based on the impersonal, individualistic, exclusionary and competitive neoliberal myth of autonomy and self-governance. It was NGOs, civic organizations and other aggressive private subjects that benefitted from the creation of this space of autonomy from the state – privatizing the public sphere, capitalizing on social participation and turning the commons good into private enclaves for capital.

The notion of participatory democracy proposed by the Italian movement of 'common goods' (movimento dei beni comuni) is based instead on a vision of state sovereignty as internally constituted by and intertwined with existing popular experiences of urban self-governance, and commoning and operating according to Micciarelli, at 'infra-governmental level' and 'in excess of state power', thus treading a fine line between co-optation and empowerment.

The public administration of De Magistris was involved in this grassroots democratic experiment from the start – first, as guarantor of the democratic form of 'management of the common good' by Asilo in order to facilitate the constituent praxis of civic use of the common good by the immaterial workers of Asilo, and second, by explicitly referring to the 'regulation of civic use and other forms of civic self-organization' drafted by the community of Asilo as the benchmark 'for the identification and management of real property assets in the city of Naples, unused or partly used, perceived by the community as Commons' (council resolution 7, 2015). In this way, the municipality made it possible for the model of 'emerging common goods' to be adopted by seven other 'liberated spaces' in Naples and potentially for a municipal asset of 50,000 square metres. The implications of the collaboration between Asilo and the City Council go beyond the mere legal aspect and point to the emergence of a new political subject that brings together part of the state and a network of urban commons.

The other remarkable aspect of the Neapolitan experience is that Asilo Filangieri now receives 'a social income' from the municipality in recognition of the social work it practises in the neighbourhood, whose value was agreed between the municipal accountants and economists and the community of Asilo. This exercise of participatory accounting led to the emergence of a non-capitalist value regime in which social relations (that is, commoning) are used as the basis for the valorization of the material asset (the building) and not the other way around as in standard forms of capitalist accounting.

Legally, these new urban commons are mixed institutions that bring together the private 'declaration of common use' by a collective private subject and its formal recognition as 'common good' by the public administration. As such, they carry with them the danger of becoming a new form of neoliberal governance 'from below' if not enclaves of capital, which is also a frequent criticism of urban commons. The second criticism normally levelled against them is that they have a narrow economistic framework derived from Elinor Omstrom's original study of natural commons, which emphasized that natural resources are scarce and satisfy basic needs; hence free access to them is a universal right. The aim of Omstrom's original study was to demonstrate that the commoning of natural resources was not only more egalitarian but also more efficient than state expropriation (nationalization) or privatization. Such economic framework failed to appreciate the relationality and openness of commons.

In fact, however, veering away from the economicist framework of the early legal struggles against the privatization of water in Italy in 1999, the legal group in Naples propose a discoursive, practical and relational understanding of the term, using the law to prefiguratively reimagine popular governance and articulate 'public' powers that the state alone can no longer exert. The group defines common goods as those goods that are explicitly declared so by a collective committed to managing them directly and democratically following the constitutional norms of horizontality, mutualism, cooperation and inclusivity. According to this definition, any park, building, school, theatre and even university can be a commons.

In this framework, common goods cannot be determined a priori. Their rights and values are relational.[26] They can be defined only in relation to an unstable, unrooted, open and continuously transforming order. Indeed, the commoners of the eight liberated centres in Naples think of themselves as 'undecided spaces' because they continually change, are open to multiple uses and subject positions, and are endlessly regenerated by the groups' constituent practices. This relational view of law-making as reflecting material acts of commoning, including their tensions and contradictions, goes against the abstract legal and economic bourgeois logic of inclusivity that drives neoliberal projects of urban fab-labs, start-ups and social entrepreneurship through which the private occupies the public or turns it into a bureaucracy in charge of policing capitalist enclaves.

Relationality is also central to the way the members of Asilo, many of whom are artists, reimagine the artistic process. For instance, the choreographer, activist and lawyer Gabriella Riccio – one of Asilo's founding members – develops performances, whose aesthetics reflects the sensuous and 'agonistic' relationality of the commons by focusing on the body as a space of negotiation between performer and spectator, and working towards the limits of this relationship.

Thus, the framework of Asilo Filangieri, where the first meeting of IRI took place, was ideal to initiate a conversation on the Post-capitalist Manifesto that I had distributed to the members (Appendix 2). I started with two questions: What is the shape of revolutionary politics in the contemporary world? What is the role of imagination in it? I emphasized the historical context in which we found ourselves. The millions of people who mobilized against state capitalism in 2011 in Greece, Spain, Egypt, New York and London, and in 2013 in Turkey, Brazil, Romania, Bulgaria and Bosnia, had been pushed back, repressed and reduced to impotence by newly emerging authoritarian states.

I presented IRI as an internationalist platform informed by the rethinking of communism in terms of the commons. I argued that in the contemporary context of identitarian fragmentation, nationalism, nativism and polarization between global North and global South it was important to create an international political platform informed by both anti-capitalism and postcolonialism. Also, there was a need to rethink class politics in relation to the complex political economy of late capitalism and also to be connected with the struggles for recognition of black, gay and feminist constituencies and of the growing armies of displaced migrants.

I hoped that within IRI these questions could be addressed not only theoretically, but also by triggering policies and direct interventions contributing to the transition into post-capitalism in the Mediterranean.

I described IRI as:

A method for instituting otherwise;
A decolonized and anti-capitalist space;
A quasi-institution and a soft infrastructure of learning, intervention and imagination.

And IRI's mission:

- To bring together art, activism and pedagogy in order to transition towards a post-capitalist society
- To work on the implementation of six steps towards post-capitalism, also intended as six forms of commoning – of money, labour, law, architecture, personhood and education
- To co-produce the institute itself as a post-capitalist institution – or 'quasi-institution'– that operates as institutional interface between universities, museums and social centres, and possibly also progressive municipalities interested in co-managing the political and cultural commons with the institute
- To create processes of mutual contamination between art institutions and political organizations – museums and social centres – for the convergence of art and life
- To refuse both statist notions of public art and the incorporation of activism inside the neoliberal museum by (1) engaging with art – its concepts, practices and competences – to experiment with activist forms of pedagogy, political economy and livelihood and (2) relying on activist networks and expert knowledge outside art to democratize art and cultural institutions and build cultural commons.

There were mixed reactions to my manifesto. Some did not like the boldness of its vocabulary, the positivist search for a better world and the modernist call to revolutionary action. Our members from Egypt emphasized how activist or even just progressive art institutions there are being shut down and silenced so that art can no longer function as a space of criticality anymore. Their vision for IRI was that it should operate like a research body, rather than being orientated towards action. Some IRI members from the South also expressed a resistance against the language of 'commons', given their rich history of mutualism, solidarity and neighbourhood-based sociality, which transcended the Western opposition between 'public' and 'private' and in the light of their current experience of authoritarianism and urban repression.

There was also a shared view that the experience of neo-municipalism in Naples, which I described above, was the exception to the general rule of repression of commons by those municipalities which, emerged from the urban mobilizations of the 2010s, subsequently turned against the very democratic platforms out of which they had developed. Municipalism had collapsed in Greece and was also under strain in Spain, where several municipalities controlled by the Podemos Party had initially strongly supported it. The Podemos-affiliated mayor of Madrid at the time, Manuela Cardena, had agreed with the prime minister, Mariano Rajoy, an austerity plan that involved cuts to welfare and social services. Backtracking from her previous support for social centres and occupied spaces, including La Ingobernable, Cardena targeted them with repeated police raids and threatened to close them down. It was thought that IRI could fill the gap emerging from the crisis of neo-municipalism, acting as a second-order platform supporting civic movements and social centres through long-term and grassroots interventions.

Manolo Borja-Villel reflected that we all had a common history in the counter-hegemonic movements of 2011, but the present was very different, given that it was marked by authoritarian, censoring and culturally backward states. We all agreed that the previously existing open and agonistic dialogue between cultural institutions and social movements was now impossible; therefore IRI should function as a parallel and underground structure connecting these two institutional levels.

His suggestion that IRI could function as an underground structure was reinforced by the mapping done by Emanuele Braga and Marco Baravalle in preparation for the meeting, which showed that the majority of IRI members belonged to political collectives but participated in IRI as independent individuals. However, I did not want IRI to be a second-order organization or a platform. How would the individual members' actions within IRI impact on the collectives they belonged to? To what extent were their voices representative of the assemblies they belonged to? This was an issue not only of political representation, but also of strategic alignment. Was it possible to keep the priorities of the collectives aligned with those of IRI? And if not, how could this divergence be ethically dealt with?

Artist Zeyno Pekünlü expressed her wish to revisit the history of the 'movement of the squares' of 2011 in Egypt, Turkey and Greece in light of their current dispersion, disbandment and ongoing repression by the state. What was the future of these urban commons in the South? Would southern Europe converge towards the Mediterranean trajectory of state authoritarianism and repression? Or could the Italian, Spanish and, to a certain extent, Greek experiments in neo-municipalism work to enliven and reactivate grassroots democracy in the Mediterranean? In the light of these global disjunctures, IRI could work as a transnational observatory for urban commons and a shared depository of information, knowledge and practices, to be used for connecting and translating experiences of struggle across different historical and geographical contexts. We agreed that the next meeting would be on European neo-municipalism and would be held in Madrid in May, in parallel with the 8M feminist mobilization.

Madrid: Master in urban commons

In Madrid, IRI co-organized, with the occupied space La Ingobernable, the six-day event '*Master En Comunes Urbanos. Debates para la Conquista del derecho al Espacio y el Derecho a la Ciudad*' (Master in Urban Commons. Debates for the Right to Space and to the City). The 'Master' in the title was a pun on the scandal that was engulfing Cristina Cifuentes, the president of the region from the Popular Party (PP), who had just resigned after it transpired that she forged her MA Law degree at the King Juan Carlos University (URJC).

The Master had two goals: (1) to share vocabularies, practices and strategies of urban commoning in Madrid and across Spain and (2) to jointly devise some mid-term and long-term actions in support of social centres and urban occupations across the nodes of IRI.

Despite the burlesque framework of the Master, the meeting wanted to be a collective reflection on the practices and central challenges experienced by 'second-generation' social centres like *La Ingobernable*. How can the non-institutionalized forms of governance of commons be made sustainable? How can transparent communication across centres be developed? How can a shared vision of rights-to-the-city and non-capitalist urban regeneration, planning and community development be co-produced by social centres? What are the practical struggles in managing commons and cooperatives? What kind of militant actions can stop the gentrification and touristification of cities? What is the best way of sharing legal knowledge and institutional strategies of commoning across cities? Can commons develop non-formal education and literacy, including feminist urban sociology and anthropology?

Secondly, the Master wanted to explore if the experience of *beni comuni emergenti* developed by Asilo in Naples could be replicated in La Ingobernable. The translation, transfer and contamination of practices and strategies across different commons create a 'epidemiological' effect that contributes to both their resilience and their openness. In this instance, the challenge was to translate the legal categories and institutional praxes adopted in Naples to the Spanish context. The case of Asilo Filangieri had been discussed in the general assembly of La Ingobernable on the previous day. The Spanish commoners supported the framework of co-management of the public good by municipalities and social centres. But several of them were also sceptical of the notion that the autonomy of social centres could be constructed by law and without state interference.

The Master took place in the building of La Ingobernable and unfolded over five days. The two full-time mentors in charge of running it put together an 85-pages-long Reader containing a mixture of legal documents, scholarly articles and activist texts. Attending the Master were the commoners from La Ingobernable and from about thirty other occupied social centres in Madrid and across Spain, as well as individual activists who had applied through the open call circulated by the organizers.

At the first session, the participants reflected on the kind of institutional space commons occupy, in relation to the fictitious capitalist realms of the 'public' and the 'private'. In the context of the ideological and institutional crisis of parliamentary politics and of traditional labour organizations, the political relevance of urban commons, as spaces of reproduction of life and of alternative economies, is growing. But as institutions for the production and reproduction of life, and 'living forms' antagonistic to the bureaucratization and commodification of life by capital, commons are difficult to stabilize and ground around a specific institutional configuration.

Indeed, institutionally commons are fluid thresholds between the private and the public and tread a fine line between autonomy and self-referential enclosure. They are porous social systems that are continuously being built and discussed, always unfinished and open – not as islands but as relational spaces that enable conflict, cooperation and negotiation. Commons are built on diversity, not identity, and by different people with common interests and needs. They cannot be individualized, yet they are not 'for everybody' – as states are supposed to be – but 'among everybody'. They are spaces of socialization, of unity in difference and of shared vulnerability. As such, they are anti-fascist spaces.

In terms of scale and temporality, commons enable grassroots urban participation and more rapid responses to political urgencies than states and the private sector, as well as greater institutional flexibility. On the other hand, the temporality of commons is uneven – that is, based on moments of great energy that easily get lost. In terms of governance, everybody is responsible for the urban commons, albeit within various forms of decentralization and nested authorities. The main goal of urban commons is to reproduce non-capitalist forms of life. When we achieve them, we learn how to protect, valorize and look after them.

Then the discussion moved onto how to valorize the collective intelligence – in the fields of public education, health, right-to-the-city, eco-feminism, mutual support and informal economy – generated by social centres and commons. This collective intelligence is situated outside both private and public enclaves and concentrated in specific neighbourhoods. Pablo Bacchiler suggested setting up the *archivos de los communes* (archive of the commons) project mapping the existing networks of social centres and commons in Madrid and collating legal material (such as formal and informal agreements with the municipality); films and visual material; oral histories and other informal visual, oral and textual data that could constitute a sort of collective memory of commoning. The *archivos de los communes* project addressed the challenge of collating, translating and transmitting across different contexts, different knowledge and different experiences of struggle, which are by their very nature autonomous and territorially grounded, as well as seeking a common, non-capitalist epistemology across occupied spaces and social centres.

One of the most inspiring moments of the Master was when the groups acknowledged the struggles commons faced on a daily base. First, there is the constant menace of the patrimonial logic of capital and the commodity form creeping back in, especially in relation to immaterial commons and consumption, for instance, of beer and recreational drug. The biggest capital threat to urban commons is the relentless advancement of the real estate market, exacerbated by urban demographic expansion. Endorsing the logic of the market, local residents blame occupied spaces for lowering the market value of their properties, while profit-orientated municipalities push urban commons and social centres to the city's outskirts, often in the form of projects of social and urban regeneration, to maximize the land value in city centres.

Moreover, commons struggling against capitalization become impermeable to the outside, resistant, self-referential and rigid, and hence unable to adapt to the multi-scalar logic of capitalism. They become fragmented and more reactive than propositional. Third, urban commons struggle to relate to the public. For instance, urban commons advocated for a public system of water management, instead of the popular governance proposed by the movement of the water commons in Italy. Fourthly, the horizontalism of commons, rather than eliminating hierarchies, creates the toxic phenomenon of 'hyper-leadership' – that is, the informal hierarchization of roles and concentration of power and knowledge around a few charismatic individuals. The inability to put in place vertical structures to counterbalance horizontality[27] generates ongoing internal conflicts, vetoes and institutional closures that delay and protract decision-making processes and ultimately lead to inertia. Lastly, even progressive municipalities are intolerant of urban commons and censor them, policing them heavily and closing them down.[288] Living conditions are deteriorating and commoners feel extremely vulnerable.

Sara Buraya, from the Reina Sofía museum, led the session entitled 'Autonomia: Towards the Collective Writing of Our Own Rules', a reflection on the existing gap between, on the one hand, the bureaucratic normativization of life embodied by states and municipal institutions and, on the other, the implicit codes of self-governance of commons, often unwritten but arising from shared modes of doing and openly self-reflexive experiences. In this session, the commoners who had been meeting and discussing in La Ingobernable for the past five days reflected together on how to formalize autonomy, through forms of collective writing and communal imagination, starting from an assessment if the Neapolitan experience of the civic use of commons could be applied to Madrid. The most established Spanish urban commons, including La Casa Invisible in Málaga, CSC Luis Buñuel in Zaragoza, Casa del Pumarejo in Seville and Astra in Guernica, attended this section. At the time, these occupied spaces were under threat of closure by municipalities and under strict police surveillance, and there was a shared desire to sketch together a collective charter for urban commons.

IRI presented itself as a 'commons in progress' and made it clear that its presence in Madrid reflected IRI's strategic goal of being embedded in its cities/nodes and establishing ongoing collaborations with the social centres and occupied spaces in these cities. There was so much that IRI could learn from the commoners who had gathered in La Ingobernable, in terms of democratic governance, common knowledge, egalitarian social relations and utopian vision. In exchange, IRI was committed to support the urban commons in Madrid and develop jointly with them some practical projects – such as a Universal Basic Income (UBI) pilot project; or a currency of the commons; or a cinema, a library, a school or a film project; or support for the 'archive of the common' project proposed by Bacchiller – in order to facilitate the emergence of a common cultural and political infrastructure across the social centres. In addition, by being connected to urban commons in Greece, Turkey, Cairo, Zagreb and Palestine, IRI could bring a different, Mediterranean, political perspective into the European debate, expressive of radically different experiences of commoning and activate networks of solidarity across these diverse political spaces.

In the evening of the last day of the Master we screened in the cinema of La Ingobernable the film *Summer School of Orientation in Zapatism* (2017) by the Chto Delat Collective. The starting point of the film is the Sixth Declaration of the Selva Lacandona by Zapatistas in Chiapas which introduced the idea of the 'Zapatistas's embassy' in which the praxis of the *encuentros* (horizontal meetings) with local people is reimagined as a transnational form of personal communication and information-sharing of the movement's struggles against neoliberalism worldwide.

The film was made in anticipation of the arrival of the Russian embassy, which never happened and was based on a two-week-long school residency led by the Chto Delat collective, where seventeen people lived in a temporary commune in the Russian countryside, discussing Zapatista ideas in reading groups, learning Spanish and developing practices of community building. What does it mean to live in a common? And how can the Zapatista way of life be practised outside the original indigenous context? One of the inspiring elements of the film is the way it experiments with Zapatista epistemology and aesthetics.

The film's anti-culmination strategy (that is, the avoidance of the classical linear narrative of commercial cinema, culminating into a cathartic ending), its irony, slow temporality and multi-perspectivism (the story is distributed across several different chapters telling different versions of the story) echo the aesthetic tradition of Third Cinema as well as the subaltern form of storytelling of Zapatista leader *subcomandante* Marcos. In addition, its polyphonic, multimodal and Brechtian formats – bringing together a parodic puppet show in which a beetle acts as alter-ego of *subcomandante* Marcos, beautiful handwoven maps depicting utopian geographies, and Zapatista texts performed by the school's residents – embody different modes of expression of the Zapatista way of life and re-enact a mesmerizing and absorbing political journey. The Zapatista film reminded me of indigenous storytelling – the multisensory, polyphonic and multi-perspectivist aesthetics, the circular and open temporality, the relational and rich epistemology and the micro-exploration of the way an ideology can be experienced as 'minor' form of politics – that is, as an embodied way of being and making together.

In addition, the film touched upon a central issue that kept coming up at the Master, and that was also central to IRI: what is the role of art in building a common 'revolutionary' culture and radical imagination, and how from such common prefigurative space can collective forms of action be developed? As well as giving a fascinating insight into Zapatista aesthetics, the film reflects the egalitarian pedagogical ethos of the Chto Delat's *Schools of Engaged Art*. It is in this doubling up of the Zapatista philosophy – as both aesthetics and as a militant form of knowledge production – that *Summer School of Orientation in Zapatism* prefigures the political horizon of the commons.

This very question arose at our first IRI meeting, after the master. What do we mean by revolutionary culture? How can we actualize historical and sociological concepts – such as communism, class struggle or feminism – in the contemporary context and across different geographies? How can we sketch a common horizon of imagination cutting across the global North and the global South?

I was specifically interested in addressing the 'discursive' political epistemology embraced by the left populist parties Podemos and Syriza, which several of us had supported in the past, in various capacities. The notion of 'discursive' politics was originally articulated by Ernesto Laclau and later popularized by the scholars Costas Douzinas and Chantal Mouffe who closely associated themselves, respectively, with Syriza in Greece and Podemos in Spain. In the 2010s, Mouffe's definition of progressive politics as performative play of opposing ('agonistic') discursive articulations – as opposed to historically determined and class-based – inspired a transversal collaboration between cultural institutions, social centres and progressive municipalities, and the neo-municipalist platforms in Barcelona and Madrid. In Greece, Douzinas's Lacanian reading of the movement of occupation of Syntagma Square as a new form of transversal democratic subjectivity was adopted by Tzipras to describe the intersectional politics of the new Greek Left. The figure of the Lacanian populist intellectual, and of culture as a discursive site of struggle, replaced the Gramscian Party intellectual and culture as a form of class struggle.

But times had changed. The agonistic dialogue between mayor Cardena and the social centres of Madrid turned into outright state repression and violence. For me, this was a sign that a capitalist state necessarily relies on class differences and speculative economies that make dialogue between municipalities and civic society lopsided and ultimately impossible. Despite the collapse of left-wing populism, Mouffe's insistence on cultural and identity politics continues to inspire the progressive Left. In her recent book *Podemos*, written with the Spanish activist Íñigo Errejón,[29] Mouffe attributes the phenomenal rise of right-wing populist parties in Europe to their better grasp of identity and cultural politics vis-à-vis the obsolete European Left which remains mired in class politics. This argument discounts the fact that capital always relies on identity politics to fragment the working class, starting from the subordination of women and people of colour, and often with the collusion of the upper strata of the white male working class. The recent successes of right-wing populist politicians such as Trump in the United States or Salvini in Italy were due to the way they re-actualized old racist and homophobic constructions of class in the contemporary context.

I thought that it was important for us to reflect on our class position – presumably we were all middle class – and on whether, through IRI, we could use culture to bring forward a broader reflection and transformation of capitalist class relations. Most of us were aware of the small social circle in which the art world existed, and with IRI we wanted to reach out to social constituencies that are normally excluded from it, forge a popular imaginary that was larger than this circle and, with such an imaginary, activate new and non-capitalist forms of relationality.

But in the discussion that followed, the group struggled to find common ground in the Western Marxist epistemology I was using. For Dmitry Vilensky, the opposition between class and identity was a false opposition, as class struggle and the struggle for representation cannot be separated. Some 'post-workerist' members of the group argued that the traditional notion of class I was using was obsolete and that class is now entirely subsumed into culture. Contemporary work is deracinated from the traditional factory and fragmented into 'the general intellect' – a productive force that operates at the biopolitical level, that is, through affective, cognitive and even chemical forces affecting the very bodies of the capitalist subject. Immaterial work, culture and even poetry are sites of such biopolitical fragmentation of capital.

Alexei Penzin's suggestion that we should jointly develop a post-Soviet epistemology, one which reimagined notions of communism and class from a postcolonial and non-Eurocentric perspective, was supported by several members of the group, especially those from the Mediterranean area who found the notions of 'class', 'work' and 'capital' I was using Eurocentric and excessively theoretical.

Sara Buraya argued that recent feminist organizations had brought together 'struggles for identity recognition and struggles for economic redistribution' (Fraser, 1995, 2018). She had been one of the organizers of the mass demonstration against domestic violence in Madrid and across Spain, sparked by the gang rape of a teenager in Pamplona the year before. On International Women's Day (8 March) that year, 5 million people across Spain – care workers, women teachers, housewives and journalists – had taken part in the *huelga feminista* (feminist strike), a nationwide stoppage of waged work, care and shopping. In Madrid 1 million people moved through the city centre in a 6-kilometre-long line, dancing and playing music. La Ingobernable and the grassroots pedagogical platform Fundación de los Comunes had been behind the movement of the 8M (8 March) since 2016, developing its network across the country, building feminist campaigns and collectives, and liaising with other groups, such as artists groups and autonomous centres. In an exceptional move, both mainstream unions (CGO and UGT) and radical unions (CGT and CNT) had supported the strike, with stoppages and walkouts.

The notion of the feminist strike is a powerful conceptual tool in the current anti-capitalist debate. It brings back the issues of labour exploitation and class formation under capitalism, which had been alienated by the current debate on income inequality and state redistribution within the liberal left, but also emphasizes the patriarchal and racist basis of capitalism. The *huelga feminista* asks: 'What kind of shop floor is the household?'; 'Can we stop caring for our loved ones?'; 'Are love, sex and even smiles instances of domestic labour?', and 'How do we strike if we are unemployed?'

The Spanish 8M movement has strong affinities with the 'Southern feminism'[30] of the #NiUnaMenos ('Not One Less') mass movement in Argentina, focused on domestic violence, femicide, anti-abortion laws; and the #PrimaveraFeminista in Brazil, sharing especially struggles against homophobia, racism and police violence. The #NiUnaMenos movement had a strong impact on European feminism – first in Poland, where it defeated a conservative anti-abortion bill in 2016; and then in Italy, where the #NonUnadiMeno brought together struggles for identity recognition and class-based claims for economic redistribution, framing the increase in domestic violence, homophobia, racism and sexism in the broader context of labour deregulation, welfare cuts and privatization by the Renzi administration. The Italian #NonUnadiMeno's manifesto, *Piano Femminista*, argued that the implementation of a Universal Basic Income (UBI) scheme, by granting economic independence to women, would undermine the patriarchal social relations normally associated with capitalism. The proposal was so popular that it was co-opted by the Five Star movement in the 2018 elections in Italy.

Because the social construction of alterity – of racialized women, migrants, queer, trans, poor and disabled – is central to capitalism, this new feminism 'for the 99 percent' (Fraser, Bhattacharya and Arruzza, 2018) is intersectional and anti-capitalist. Moreover, unlike the liberal feminism represented by the #MeToo movement, which advocates for women's greater participation in the capitalist plunder, anti-capitalist feminism advocates women's (and men's) liberation from it. Through the debates, workshops and activities organized by Sara Buraya and Ana Longoni (the director of the museum's programme) the Reina Sofia Museum established itself as an intellectual and logistical meeting point for international scholars, feminist organizations and art collectives working together towards sustaining and reinforcing the new 'feminist wave' (*marea feminista*) across Europe and Latin America.

In the afternoon of that day, we brainstormed the possible interventions IRI could develop in relation to the strategic needs highlighted in the Master. It was decided that there was an urgent need to set up an archive of the commons, storing knowledge to be used by social centres across Spain and the rest of Europe. Pablo Bacchiler, Sara Buraya and Elena Lasala proposed the project *Archivo sobre Comunes, Derecho a la Ciudad* (Archive on Commons, Rights to the City), an online platform aiming at archiving material on urban commons relative to the collective experiences of social centres in Madrid in the last ten years. The archive will bring together material of different kinds, including textual material such as formal agreements between municipalities and occupied spaces, legal frameworks, urban planning documents, theoretical and political documents, experiential material such as video and audio interviews, films, photos and also more experimental and experiential material such as diaries and conversations; and journalistic material such as reports, newsletters, petitions and calls to action.

In the afternoon, we discussed how to implement forms of collective governance and decision-making in IRI. Currently the general assembly collectively takes strategic decisions (for instance, which projects to start and what resources to allocate to these projects); the operative groups of the different nodes act upon these decisions and develop projects autonomously; and a small coordinating group deals with logistics and administration. In the process the operative nodes liaise with the coordinating group and periodically give feedback on the development of their projects to the general assembly.

The alternative model of having the operative and regional nodes independent from IRI was also discussed. In this context, the general assembly of IRI would continue to be the main decision-making body, but IRI and the operational nodes would collaborate only on a projects/action basis. The relationship between IRI and the nodes would be more contractual, and the function of IRI would be limited to decision-making, storage of archival material, internal and external communication, and resource redistribution. Some members argued that this second model risked replicating the neoliberal project-based and redistributive logic, and we decided instead to continue to operate jointly and work on developing a common intelligence.

The second part of the meeting discussed IRI's economy and sustainability. IRI will be funded by the FfAI (Foundation for the Arts Initiative) until 2021. But how can IRI be sustainable beyond that? How do we establish alternative economies and diverse forms of valorization of our contributions, contaminating, deflating and demonetizing the capitalist economy? What kind of economy is the economy of commons? Can commons rely just on reciprocity or on state redistribution, as in Naples? How do we avoid precarizing our labour? Can the market be used in a non-capitalist way? Emanuele Braga suggested the creation of a commons fund sustained by the different nodes of IRI. This commons fund would function both as a form of mutual aid and as a redistribution network. It would be fed through individual cash contributions or in kind – that is, through labour that contributes towards the activities of IRI, as well as being generated through a Universal Basic Income (UBI) pilot project. In this light, IRI could function as a small laboratory for an alternative economy, subsequently contaminating and de-commodifying the social relations each of us had outside our commons. Currently, IRI operates with a system which remunerates the members' contributions with tokens which they can convert into money, keep as credit or donate to other members.

At the end of our Madrid experience, inspired by the Zapatista project, we decided that our next step would be to work together on shared epistemologies and common pedagogical practices. The chosen location for this project was Athens, where IRI had strong links with the solidarity school network.

Athens

In the context of the worldwide attack on education – either through extreme marketization, as in the UK and United States, or through state censorship and direct repression, as in Brazil, Turkey and Hungary – IRI's role as producer of anti-capitalist knowledge and epistemology of the commons seemed extremely urgent. There is already a rich established tradition of radical and anti-institutional pedagogy – from Freire's pedagogy of the oppressed to Ivan Illich's de-schooling practice – in addition to the 'decolonizing the curriculum' movement currently sweeping across Mexico, Latin America and South Africa, as well as in the United States and UK, where, nonetheless, calls for a decolonized pedagogy and post-disciplinary education are partly market-driven and aimed at deskilling Higher Education workers.

I thought it was important for IRI to kick-start its own pedagogical project rather than transplant practices and vocabularies from other contexts. I was interested in sketching some cross-cultural, if not-universal, principles of how to generate and share knowledge about life in common in non-hierarchical, non-commodified and non-institutionalized ways. But instead of dismissing the notion of expert knowledge altogether – as in the current post-disciplinary trend – I was interested in the way some expert knowledge is preserved, valorized and transmitted across generations and social constituencies, through rituals and protocols that reinforce the commons, rather than being exclusionary or elitist.

The chance came when Zeyno Pekünlü and I started a project on solidarity education in Turkey, founded by the art organization COUNCIL (Paris), in which we mapped the pedagogical practices developed by academics for peace – the signatory academics from Higher Education who were sacked and banned for life by the Erdogan government.[31] Some of these solidarity academies functioned as street universities, and others like social centres. On the basis of their exilic conditions, these academies had developed methodologies, such as collective teaching or co-production of curricula, aimed at democratizing teaching and reaching out to constituencies who would not normally be involved in education. The situation in Istanbul was different from that of solidarity schools in Greece, which, unlike academics for peace, were not illegal and were self-sustaining. As part of the project, Pekünlü and I had commissioned the academics for peace a report on solidarity education, as well as bringing them into conversation with the Solidarity School Network in Greece, with which we had both collaborated in the past.

Thus, with this IRI intervention we wanted to develop further our understanding of solidarity education – which I describe here as a set of pedagogical practices developed outside the state in self-organized, grassroots and egalitarian ways, by communities either persecuted by the state or critically positioned outside it – and build a dialogue between academics for peace in Istanbul, the Solidarity School of Mesopotamia and the Piraeus Open School of Immigrants in Athens.

The Solidarity School of Mesopotamia started in 2013 as part of the Greek Time Bank Network, a demonetized exchange network in which educational services were exchanged with other public services, mainly food and medical treatment. The Time Bank Network began at the peak of the economic crisis in 2013, when unemployment was at 30 per cent, the state was heavily cutting down its social services, and there were approximately 350 solidarity centres across the country. The Solidarity School of Mesopotamia started with no funding and with thirty students. Today it has 350 students, 50 teachers and 60 classes. In 2015, the Solidarity School of Mesopotamia led a process of institutional consolidation, creating the Solidarity School Network (SSN), which currently has ten affiliated solidarity schools. The Mesopotamia Solidarity School was unofficially 'donated' by the municipality of Moscato to the 'citizens' movement of Mesopotamia' in 2007. The school is located close to the touristic port of Piraeus and is also part of an anti-gentrification and ecological platform that opposes major tourist developments along the coast and demands free access to the beach. The school does not have any legal form and operates through open weekly school assemblies and SSN's monthly general assemblies.

Lower-middle-class and working-class families in Greece struggle to find extra money for private tuition in those subjects (Maths, English and Ancient Greek) that are mandatory entrance requirements for public universities. So, despite the fact that primary and secondary education are public in Greece, access to universities ultimately relies on the expanding private tuition sector. Because of the growing demand for extra tuition for the children of the Moscato neighbourhood, the Time Bank School became the Mesopotamia Solidarity School.

According to Christos Korolis, the founder of the Mesopotamia school and the SSN, solidarity schools have no utopian goals but are grounded in the needs of the community. At the same time, however, they want to change the logic of public education through (1) the participation of parents, students and teachers in the Time Bank, which creates horizontal relationships among them; (2) the participation of parents, students and teachers in non-hierarchical assemblies every three months; and (3) the co-production of non-standard school curricula and seminar formats.

Solidarity schools within the SSN share information, knowledge and best practices around solidarity education on the basis of their shared belief that they do not want to get rid of the state, but instead they want to radically transform the public system by introducing democratic practices and curricula. They don't see themselves as being 'between' public and private education – in fact, they strongly oppose privatization. Moreover, they don't consider themselves as pedagogical movements but as political ones, although they are not associated with any political party. Their aim is to democratize the school system in the broader project of the democratization of society. In addition, solidarity schools in Athens are deeply intertwined with the local solidarity economy network, which includes housework (help at home, decoration, refurbishment, help with pets), health (nursing, first aid, alternative medicine and medical information) and legal consultancy. Hence, they partake to the broader process of demonetization of the economy and operate according to a post-capitalist logic.

The Piraeus Open School for Immigrants emerged in 2005 to provide educational support for immigrants and refugees. The school's annual programme includes lessons in English, Spanish, Italian and German at all levels, and an intensive Greek writing and reading course necessary to obtain the advanced language certificate at A and B levels. The school also offers classes in photography, theatre and traditional folk dances across the world. In addition, the school is strongly engaged in defining and upholding the rights of immigrants and refugees, especially health and labour rights, and in facilitating citizen status. In fact, through the school's advanced Greek language certificates, migrants do acquire legal citizenship status.

The Open School Piraeus's volunteers also provide clothing, footwear and personal hygiene items to refugee camps, detention centres and nursing homes throughout the year and give crucial health support in the detention centre of Amigdaleza, in liaison with the solidarity clinic KEELPNO. For instance, they update and organize the detainees' medical files, which are often incomplete or missing; run a social pharmacy inside the centre; and provide transport for emergency transfers to the hospital. After October 2015, when thousands of refugees got trapped in the port of Piraeus, the volunteers from the Piraeus Open School worked full-time in the social clinic inside the port.

In 2016, the Piraeus Open School devised, with Syrians, Afghani and Kurdish refugee teachers, a common educational programme including Maths, Greek and English classes, in their mother tongues – Arabic, Kurdish and Farsi – running from 9 a.m. to 5 p.m. every day, for six days a week. The 'School of Hope' is the first solidarity structure in Greece self-organized by refugees themselves in their camps and based on pedagogical principles and material from their home countries. Volunteer teachers give daily evening lessons (from 5 p.m. to 8 p.m.) to teenagers and adults in Greek, Spanish, French and English. There are currently over 630 registered children between the ages of 5 and 13 at the daytime lessons and 340 teenagers and adults at the evening lessons. The Piraeus Open School is free of charge. It is not an NGO, and it is run entirely by volunteers.

In December 2018, IRI conducted a workshop with the Piraeus Open School and Mesopotamia Solidarity School exploring their legal, economic and political challenges in the political context of the time. Despite their growth and consolidation, these schools were threatened by the steep rise of far-right groups and the conservative New Democracy Party, which intended to break the solidarity economy network, because its neoliberal view was that the way to reactivate the Greek economy was to unleash private capital. Thus, the Solidarity Schools Network needed to acquire legal status before the forthcoming October elections, when Syriza was very likely to lose and the New Democratic Party to gain power. Thus, IRI assembled a group of lawyers, activists and experts, charged with the task of devising a legal framework for the solidarity schools to present to the Syriza government in September 2019.

For human rights lawyer Margherita D'Andrea, solidarity schools such as the Open School Piraeus were points of contact between illegal migrants and refugees and local communities in which informal social contracts were drawn up and new forms of citizens' rights established. D'Andrea suggested that in the new legal set-up of the Open School Piraeus should also be included basic immigrants' basic rights – to education, health and political representation – as they *emerged* through the activities of the schools. Just as the legal institution of 'public good' in Asilo in Naples had been formulated starting from the grassroots activities of commoning taking place in social centres, D'Andrea suggested that solidarity schools could be spaces in which denizens' rights were upheld and legally formalized. Korolis was keen to develop the Neapolitan framework for the Solidarity School Network so that solidarity schools could receive a social income and be formally recognized as part of the public education system, albeit not entirely internal to the state but, rather, in productive tension with it.

The IRI working group on solidarity education also included members of the Argentinian Bachilleratos Populares (BP) – secondary schools for young people and adults inspired by the principles of Popular Education (EP) developed by Brazilian educator and activist Paulo Freire, which combines radical pedagogy, and feminist and anti-capitalist activism, in Latin America. BP developed in the early 2000s in the city and province of Buenos Aires, as part of the wider protest movement against neoliberalism taking place in working-class districts, recovered factories, unemployed workers' organizations, trade unions, cooperatives and neighbourhood-based organizations.

Popular Education considers education to be a practice of struggle for popular emancipation based on dialogue, inclusion and active participation. Since 2015, BPs have been strongly involved in the feminist movement *Ni Una Menos*, including International Feminist Strikes and the campaign for the decriminalization and legalization of abortion in 2018. The BP's pedagogy of popular feminism (*feminismos populares*) opposes the formal, elitist and identity-based feminism of academics and middle-class activists and addresses women from working-class and poor backgrounds in simple and direct language. The core principle of BPs is to be accessible (lessons take place from Monday to Friday outside working hours, between 6 p.m. and 10 p.m.) and self-managed – they are based on non-hierarchical assemblies of teachers and between teachers and students. As well as developing innovative methodologies – for instance, student-led workshops and collective teaching – the strength of BP is that since 2011, they have been officially recognized by the municipality and the state. Their teachers are fully paid, and their students are fully funded. With their strong links with *piquetera* (movement of unemployed workers) and trade unions, BPs consider their work not as an alternative to the state, but working towards an emancipatory dimension of the public, which both encompasses and transcends the state realm.

After the catastrophic European referendum, in July 2019 Syriza lost power to the New Democracy Party. This halted IRI's project of developing a legal framework for the Solidarity School Network to propose to the Syriza government. The referendum saw the collapse of left-wing parties and the consolidation of right-wing forces within national governments and municipalities across Europe, most dramatically in Spain and Italy. At the time of writing, IRI's challenge is to organize a common imaginary of resistance and solidarity across its nodes at a moment of deep political and economic crisis.

In September 2019, I returned to Istanbul to meet the members of BIRARADA ('all together'), the umbrella association of all solidarity academies in Turkey. The tense atmosphere that had accompanied my previous visits had partly lifted after the candidate for the Republican Peoples Party (CHP), Ekrem Imamoglu, defeated Erdogan's candidate in a heavily charged municipal electoral rerun. I was captivated by the spirit of that meeting, which consisted of just eight women, and I. It was noted at the beginning of the meeting that men are around only when they can reap the benefit of victory, as in the Gezi Park uprising, but when the movement is dispersed and demoralized, they disappear. Then, it is up to women to fill the gap – to mend, heal and start the labour of reconstruction.

The eight academics for peace talked about their activities. The Ankara Solidarity Academy (ADA) runs courses for human rights activists, including on how to research and collect documentation on human rights violation and advocacy training; the Kocaeli Academy for Solidarity (KODA) organized a very popular summer school on authoritarianism in an island in the Aegean with forty women and their families; and the 'Academics without Campus' (*Kampüssüzler*) developed workshops and course collectives in deprived neighbourhoods across the city, with women's societies, residents' organizations and people from very different backgrounds – gardeners, domestic workers, poets, bakers and butchers – collectively developing curricula on feminism, labour history and capitalism. Most of these schools were iterant and nomadic, bringing education into the streets, reframing the right to education as right-to-the-city, and developing pedagogies that also socialized the urban space.

When I was told that all solidarity academies supported a post-disciplinary methodology, I felt sceptical, as I automatically associated the word 'post-disciplinary' with the deskilling of academics and the commodification of curricula (through their repackaging into small, light in content and digitalized courses) in higher education in UK and US academies.

From the perspective of these Turkish academics, however, the word 'post-disciplinary' made perfect sense. Their Marxist model of organic, integrated and collaborative epistemology, in which both educators and learners engage in non-professionalized and non-bureaucratic processes, was systematically negated by fragmentation and verticalization of the higher education sector in Turkey. I was told that in the previous year *Kampüssüzler* had invited a baker as mentor in the 'History of Capitalism' course, and his lectures were the most popular on the entire course.

But the term 'post-disciplinary' made also sense in a more personal way. From one day to the next, all the women at our meeting were dispossessed of their knowledge and skills and silenced by the state. But out of this personal experience of loss, they built together a common ground, a common language and a form of producing knowledge in common, with ordinary people, nonprofessionals or other people like them, who felt they had something to give and share. This is when I appreciated the great potential of constructing education as a commons, based on reciprocal exchanges between educators and learners, and rooted in the spaces and economies of the neighbourhood, unlike the equally dissatisfying models of top-down professionalized lecturing of public and civil servants, or the market delivery of just-in-time courses for students-clients.

As I was listening to their conversation, I realized that they were following a shared pattern – reinforcing each other, referring to each other, witnessing each other, but also straying a little, expanding just slightly, and challenging what was being said, and then returning to their common repertoire. That empathy, mutual respect and pragmatic creativity reminded me of Miriam Toew's extraordinary book *Women Talking*, in which eight women from a Mennonite community in Bolivia, who had been repeatedly drugged and raped in their sleep by their men, meet in a hayloft to decide what to do next. The book is about resilience in the face of trauma and about the building of a commons – a relational space of reciprocity and beauty – out of simple words and utterances exchanged in defiance of male violence, and for the purpose not only of healing and reparation but also of making the world anew. I mentioned to the group that this gathering reminded me of Toew's book. Most of them had read it and felt the same. The space that I was witnessing, and that they were making together, was a space of personal and political reconstruction – a space of commons.

Conclusion: Part II

Life is movement. Movement of the cosmos and of the earth, of the vital forces and elements in them, and of the humans who appropriate and reproduce the world around them and make up images and stories – immortal and imperishable – in their short journeys through it. To acknowledge movement means to challenge the containment, entrapment, autonomy, purity and linearity of Western capitalocentric ontologies and economies of life, and the stillness generated by the movement and continuous growth of the commodity form.

In the first part of this book, I have argued that the 'artistic mode of production' – based on the capture, commodification and the mechanical circulation of images (mental, or embodied in physical media); individualized notions of human agency and skills; externalized and simplified epistemologies of doing, giving and receiving; and ontologies of unrelatedness between humans, objects and environments – has led to the progressive entrapment of people and objects into the separate realms of art, economy and politics: 'the great capitalist transformation' described by sociologist Karl Polanyi (1944).

I have also argued that the social formations at the margins of capitalism make movement central to how they get to know, organize and imagine life, simultaneously in their epistemology, politics and aesthetics. I suggested that the space of the commons, where art, politics and epistemology come together, is not only non-anthropocentric and non-Eurocentric. It is also the horizon of communism.

Politically, the commons is the coming together of people who explicitly acknowledge movement[1] and are committed to nurture it and live in it together. Life in commons makes the Western and capitalist notion of politics – the virtuous, singular and time-specific gestures of heroic individuals – irrelevant. Instead, commoning is the ongoing listening and dwelling, the tuning in and out of the varied rhythms and spaces of the world in movement.

In terms of praxis, commoning is a form of doing from below,[2] of sharing and cooperating in situation of precariousness. It is how the poor, the working class, the disenfranchised, and those living at the margins of capitalism or in non-capitalist zones make their lives anew – all day, every day.

As ontology, the commons is a specific way of embracing, re-enacting and facilitating movement through artefacts, institutions and rituals that direct it towards the community – putting things in motions, fighting for the freedom of movement of people and objects, and breaking *man*-made enclosures. This kind of movement is not the same as the movement of the free market, which is merely fictional and, in fact, is based on private enclosures and frozen life forms enforced by capitalist states and their experts – the political leader, the lawyer, the economist, the public curator or the artist. Nor can such a movement be confined to the macropolitical movement of class struggle; it has to be a 'micropolitical insurrection' – a resurrection of the subject's vital force (Rolnik, 2017).

In making the strong case that the commons is an anti-Eurocentric and anti-capitalocentric space, I am aware of the risks of exoticization and ontological reification. My intention is to use the commons as a method of immanent critique against and beyond capitalism, a method that also acknowledges the historical specificity of the concept and ultimately aims at its dissolution, under the new condition of communist life.[3]

I have also argued in the first part of this book for the abolition of the Western notion of art: because it both partakes of and reproduces the capitalist mode of production, and because it enslaves the so-called artists who spend most of their existence dependent on dealers, curators and gallerists and make no money out of their work.

But this does not mean that I advocate for their disappearance altogether. Rather, I believe that artists have a central role in prefiguring knowledge, processes and ontologies that negate the generalized condition of enslavement associated with racial and patriarchal capitalism and bring into existence communist ways of thinking and living. But instead of calling them artists, we could call them 'storytellers', 'mediators', 'healers', 'guardians of collective knowledge', 'cosmopolitical leaders' or 'magical choreographers'.

The autoethnography in the second part of the book describes my attempts to establish the commons as aesthetics in the making of *Steel Lives*, as instituting praxis in curating the Athens Biennale and as epistemology by setting up IRI. I had not planned that each project would engage with separate realms of commoning – as aesthetics, politics and praxis – and the very fact that these separated and reified realms emerged explains why some of them – at least partially – failed.

The reader will ask: 'How do these projects relate to art at all?' Rather than calling it art, I suggest calling these experiments 'reproductive' or 'relational' or 'existential' labour: that is, actions concerned with the making and remaking of communities, the socialization of expert knowledge, and the re-enactment and valorization of the forms of the collective. In other words *Art/Commons* is a way of doing, knowing and relating to the other that sustains a non-alienated and good life. This is not the same as the 'decommodification of labour' by the historical avant-garde or by contemporary socially engaged artists or 'social work' (Jackson, 2011) – all notions that end up reproducing the capitalist mytho-logics and its rarefied realm of the uncommodifiable.

Rather, these are actions that set in motion material processes, forms of knowledge and ontologies that transcend and negate the cultural logic of capitalism, as they also concretely build alternatives to it. In other terms, art/commons is the power of art to sustain non-alienated and good forms of life.

Below, I briefly sketch how I tried to articulate art/commons in the realms of aesthetics, politics and epistemology.

Art as a living form (Steel Lives)

What is the form of militant images? What are the patterns and rhythms of the movements that reveal the living agency and animacy of humans and non-humans? With *Steel Lives* I wanted to create images that were at the same time critical and empathic and set up a sensuous threshold between the flow that erases differences and liberates people, and the frame that protects and occupies spaces and freezes their movements. I also wanted to re-create the form of Castoriadis's magma – based on forms that are also formless; closures that remain open; collectives sharing autonomy and a movement that never ceases or disperses – a form that could speak 'with' rather than 'on behalf' of a working class that had been fragmented, dispersed, relocated, exhausted and immobilized, but which, nonetheless, remained resilient, united, spatially grounded and in motion. I wanted to craft a critical space in which the hallucinatory world of capitalism appeared both real and surreal and to convey the working-class experience as both a sociological category and an existential vessel – both the funerary mask and the missing body. I wanted to capture the consciousness of labour in movement, existing both inside and outside the frame, and the form of this movement, despite capitalism.

Art as ritual gesture and fieldwork (Athens Biennale)

Directing the Athens Biennale, I veered away from the notion of the curator as activist and organizer (*à* la Nato Thompson) and followed instead the social processes of urban commoning, sharing, co-producing and co-living that were already taking place in Athens, just as which I would follow my informants during an anthropological fieldworks, treating these informal processes as rituals and performative gestures, and remoulding and recontextualizing them in the institutional format of the international art biennale. That is to say, I treated curating as anthropological fieldwork and the art system as a system of ritual gestures and performative work.

Curating as fieldwork is the irruption by foreign bodies that complicates the politics of inclusion and exclusion, of cultural appropriation and of the right to appear. It is becoming a foreigner (rather than a native) – an exilic and haunted presence which makes each social encounter unique and valuable. It is the building of social relations and spending time together, developing common vocabularies and support structures, understanding each other, mirroring, exchanging and acting in common. Curating as fieldwork is the exchange among people who are committed to being together in the long term and relationally. It is re-enactment of life's affective movements – both the coming close of empathy and the distance of alienation.

Art is the performative gesture of abstraction, cutting loose and freedom from existing social relations; the play of exploration and confusion of boundaries between self and other, work and leisure, the public and the market, movement and stillness, and entrapment and freedom. Artists as leaders and servants of their community. Artists as humans in solidarity with the non-human and the alien. Theirs is an art of movement – of sensuous connection, threading and mediation between natural, human and supernatural worlds in movement. Art as labour, reproductive yet useful, non-commodifiable yet valuable, self-directed yet collective, sustainable and antagonistic. Art as labour is the ontological stance and the everyday practice through which humanity both reproduces and transcends itself.

Art as militant research, knowledge and prefiguration (IRI)

With IRI I wanted to experiment with art as militant research – partisan, dialogical, relational, sensuous, affective, experiential and open to other perspectives and other positionalities, including the stories of its research subjects. Art as militant research is the undoing, the unmaking and the unfolding of singular issues and subjects into knots, relationships, greater configurations and cosmologies of relations. It is the praxis and the rituals that acknowledge the sacred space that both separates people and brings them together. It is agency upon the world and, at the same time, self-intervention, self-critique and self-knowing. It is embodied knowledge – sensuous, silent, implicit, colourful, transgenerational and trans-human – non-professional and yet crafted. It is dwelling, feeling, drifting and listening. Art is the epistemology of movement, which postcolonial philosophers Senghor[4] opposes to the analytical and distant intelligence of the West, which divides, distinguishes and freezes entities from life. Art is knowledge in movement: movement in-between the proximity that turns entities into relationships and the distance from which different subject positions come to articulate the point of the collective. Art is an exilic and nomadic knowledge position, always on the move – based on partial failures and momentary achievements. Art is prefiguration – practice-driven, performative and open-ended political praxis based on experimentation, ex-post conceptualization and a constant engagement on two fronts: one of struggle and critique of the hegemonic forces of capitalism; the other of epistemological and discursive construction of a new post-capitalist imaginary, including new form of dramaturgy in which art and politics inform each other. Art as non-alienated knowledge – at one and the same material, cosmological and political.

Indigenous researcher Shawn Wilson (2008) describes research as a ceremony in which the researcher sets the stage, acknowledges the sacred space, then connects all the participants and works towards eliminating such a space, thus triggering a collective self-transformation towards greater interrelatedness. For Wilson indigenous research is simultaneously a 'relational Way of Being, Way of Knowing and Way of Doing'.

The autoethnography contained in the second part of this book shows that my attempt to develop imaginaries and institutions of commoning has also been a journey of self-transformation towards greater relational involvement, a journey during which my position shifted from 'writing about the other' to 'writing with the other', and being more a witness than an author. Moreover, as for indigenous research, in which place is central, I have progressively shifted the focus of my search for the commons towards my home – the Mediterranean – an ancient space of cosmopolitan knowledge, informal trade routes, spirituality, early empires and revolutionary movements which today is again a battleground for the definition of the rights of movement of dispossessed people, illegal commodities, migrant labour and global capital. The knowledge I discuss in this book is neither mine, nor it is addressed to a specific public. It is a fragment of an old story that people have used for centuries – for recreation, survival or political warfare – a story that we are just looking after and preserving for the next generations.

EPILOGUE

Started in the Chinese town of Wuhan in December 2019, the severe acute respiratory syndrome coronavirus 2 (Covid-19) turned into a global pandemic which claimed more than 500,000 deaths worldwide at the time of writing. One thing is sure: if just briefly, the pandemic stroke at the heart of capitalism. It paralysed the economy, broke the bureaucratic machine of old and new nation states, and forced conservative governments worldwide to discuss post-capitalist policies which, only a few months earlier, were considered too radical even for the radical left: the renationalization of public utilities, the rolling out of universal basic income schemes, debt defaults and rent freezes, and heavy recapitalization of the public sector. As the top layers of the state broke down, and lost their connection with/control over civil society, from gestures of radical care, reciprocal exchange and commoning a new political economy of life emerged. The sudden de-growth, demonetization and socialization of life opened up new possibilities for relearning, regathering and redoing from below. Carbon emissions plummeted, the price of oil went below zero and the global economy contracted by 20 per cent the greatest recession since the Great Frost of 1709.

But capital's loss of control was only temporary. Only a few weeks into the crisis, capitalism mutated with the virus, taking advantage of the new forms of sociability and the new economy of circulation and movement, the uneven boundaries, borders and enclosures generated by the lockdown. Soon it became evident that the pandemic had accelerated the 'externalities' of late capitalism, as deaths and dispossession disproportionally fell upon black, women and the elderly; the necro-politics of capitalist enclosures rehearsed its new powers in nursing homes, immigration camps, prisons, factories and patriarchal households; and new technologies of immunization, isolation and extermination prefigured a biopolitical and anthropological regime shift, unimaginable and unpredictable and yet terrifying. While the rich hide in nuclear bunkers, countryside homes or gated urban mansions, nursing homes, hospitals, busses and schools turned into exterminations camps.

The pandemic accelerated the urgency of what black philosopher Christina Sharpe calls 'wake work': 'to recognize the ways that we are constituted through and by continued vulnerability to overwhelming force though not only known to ourselves and to each other by that force'[1] (Sharpe, 2016: 64). Dwelling in the wake, I witnessed the enclosures, the spectral accounting, 'the mathematics of black lives' (McKittrick, 2014), and the cold trade-offs between money and deaths, upon which patriarchal and racist capitalism is built.

I witnessed how the movement of capitalist economies relies on 'anti-value' (Harvey, 2018), that is, the extermination of those people who produce movement and allow other people to move and be alive – those people whose movement will be once again constrained, annihilated and incorporated, as spectral presences, into 'the new normal'. The statistics[2] are clear: people of colour and blue-collar workers are more than twice as likely to die of Covid-19 than the white, white-collar population. They are the nurses, the care workers, the cleaners, the taxi drivers, the bus drivers who keep goods and people in movement. They sustain and reproduce lives with their own bodies and with their own lives – I recall a passage from Joao Reis's description of urban Bahia in 1850: '[W]herever there was movement of people or goods, there were slaves sustaining that movement.'[3]

The invisible offshore economies, the abstract algorithms of global finance, and the subterranean economy and informal livelihood of the surplus population are already a thing of the past. Capitalism's spectral economy is becoming increasingly vivid, visible and realist – and magically so, in its baroque combination of movement and stillness. The journal *The Economist* coined the term '90% economy' for it. As wage work will be rendered obsolete, automated and de-functionalized in virtual factories, the new modes of dwelling and living of the surplus population will constitute the phantom limb, the missing 10 per cent of a truncated capitalism, repurposed as spectral presence or living absence of (white) skilled labour, but more importantly, as deadly labour, whose debt remains unpayable (Denise da Silva, 2020).

But as the death by asphyxiation of George Floyd, a 46-years-old black man, by the hand of white police officer Derek Chauvin in Minneapolis trigged a wave of anti-racist demonstrations across the world reminiscent of the civil right era, a new movement is breaking through the carceral institutions of capitalism. The police force of

Minneapolis has been defunded and the campaign to reform or even abolish the prison system is spreading across the United States. As of today, the enclosures of culture and art – universities and museums – remain closed to the public, to be soon repurposed as sites of long-distance learning, that is, as digital enclosures. It is clear that the abolition of all capitalist carceral institutions, including of art and culture, and their repurposing as commons, is essential to keep this movement alive.

In response to capitalism's latest mutation, IRI is currently running 'the School of Mutation', free to everyone, with open and collective curricula, and operating both transnationally and in the different nodes of the institute. Our 'School of Mutation' is a space of co-production of knowledge, an institution of commons praxis and a form of reconfiguration of our social commons in relation to the conditions of physical restriction, temporary unemployment and anxiety, both in our group and outside, generated by the global pandemic.

NOTES

Prologue

1   Nail (2019). Nail's kinaesthetic theory of images is validated by research in comparative psychology, which shows that animism and movement are hardwired in human beings, as well as being celebrated in all major non-Western ontologies.

2   Belting (2011).

3   I follow Jaeggi's notion of the non-alienated self as (1) pragmatic and 'as doing' (2) relational (3) fluid and in the making (4) both internal and external (2014: 164–5). Uruguayan political ecologist Eduardo Gudynas talks about *buen vivir* (good life).

4   Povinelli (2016).

5   For an analysis of the relationship between Kantian aesthetics and colonialism, see Loyd (2018); Moten (2018b); Scott (2004).

6   For the historical entanglement between capitalist fetishes and black fetishes, see Matory (2018).

7   According to Goodhart (2016) in post-Brexit UK the new political fault line is between the affluent, cosmopolitan, pro-globalization, progressive and *mobile* elite (the 'anywheres') and the conservative, nationalist, impoverished, nativist and *immobile* working class (the 'somewheres').

8   Meillassoux (1972) argues that in domestic communities there is a congruence between the productive cycle and the reproductive cycle.

9   In mercantilist Europe in the thirteenth century, capital was seen as money and as storable valuable objects – or wealth. In classical political economy, capital was considered physical and productive, embodied in human labour. Marx shows instead that capital is a relationships between people and things.

10   I refer to Mauss's distinction between 'individual' and 'person' (1935).

11   De Angelis (2007).

12   Chari (2015: 114).

13   Martin describes Adorno's view that art is a threshold space between the absolute artwork and the absolute commodity (2007).

14   Gell (1998).

15   On the relationship between Elizabethan theatre and capitalism, see Agnew (1986).

16   Diderot ([1883] 2010: 100) in Jackson (2012).

17   See also Beller (2006).

18   See also Kunst (2015) and Jackson (2012).

19   Is the ceremonial exchange conducted in the Milne Bay province of Papua New Guinea famously discussed by anthropologist Bronislaw Malinowski (1922).

20 Art historian Carl Einstein discusses how European avant-gardes used the multi-perspectivist aesthetics of African art.
21 See Alberro (2017).
22 Tuzin (2006).
23 See Souleymane (2012).
24 For the relationships between bodies, movement and black radical art, see Jafa and Campt (2017) and Campt (2019).
25 Bennett (1995).
26 See also Graeber (2002). Lambek (2013) also distinguishes between these two orders of actions. But Lambek distinguishes between actions (with ethical value) and labour, whereas I consider all actions as imbued with both ethical and material values.
27 For instance, animal traps among the Fang people of West Africa enchant because they connect the physical and the mental universe of the hunter and of the victim, the prey animal, and 'embody a scenario which is the dramatic nexus that binds these two protagonists together and which aligns them in time and space' (Gell 1998: 27). In other words, traps embody a fantastical world where animal and humans are entangled, and yet they remain unequal.
28 Parry and Bloch (1989).
29 Carsten (1989).
30 Parry (1989).
31 Mollona (2020).
32 Veblen (1899).
33 For the anthropological discussion about the unconscious and capitalism, see Graeber (2007) and Kapferer (2005).
34 Bateson (1958).
35 Men are artists – woodcarvers and makers of homes and canoes – and theatrical performers. Women are the main producers – they produce 80 per cent of subsistence fish and nets, basket and cooking.
36 The case is extensively described in Morphy (1992).
37 I am referring to Reddy (1987).
38 On art and slavery, see Loyd (2018).
39 It was the art historian Carl Einstein (1915) who argued that the fluidity of forms of futurist and cubist paintings reflected the ontology of movement of African art.
40 See Lenin's discussion on imperialism and finance (1916) and Lazzarato's (2014) reading of it.
41 Performances artists Andrea Fraser, Carolee Schneemann and Marina Abramovich explore the commodification of bodies from a feminist perspective.
42 For a critical reflection of the relationship between slavery and capitalism, see Graeber (2006), Matory (2018) and Robinson (2001).
43 See Federici (1998).

44 See Buck-Morss (2000). Besides, Matory (2018) argues that Marx and Freud disguised the experience of slavery under capitalism through the theories of respectively, class consciousness and the unconscious.

45 Here I refer to Flusser's (1999) notion of gesture as a form of symbolical and performative externalization of affective impulses.

46 Buck-Morss (1992).

47 In Moten (2008a).

48 The title was inspired by Alexander Solzhenitsyn's famous quote: 'Once you have taken everything away from a man, he is no longer in your power. He is free.'

49 Varnedoe (2006).

50 Mies and Bennholdt-Thomsen (1999).

51 His real name is Peter Lamborn Wilson.

52 Fraser (2005: 280).

53 This narrative underpins much of Hito Steyerl's latest work (2017). See also Nick Dyer-Whiteford (2015).

54 I am referring to the genre of 'art of work' analysed extensively by Julia Bryan-Wilson (2009). See also Danielle Child (2019).

55 Raunig (2007) and MIL Collective (2018).

56 https://www.arte-util.org/about/activities/, accessed 1 October 2020.

57 See Ross (2015) and MIL Collective (2018).

58 For MACBA, see Expósito (2016).

59 MIL Collective (2018).

60 For the targeting of women in Bolivia, see Maria Galindo (2011).

61 De Oliveira (2005).

62 For such romanticization of the slums see Gaitán (2013).

63 See Kortun (2017).

64 Regarding the reappropriation of 'abstractionism' by the black tradition, see Harper (2015).

65 Gell (1992).

Chapter 1

1 I discuss this research in my monograph (Mollona, 2020).

2 For a detailed analysis of working-class cinema in the UK, see Mollona (2020).

3 On the dangers of labour representations, see art theorist and philosopher John Roberts (2012).

4 As per German filmmaker Harun Farocki (2002).

5 Lange (1974).

6 Roberts call this 'dialectical realism' (1998) and 'alter-realism' (2015).

7 On these different views of left-wing melancholia, see Traverso (2016) and Brown (1999).

Chapter 2

1 Aberro (2017).
2 McKee (2016).
3 See Expósito (2016).
4 For the notion of *commonfare*, see Fumagalli et al. (2019).
5 This is the term used especially in the media to refer to the decision group formed by the European Commission (EC), the European Central Bank (ECB) and the International Monetary Fund (IMF).
6 Maurizio Atzeni, Dario Azzellini, Sharyn Kasmir, Andrea Fumagalli, Tiziana Terranova, Maria Hlavajova, Emily Petlick, Adam Szymczyk, Leo Panitch, Hilary Wainwright, Athena Athanasiou, Angela Dimitrakaki, Costas Douzinas, Oliver Ressler, Kostis Stafylakis, Margarita Tsomou, Angela Melitopoulos, Emanuele Braga from Macao (Milan, Italy), Federica Giardini, the workers-run company Fralib (Marseilles, France); Teatro Valle (Rome); Comunita' dei Frutti minori (Castiglione, Italy).
7 See the reviews of OMONIA by Tarasoff (2015) and Drake (2015).
8 The term coined by artist Tania Brugueira indicates socially engaged artists.
9 I am referring to Mouffe's (2013) notion of agonism as pluralistic and democratic space.
10 See Braga and Fumagalli (2015).
11 Szreder (2014).
12 Subsequently the documenta 14 board accused him of financial misconduct.
13 For an insider's criticism of the operations of documenta 14 in Athens, see Fokianaki (2017).
14 For detailed discussion of the project, see Rikou and Yalouri (2018).
15 *South as a State of Mind* was the title of a magazine founded by Marina Fokidis in Athens in 2012, which in 2015 temporarily became documenta 14 journal, publishing four special issues edited by Quinn Latimer and Adam Szymczyk.
16 Foster (1995).
17 For Brugueira 'Useful Art' has the following characteristics: (1) propose new uses for art within society, (2) use artistic thinking to challenge the field within which it operates, (3) respond to current urgencies, (4) operate on a 1:1 scale, (5) replace authors with initiators and spectators with users, (6) have practical, beneficial outcomes for its users, (7) pursue sustainability, and (8) re-establish aesthetics as a system of transformation. https://www.arte-util.org/about/colophon/
18 The Decolonize This Place (DTP) Collective (2018).
19 The system workers to so-called sponsorship by their employer, meaning they cannot move jobs or leave the country without the employer's approval.

20   The acknowledgement of the sacred space of relationality in which
     humans are entangled is central to indigenous ontologies and
     epistemology. Wilson,
21   https://instituteofradicalimagination.org/?s=of , accessed 1 October 2020.
22   De Angelis (2007: 232).
23   Cinema Palazzo e Teatro Valle in Rome; Teatro Garibaldi and L'Assemblea
     Montevergini in Palermo; Teatro Rossi Aperto in Pisa; Sale Docks
     in Venezia; La Cavallerizza Imperiale in Tourin, the Teatro Pinelli in
     Messina.
24   Details of the process can be found on Asilo's website. http://www.
     exasilofilangieri.it
25   Micciarelli (2018).
26   Micciarelli (2018: 58). Riccio (2017a and b).
27   On the problems of horizontalism, see Mark Fisher (2013).
28   In November 2019, the major of Madrid Manuela Cardena, from the
     Podemos Party, ordered the eviction of La Ingobernable, which took place
     at 3 a.m., with a coordinated action involving around 130 policemen.
29   Mouffe (2013).
30   See Fraser, N. Bhattacharya, T. and C. Arruzza (2018).
31   In 2017 there were around 500 of such academics.

Conclusion

1   Zibechi describes the contemporary popular social movements operating
    bottom-up 'societies in movement' (2010: 11); see also Stavrides (2016: 95).
2   On the emancipatory power of doing, see Holloway (2016: 245–50).
3   I thank Max Haiven for pointing this out to me.
4   Senghor (1956: 211–12).

Epilogue

1   Sharpe (2016: 64).
2   ONS. Office for National Statistics, 'Coronavirus and the Latest Indicators
    for the UK Economy and Society', 21 May 2020.
3   Reis (1993: 30).

BIBLIOGRAPHY

Adorno, T. (1970) *Aesthetic Theory*, Bloomsbury, London.

Agnew, J. C. (1986) *Worlds Apart. The Market and the Theatre in Anglo-American Thought, 1550–1750*, Oxford University Press, Oxford.

Alberro, A. (2017) *Abstraction in Reverse. The Reconfigured Spectator in Mid-Twentieth-Century Latin American Art*, Chicago University Press, Chicago.

Alexievich, S. (2016) *Second-Hand Time*, Fitzcarraldo, London.

Arendt, A. (1958) *The Human Condition*, University of Chicago Press, Chicago.

Bateson, G. (1958) *Naven. A Survey of the Problems Suggested by a Composite Picture of the Culture of a New Guinea Tribe Drawn from Three Points of View*, Stanford University Press, Stanford.

Bateson, G. and M. Mead (1942) *Balinese Character: A Photographic Analysis*, Special Publications of the New York Academy of Science, Wilbur Valentine, New York.

Beech, D. (2019) *Art and Post-capitalism: Aesthetics, Labour, Automation and Value Production*, Pluto Press, London.

Beller, J. (2006) *The Cinematic Mode of Production. Attention Economy and the Society of the Spectacle*, University Press of New England, Hanover and London.

Belting, H. (2011) *An Anthropology of Images: Pictures, Medium, Bodies*, Princeton University Press, Princeton.

Bennett, T. (1995) *The Birth of the Museum. History, Theory, Politics*, Routledge, London and New York.

Bergson, H. (1911) *Laughter, an Essay on the Meaning of the Comic*, Macmillan, London.

Bishop, C. (2013) *Radical Museology, or, What's Contemporary in Museums of Contemporary Art?* Cornerhouse, Manchester.

Bishop, C. (2019) Rise to the Occasion, *Artforum*, May, Vol 57(9), pp: 198–204.

Boltanski, L. and Chiapello (2007) *The New Spirit of Capitalism*, Verso, London.

Bookchin, M. (2005) *The Ecology of Freedom. The Emergence and Dissolution of Anarchy*, AK Press, Oakland.

Bourriaud, N. (1998) *Relational Aesthetics*, Les Presses Du Reel, Paris.

Braga, E. and A. Fumagalli (eds.) (2015) *La Moneta del Comune. La sfida dell'istituzione finanziaria del comune*, Derive e Approdi, Milano.

Brown, W. (1999) Resisting Left Melancholy, *Boundary*, Vol 26(3), pp: 19–27.

Brugueira, T. (2019) Notes on Political Timing Specificity, *Artforum*, May, Vol 57(9), p: 205.

Brugueira, T. Asociación Arte Útil (AAU). https://www.arte-util.org/about/activities/, accessed 27 January 2020.

Bryan-Wilson, J. (2009) *Art Workers: Radical Practice in The Vietnam War Era*, University of California Press, Berkeley.

Bryan-Wilson, J. (2012) Occupational Realism, *TDR. The Drama Review*, Vol 56(4), pp: 32–48.

Buck-Morss, S. (1992) Aesthetics and Anaesthetics: Walter Benjamin's Artwork Essay Reconsidered, *October*, Vol 62, Autumn, pp: 3–41.

Buck-Morss, S. (2000) Hegel in Haiti, *Critical Inquiry*, Vol 6(4), pp: 821–65.

Bürger, P. (1974) *Theory of the Avant-Garde*, University of Minnesota Press, Minneapolis and London.

Campt, T. (2019) Black Visuality and the Practice of Refusal, *Women& Performance: A Journal of Feminist Theory*, Vol 29(1), pp: 79–87.

Carrier, J. (1992) Emerging Alienation in Production: A Maussian History, *Journal of Royal Anthropological Institute*, Vol 27(3), pp: 539–58.

Carsten, J. (1989) Cooking Money: Gender and the Symbolic Transformation of Means of Exchange in a Malay Fishing Community, *Money and the Morality of Exchange*, Parry and Bloch (eds.), Cambridge University Press, Cambridge, pp: 117–41.

Castoriadis, C. (1994) The Logic of Magmas and the Question of Autonomy, *Philosophy and Social Criticism*, Vol 20(1–2), pp: 123–54.

Chari, A. (2015) *A Political Economy of the Sense. Neoliberalism, Reification, Critique*, Columbia University Press, New York.

Child, D. (2019) *Working Aesthetics. Labour, Art and Capitalism*, Bloomsbury, London.

Clastres, P. (1974) *Society against the State: Essays in Political Anthropology*, Zone Books. MIT Press, Cambridge, MA.

Clifford, J. (1981) On Ethnographic Surrealism, *Comparative Studies in Society and History*, Vol 23(4), pp: 539–64.

Collective, M. T. L. (2018) From Institutional Critique to Institutional Liberation? A Decolonial Perspective on the Crises of Contemporary Art, *October*, Vol 65, pp: 192–227.

De Angelis, M. (2007) *The Beginning of History. Value Struggles and Global Capital*, Pluto Press, London.

De Angelis, M. (2017) *Omnia Sunt Communia. On the Commons and the Transformation to Postcapitalism*, Zed, London.

De Landa, M. (2002) *Intensive Science and Virtual Philosophy*, Bloomsbury, London.

De Oliveira, F. (2005) *Crítica à razão dualista/O ornitorrinco*, Boitempo, São Paulo.

Diderot. (1883) [2010] *The Paradox of Acting*, Kessinger Publishing, New York.

Didi-Huberman, D. (2018) *The Eye of History: When Images Take Position*, MIT Press, Cambridge, MA.

Dockx, N. and P. Gielen (eds.) (2018) *Commonism. A New Aesthetics*, Antennae Arts, Ghent.

Drake, C. (2015) 5th Athens Biennale, *Frieze*, 27 November.

Einstein, C. (1915) *Negerplastik*, Leipzig, Germany.

Errejón, I. and C. Mouffe (2016) *Podemos: In the Name of the People*, Lawrence and Wishart Ltd, London.

Expósito, M. (2016) *Conversación con Manuel Borja-Villel*, Turpial, Madrid.

Fanon, F. (1952) *Black Skin, White Masks*, Grove Press, New York.

Farocki, H. (2002) Workers Leaving the Factory, *Senses of Cinema*, Vol 21. http://sensesofcinema.com/2002/harun-farocki/farocki_workers/, accessed 25 June 2020.

Federici, S. (1998) *The Caliban and the Witch: Women, The Body and Primitive Accumulation*, Autonomedia, New York.

Federici, S. (2012) *Revolution at Point Zero: Housework, Reproduction, and Feminist Struggle*, Autonomedia, New York.

Federici, S. (2018) *Re-enchanting the World: Feminism and the Politics of the Commons*, Autonomediam, New York.

Ferreira da Silva, D. (2020) *Unpayable Debt*, MIT Press, Cambridge, MA.

Fisher, M. (2013) Indirect Action. Some Misgivings about Horizontalism, *Institutional Attitudes. Instituting Art in a Flat World*, Gielen, P. (ed.), Valiz, Amsterdam, pp: 104–14.

Flusser, V. (1999) *Gestures*, University of Minnesota Press, Minneapolis.

Fokianaki, I. (2017) Documenting Dcuemnta14 Athens, *Metropolis M*. https://www.metropolism.com/en/opinion/31387_documenting_documenta_14_athens

Foster, A. (1995) The Artist as Ethnographer? *The Traffic in Culture. Refiguring Art and Anthropology*, Marcus, G. and F. Myers (eds.), University of California Press, Berkeley, LA and London, pp: 302–9.

Fraser, A. (2005) From the Critique of Institution to an Institution of Critique, *Artforum*, Vol 44(1), pp: 278–88.

Fraser, N. (1995) From Redistribution to Recognition? Dilemmas of Justice in a Post-Socialist Age, *New Left Review*, 212 July/August, pp: 68–93.

Fraser, N., T. Bhattacharya and C. Arruzza (2018) Notes for a Feminist Manifesto, *New Left Review*, 114 (November/December), pp: 113–34.

Fumagalli, A., A. Giuliani, S. Lucarelli and C. Vercellone (2019) *Cognitive Capital, Welfare and Labour. The Commonfare Hypothesis*, Routledge, Oxford.

Gago, V. (2017) *Neoliberalism from Below: Popular Pragmatics and Baroque Economies*, Duke University Press, London and Durham.

Gaitán, J. (2013) *Self-Organized*, ed. Ault, J. and M. Borgen, Open Editions, London.

Galindo, M. (2011) La Pobreza, un gran Negocio, *Mujer Publica* n. 7 (December), pp: 111–12.

Gell, A. (1992) The Technology of Enchantment and the Enchantment of Technology, *Anthropology, Art and Aesthetics*, Coote, J. and A. Shelton (eds.), Clarendon Press, Oxford, pp: 40–63.

Gell, A. (1996) Vogel's Net. Traps as Artworks and Artworks as Traps, *Journal of Material Culture*, Vol 1, pp: 15–38.

Gell, A. (1998) *Art and Agency. An Anthropological Theory*, Oxford University Press, Oxford.

Gillick, L. (2011) Abstract, *Microhistorias e Macromundos, Vol 3 – Abstract Possible*. Lind, M. (ed.), Instituto Nacional de Bellas Artes Y Literatura, Mexico City, pp: 157–67.

Gombrich, E. H. (1960) [2002] *Art and Illusion. A Study in the Psychology of Pictorial Representation*, Princeton University Press, Princeton and Oxford.

Goodhart, D. (2016) *The Road to Somewhere: The Populist Revolt and the Future of Politics*, Hurst & Co. Publisher, London.

Gorz, A. (1985) *Path to Paradise: On the Liberation from Work*, Pluto Press, London.

Graeber, D. (2002) *Towards and Anthropological Theory of Value. The False Coin of Our Own Dreams*, Palgrave, New York.

Graeber, D. (2004) *Fragments of an Anarchist Anthropology*, Prickly Paradigm Press, Chicago.

Graeber, D. (2006) Turning Modes of Production Inside Out. Or Why Capitalism Is a Transformation of Slavery, *Critique of Anthropology*, Vol 26(1), pp: 61–85.

Graeber, D. (2007) *Possibilities. Essays on Hierarchies, Rebellion and Desire*, AK Press, Oakland.

Grincheva, N. (2019) *Global Trends in Museum Diplomacy*, Routledge, London and New York.

Groys, B. (2016) *In the Flow*, Verso, London.

Groys, B. (2017) Towards a New Universalism, *e-flux#* 86.

Haiven, M. (2018) *Art after Money, Money after Art*, Pluto Press, London.

Hantelmann, D. (2019) *The Shed. What Is the New Ritual Space for the 21st Century?* https://theshed.org/program/series/2-a-prelude-to-the-shed/new-ritual-space-21st-century

Harper, P. B. (2015) *Abstractionist Aesthetics. Artistic Form and Social Critique in African American Culture*, New York University, New York.

Hartman, S. (1997) *Scenes of Subjection: Terror, Slavery and Self-making in Nineteen-century America*, Oxford University Press, Oxford.

Harvey, D. (2012) *Rebel Cities: From the Right to the City to the Urban Revolution*, Verso, London.

Harvey, D. (2018) *Marx. Capital and the Madness of Economic Reason*, Profile Books, London.

Holloway, J. (2016) *In, Against and Beyond Capitalism: The San Francisco Lectures*, PM Press, Los Angeles, CA.

Jackson, S. (2011) *Social Works: Performing Art, Supporting Public*, Routledge, London.

Jackson, S. (2012) Just-in-Time. Performance and the Aesthetics of Precarity, *TDR: The Drama Review*, Vol 56(4), pp: 10–31.

Jaeggi, R. (2014) *Alienation*, Columbia University Press, New York.

Jafa, A. and T. Campt (2017) Love Is the Message. The Plan Is Death, *e-flux.* #81.

Kapferer, B. (2005) *Sorcery and the Beautiful: A Discourse on the Aesthetic of Ritual. Aesthetics in Performance: Formations of Symbolic Construction and Experience*, Hobart, A. and B. Kapferer (eds.), Berghahn Books, New York, pp: 129–60.

Kapferer, B. (2013) Montage and Time: Deleuze, Cinema and a Buddhist Sorcery Rite, *Transcultural Montage*, Suhr, C. and R. Willerslev (eds.), Berghahn Book, Oxford, pp: 20–39.

Kortun, V. (2017) In Turkish the Word 'Public' Doesn't Exist, Warsza, J. (ed.) *I Can't Work Like This. A Reader on Recent Boycotts in Contemporary Art*, Sternberg Press, Salzburg, pp: 133–9.

Kunst, B. (2015) *Artists at Work. Proximity of Art and Capitalism*, Zero Books, London.

La Berge, L. C. (2019) *Wages against Artwork. Decommodified Labor and the Claims of Socially Engaged Art*, Duke University Press, London and Durham.

Lambek, M. (2013) The Value of (Performative) Acts, *HAU: Journal of Ethnographic Theory*, Vol 3(2), pp: 141–60.

Lamborn Wilson, P. (1992) *Immediatism*, Libertarian Book Club, New York.

Lazzarato, M. (2014) *Marcel Duchamp and the Refusal of Work*, trans. Jordan, J., CA: Semiotext (e), Los Angeles.

Lenin, V. (1916) [2010] *Imperialism: The Highest Stage of Capitalism*, Penguin, London.

Loyd, D. (2018) *Under Representation. The Racial Regime of Aesthetics*, Fordham University Press, New York.

Lukács, G. (1930) [1983] *Essays on Realism*, ed. and trans. Livingstone, R., MIT Press, Cambridge, MA.

Lukács, G. (1968) *History and Class Consciousness*, trans. Livingstone, R., Merlin Press, London.

Martin, S. (2007) The Absolute Artwork Meets the Absolute Commodity, *Radical Philosophy*, Vol 146 (November–December), pp: 15–25.

Marx, K. (1976) *The Capital Vol.1. The Process of Production of Capital*, Penguin, London.

Matory, J. L. (2018) *The Fetish Revisited. Marx, Freud and the Gods Black People Make*, Duke University Press, Durham and London.

Mauss, M. (1935) [1973] Techniques of the Body, *Economy and Society*, Vol 2, pp: 1–88.

Mauss, M. (1950) [2002] *The Gift: The Form and Reason for Exchange in Archaic Societies*, Routledge, London.

McKee, Y. (2016) *Strike Art. Contemporary Art and the Post-Occupy Condition*, Verso, London.

McKittrick, K. (2014) Mathematics Black Lives, *The Black Scholar*, Vol 44(2), pp: 16–28.

Meillassoux, C. (1964) *Anthropologie economique des gouro de Coite D' Ivoire*, Mouton, Paris.

Meillassoux, C. (1972) From Reproduction to Production, *Economy and Society*, Vol 1(1), pp: 93–105.

Meillassoux, C. (1981) *Maidens, Meal and Money: Capitalism and the Domestic Community*, Cambridge University Press, Cambridge.

Meillassoux, C. (1986) *Anthropologie de 'esclavage: Le ventre de fer et d'argent*, Presses Universitaires de France, Paris.

Micciarelli, G. (2018) La Rifondazione degli ex luoghi: pratica politica e diritto nell'autogoverno dei beni comuni, *I Beni Comuni. L'inaspettata Rinascita degli Usi Collettivi*, Rodotà, S., G. Preterossi and N. Capone (eds.), La Scuola di Pitagora, Napoli, pp: 103–13.

Mies, M. and V. Bennholdt-Thomsen (1999) *The Subsistence Perspective. Beyond the Globalized Economy*, Zed, London.

Mies, M. and V. Shiva (2014) *Ecofemminism. (Critique. Influence. Change)*, Zed, London.

Mollona, M. (2009) *Made in Sheffield: An Ethnography of Industrial Work and Politics*, Berghahn Books, New York and Oxford.

Mollona, M. (2020) *Brazilian Steeltown. Machines, Land, Money and Commoning in the Making of the Working Class*, Berghahn Books, New York and Oxford.

Mollona, M. (2020) Working-class Cinema in the Age of Digital Capitalism. *Beyond Digital Capitalism: New Ways of Living*. Leo Panitch and Greg Albo (eds.), Merlin Press, London, pp: 153–74.

Morphy, H. (1992) From Dull to Brilliant. The Aesthetics of Spiritual Power among the Yolngu, *Anthropology, Art and Aesthetics*, Coote, J. and A. Shelton (eds.), Clarendon Press, Oxford, pp: 181–208.

Morton, T. (2017) *Humankind. Solidarity with Non-Human People*, Verso, London.

Moten, F. (2008) The Case of Blackness, *Criticism*, Wayne State University Press, Detroit (2): 177–218.

Moten, F. (2018a) *The Universal Machine*, Duke University Press, London and Durham.

Moten, F. (2018b) *Stolen Lives*, Duke University Press, London and Durham.

Mouffe, C. (2013) *Agonistics. Thinking the World Politically*, Verso, London.

Mulvey, L. (2005) *Death 24X A Second: Stillness and the Moving Image*, Reaktion Books, London.

Munn, N. (1973) *Walbiri Iconography. Graphic Representation and Cultural Symbolism in a Central Australian Society*, University of Chicago Press, Chicago.

Myers, F. (1991) *Pintupi Country, Pintupi Place. Sentiment, Place and Politics among Western Desert Aborigines*, University of California Press, Berkeley.

Neil, T. (2010) *Theory of the Image*, Oxford University Press, Oxford.

Nick Dyer-Whiteford, N. (2015) *Cyber-Proletariat: Global Labour in the Digital Vortex*, Plutom, London.

O'Hanlon, M. (1992) Unstable Images and Second Skins: Artefacts, Exegesis and Assessment in the New Guinea Highlands, *Man*, Vol 27(3), pp: 587–608.

Overing, K. J. (1975) *The Piaroa: A People of the Orinoco Basin – A Study in Kinship and Marriage*, Clarendon Press, Oxford.

Overing, K. J. (1989) The Aesthetics of Production: The Sense of Community among the Cubeo and Piaroa, *Dialectical Anthropology*, Vol 14, pp: 159–75.

Parry, J. (1989) On the Moral Perils of Exchange, *Money and the Morality of Exchange*, Parry, J. and M. Bloch (eds.), Cambridge University Press, Cambridge, pp: 64–93.

Parry, J. and M. Bloch (eds.) (1989) *Money and the Morality of Exchange*, Cambridge University Press, Cambridge.

Pendelton, A. (2017) *Black Dada Reader*, Koenig Books, New York.

Piper, A. (1987) Flying, *Adrian Piper: Reflection 1967–1987*, Curated by Farver, J., Alternative Museum, New York, p: 20.

Polanyi, K. (1944) *The Great Transformation. The Political and Economic Origins of Our Time*, Beacon Press, Boston, MA.

Povinelli, E. (2016) *Geontologies. A Requiem to Neoliberalism*, Duke University Press, London and Durham.

Raunig, G. (2007) *Art and Revolution: Transversal Activism in the Long Twentieth Century*, Semiotext(e), Los Angeles.

Reddy, W. (1987) *Money and Liberty in Europe. A Critique of Historical Understanding*, Cambridge University Press, Cambridge.

Reis, J. (1993) *A Greve Negra de 1857 na Bahia*, Revista USP, Sao Paulo.

Riccio, G. (2017a) Il Corpo e la Scena. Territori dell'Esperienza Estetico-Conoscitiva Nella Pratica Artistica della Danza. Kaiak, *A Philosophical Journey*, Vol 4, pp: 1–3.

Riccio, G. (2017b) La Pratica dell'uso civico come scelta etica ed estetica e political per il sensibile commune. *I Beni Comuni e l'imaspettata riscoperta degli usi collettivi*, Rodotà, S. (ed.), La Scuola di Pitagora Editrice, Napoli, pp: 129–36.

Rikou, E. and E. Yalouri (2018) Documenta 14 learning from Athens. The response of the 'learning from documenta' research project. FIELD. Issue 11. http://field-journal.com/issue-11/documenta-14-learning-from-athens-the-response-of-the-learning-from-documenta-research-project

Roberts, J. (1998) *The Art of Interruption. Realism, Photography and the Everyday*, Manchester University Press, Manchester.

Roberts, J. (2007) *The Intangibility of Forms: Skill and Deskilling in Art after the Readymade*, Verso, London.

Roberts, J. (2012) The Missing Factory, *Mute*. https://www.metamute.org/editorial/articles/missing-factory/, accessed 25 June 2020.

Roberts, J. (2015a) Aporetischer Realismus: Der Realismus als philosophisches Problem und kritischer Horizont der Kunst. *Lettre International*, Vol 109, pp: 86–91.

Roberts, J. (2015b) *Revolutionary Time and the Avant-Garde*, Verso, London.

Robinson, C. (2001) *An Anthropology of Marxism*, Pluto Press, London.

Rogoff, I. (2016) Starting in the Middle. NGOs and Cultural Institutions, *Public Servants Art and the Crisis of the Common Good*, Burtin, J., S. Jackson and D. Willsdon (eds.), MIT Press, Cambridge, MA, pp: 10–24.

Rolnik, S. (2006) The Geopolitics of Pimping, *Transversal Texts*. https://transversal.at/pdf/journal-text/466/, accessed 1 February 2020.

Rolnik, S. (2017) The Spheres of Insurrection: Suggestions for Combating the Pimping of Life, *e-flux*. # 86.

Rosler, M. (2012) The Artistic Mode of Revolution. From Gentrification to Occupation, *e-flux*. #33.

Ross, A. (2015) *The Gulf: High Culture/Hard Labor*, OR Books, New York and London.

Sahlins, M. (1972) *Stone Age Economics*, Routledge, New York.

Sassen, S. (2014) *Expulsions: Brutality and Complexity in the Global Economy*, Harvard University Press, Cambridge, MA.

Schumacher, E. (1975) *Small Is Beautiful. A Study of Economics as If People Mattered*, Penguin, London.

Scott, D. (2004) *Conscripts of Modernity. The Tragedy of Colonial Enlightenment*, Duke University Press, Durham and London.

Senghor, L. (1956) *L'Esthetique négro-africaine*, Gallimard, Paris.

Sharpe, C. (2016) *In the Wake. On Blackness and Being*, Duke University Press, Durham and London.

Sholette, G. (2010) *Dark Matter*, Pluto Press, London.

Simmel, G. (1918) [2010] *The View of Life: Four Metaphysical Essays with Journal Aphorisms*, trans. Andrews, J. A. Y. and D. N. Levine, Chicago University Press, Chicago.

Small, I. (2009) Morphology in the Studio: Helio Oiticica at the Museu Nacional, *Getty Research Journal*, Vol 1, pp: 110.

Solanas, F and O. Getino (1997) Towards a Third Cinema: Notes and Experiences for the Development of a Cinema of Liberation in the Third World, *New Latin American Cinema: Volume One: Theory, Practices, and Transcontinental Practices*, Martin Michael (ed.), Wayne State University Press, Detroit, pp: 33–58.

Souleymane, D. (2012) *African Art as Philosophy. Senghor, Bergson and the Idea of Negritude*, Seagull Books, Chicago.

Srnicek, N. (2016) *Platform Capitalism*, Polity Press, London.

Standing, G. (2014) *The Precariat: The New Dangerous Class*, Bloomsbury, London.

Stavrides, S. (2016) *Common Space. The City as Commons*, Zed, London.

Steyerl, H. (2009) Is a Museum a Factory? *e-flux*. # 07.

Steyerl, H. (2013) Freedom from Everything. Freelancers and Mercenaries, *e-flux*. # 41.

Steyerl, H. (2017) *Duty Free Art*, Verso, London.

Szreder, H., M. Kozlowski and J. Sowa (2014) *The Art Factory. The Division of Labour and Distribution of Capitals in the Polish field of Visual Art*, The Free/Slow University of Warsaw, Warsaw.

Tarasoff, S. (2015) An Artless Biennale. *Flash Art*, Vol 305, pp: 10–15.

Tible, J. (2018) *Marx Selvagem*, Autonomia Literária, Sao Paulo.

Traverso, E. (2016) *Left Wing Melancholia. Marxism, History and Memory*, Columbia University Press, New York.

Tuzin, D. (2006) Art, Ritual and the Crafting of Illusion, *The Asia Pacific Journal of Anthropology*, Vol 3, pp: 1–23.

Ure, A. (1829) *A New System of Geology*, Longman Press, London.

Ure, A. (1835) *The Philosophy of Manufactures. Or an Exposition of the Scientific, Moral and Commercial Economy of the Factory System*, Charles Knight, London.

Varnedoe, K. (2006) *Pictures of Nothing: Abstract Art since Pollock*, Princeton University Press, Princeton.

Veblen, T. (1899) [1994] *The Theory of the Leisure Class: An Economic Study of Institutions*, Macmillan, New York.

Vettese, T. (2018) To Freeze the Thames, *New Left Review*, pp: 63–86.

Vilensky, D. (2007) *Newspaper of the Platform 'Chto Delat?'* n. 23 pp: 10–25.

Vishmidt, M. (2018) *Speculation as a Mode of Production: Forms of Art Subjectivity in art and Capital*, Brill, Leiden.

Viveiros de Castro, E. (1982) *From the Enemy's Point of View*, The University of Chicago Press, Chicago.

Viveiros de Castro, E. (2009) *Cannibal Metaphysics*, University of Minnesota Press, Minneapolis.

Weeks, C. (2011) *The Problem with Work. Feminism, Marxism, Anti-Work Politics and Postwork Imaginaries*, Verso, London.

Wilson, S. (2008) *Research Is Ceremony: Indigenous Research Methods*, Fernwood publishing, Black Point, NS Canada.

Wood, C. (2018) *Performance in Contemporary Art*, Tate, Publishing, London.

Worringer, W. (1908) [1997] *Abstraction and Empathy. A Contribution to the Psychology of Style*, Elephant Paperbacks, Chicago.

Worth, S. and J. Adair (1969) Navajo Filmmakers, *American Anthropologist*, Vol 9, pp: 34.

Wynter, S. and K. McKittrick (2015) Unparalleled Catastrophe for Our Species? Or, to Give Humanness a Different Future: Conversations, *Sylvia Wynter: On Being Human as Praxis*, McKittrick, K. (ed.), Duke University Press, Durham, pp: 9–89.

Xavier, I. (1993) *Allegories of Underdevelopment. Aesthetics and Politics in Modern Brazilian Cinema*, University of Minnesota Press, Minneapolis.

Zibechi, R. (2010) *Dispersing Power: Social Movements as Anti-State Forces*, AK Press, Oakland.

FILMOGRAPHY

Berwick Street Collective. (1975) *The Nightcleaners*. (1h 30'). UK.

Cavadini, A. and C. Strachan. (1982) *Two Laws: A Film in Four Parts*. (2h 10'). UK.

Chto Delat. (2017) *Summer School of Orientation in Zapatism.*

Farocki, H. (1995) *Workers Leaving the Factory.* (Arbeiter verlassen die Fabrik).

(36′) Germany.

Lange, D. (1974) *A Documentation of Bradford Working Life.* (2h 25′). UK.

Loach. K. (1969) *Kes.* (1h 52′). UK.

Loach, K. (2001) *The Navigators.* (1h 36′). UK.

Lumiere L. (1895) *Workers Leaving the Lumière Factory in Lyon* (La Sortie des Usines Lumière à Lyon).

Mollona, M. (1999) *Steel Lives.* (50′). UK.

APPENDIX 1

Chaired by Sharyn Kasmir, the *Cooperative* group made the following proposals for the biennale: (1) to be a translator between international cooperatives both in terms of language and in terms of personal experience also in regard to artists' initiatives; (2) to be a facilitator of different solidarity economy experiences, for instance, the creation of database of products, the financialization or re-investments of coops; or the creation of distributive or solidarity capital; (3) to map value chains and green connections; (4) to organize a Workers Film festival; (5) to turn the Bageion into a space for hosting refugee after the end of OMONIA.

Chaired by Margerita Tsomou, the *Solidarity Network* group made the following proposal for the biennale: (1) to be a space for mutual care and face-to-face communication, a transnational space and an open public space; (2) to map the solidarity initiatives in Athens; the empty building and alternatives to Airbnb which is destroying the economy of Athens; (3) to function as a laboratory/research centre opened to the city and working through open calls to scholars and the public and workshop series.

Chaired by Sylvia de Fanti, the *Commons* group proposed: (1) to develop free Wi-Fi networks in the countryside for rural communities; (2) to support local ecological struggles including the network of squat gardens across Athens, the struggles against the privatization of water in Greece, and develop research on food sovereignty; (3) to function as an international cultural commons liaising across different local experiences; (4) to liaise and support the solidarity network of health clinic, food market, schools and refugees in Athens; (5) to develop grassroots and self-organized universities in Athens and Berlin.

Coordinated by Tiziana Terranova, the *Alternative Economies* group proposed: (1) to establish an independent and free Wi-Fi network of rooftop antennas through the city; (2) to create an alternative encrypted currency (FairCoin and FairLoan) based on the model of BitCoin but relying on an established international network of shops, businesses, individuals and groups and with the aim of developing a democratic and demonetized economy; (3) to set up an infopoint of alternative currencies during all the time of OMONIA including with a BitCoin/ FairCoin vending machine (ATM); (4) to set up an international cooperative network, linking existing cooperatives in Greece and Athens.

Other propositions of the groups included: (1) the collective drafting of a programme for the biennale; (2) building a shared vocabulary and understanding of commons; (3) developing a fair economy of art; (4) building digital platforms and hotspot; (5) running an autonomous radio and YouTube education channel.

APPENDIX 2

POST-CAPITALIST MANIFESTO

6 Post-capitalist stations

a) Digital currency/parasitical finance and sharing economy
b) De-commodification of work and labour commoning
c) Legalization of the commons
d) Rethinking citizenship
e) Architecture of commons
f) Alternative education.

34 Routes/journeys

In the section on IRI, I have described the thirty-four possible projects/ routes for the creation of IRI as interface between art/knowledge production/activism. Each route/project will generate human communities (for instance recipients of Universal Basic Income pilot projects or artists' communities experimenting with digital currencies), modes of action or policies (on human right, informal labour or credit) which will become part of the human and non-human network of the institute. So these journeys are constellations of relationships in ongoing transformations.

93 Experts/dreamers

Each route relies on specific experts.

10 Operative nodes

S. A. Le Doc (Venice); Macao (Milan), Asilo Filangieri (Naples), Laboratory for the Urban Commons (LUC) Athens; Reina Sofia

(Madrid), Townhouse (Cairo), SALT (Istanbul). Our Commons (Istanbul); Fundacion de los Communues (Madrid).

3 Institutional frames

Art, activism and pedagogy.

INDEX